Software Order Form

Pascal: An Interactive Text

Software forms an essential part of this *Computer Illustrated Text*. It is integrated with 50 activities in the text and is designed to save time in keying programs to allow more time to be given to hands-on experience of working in Pascal.

Software is available for MS-DOS machines on 5¼ disc at £32.50 (inc VAT) per disc

To receive your software complete this form and return with your remittance to: ESM, Duke Street, Wisbech, Cambs PE13 2AE. Telephone 0945 63441

Telephone orders are accepted from customers paying by credit card

Please send me software for *Pascal: An Interactive Text* by S J Abas and J R Mondragon on

☐ MS-DOS disc

I enclose my cheque for £________ payable to ESM

Please charge to my Access/Visa card number

☐☐☐☐☐☐☐☐☐☐☐☐☐☐☐☐ Expiry date ________

Name________________________ **Signature** ________________________

Address ____

____

Pascal: an Interactive Text

Other Titles in the Series

An Introduction to Groups
D Asche

Introduction to Statistics
A W Bowman and D R Robinson

Introduction to Regression and Analysis of Variance
A W Bowman and D R Robinson

An Introduction to the Digital Analysis of Stationary Signals
I P Castro

Introductory Quantum Mechanics
R C Greenhow

Fourier Series and Transforms
R D Harding

A Simple Introduction to Numerical Analysis
R D Harding and D A Quinney

A Simple Introduction to Numerical Analysis
Volume 2: Interpolation and Approximation
R D Harding and D A Quinney

From Number Theory to Secret Codes
T Jackson

A Simple Introduction to Unconstrained Optimisation
J J McKeown, D Meegan and D Sprevak

Introduction to Probability
D R Robinson and A W Bowman

Of Related Interest

Scientific Programmer's Toolkit: Pascal Edition
M H Beilby, J R Harding and M R Manning

A Computer Illustrated Text

PASCAL: AN INTERACTIVE TEXT

S J Abas

and

J Rangel Mondragon

School of Mathematics, University College of North Wales, Bangor

Adam Hilger, Bristol and New York

ESM, Cambridge

British Library Cataloguing in Publication Data

Abas, Jan
Pascal: an interactive text (A Computer illustrated text)
1. Computer systems, programming languages. Pascal language.
I. Title II. Mondragon J. R. (Jaime Rangel) III. Series
005.133

ISBN 0-7503-0020-5 (Text)
ISBN 0-7503-0021-3 (IBM Disk)
ISBN 0-7503-0022-1 (Text and Disk)
ISBN 0-7503-0023-X (Network)

Library of Congress Cataloging-in-Publication Data are available

Series Editor: **R D Harding**, University of Cambridge

Published by: IOP Publishing Ltd, Techno House, Redcliffe Way, Bristol BS1 6NX, England
335 East 45th Street, New York, NY 10017-3483, USA
ESM, Duke Street, Wisbech, Cambs PE13 2AE, England
Published under the Adam Hilger/ESM imprint

Printed in Great Britain by J W Arrowsmith Ltd, Bristol

This book is dedicated to Niklaus Wirth and Philippe Kahn, the two who have done most to make Pascal available to the computing community.

〉 Contents

〉 Preface

This book is mainly intended as a textbook for the teaching of ISO Pascal to students in universities and polytechnics. It will also be particularly well suited for those learning Pascal through self-study or distance learning. No previous knowledge of programming is assumed.

There are of course a substantial number of books on Pascal already on offer and to produce yet another volume demands considerable justification. This we shall now do.

The main motivation for writing the book springs from our desire to exploit a relatively new but now commonly available technology to respond to something which is part of every teacher's experience. This being that programming, like any other worthwhile skill, cannot be learnt passively by merely reading a book, no matter how good the book. It must be learnt actively through problem solving and through accumulating experience. As Confucius is reputed to have said, 'I hear and I forget. I see and I remember. I do and I understand.'

In our view the traditional paper-based book, which has served as the basic educational medium for several centuries, is not the best medium that we have to offer our students any more. A concise textbook, integrated with tutorial material supplied on disk, now constitutes a vastly superior medium to promote learning through doing. Educators have so far not utilised the potential of this combination to any great extent.

Our book sets out to provide an introduction to Pascal in an interactive way using a book/disk combination. Our central strategy is to give the student a vastly extended hands-on experience by providing a substantial collection of pre-written programs and program shells.

In our experience, a great deal of teaching time in computing courses is presently spent doing nothing more productive than typing in programs. An immediate advantage of the book/disk combination is that this essentially trivial activity can be very substantially pruned and time spent instead on problem solving. There are many other advantages that the tutorial material on a disk provides.

The traditional book is frozen and static. By contrast, the material contained on a disk is 'live'. It can grow and change. It can be readily added to and subtracted from as experiences and insights are gained. For example, whereas one would not encourage a student to scribble in a book, we expect our students to write their own comments in the pre-written programs that we supply. Similarly, we expect the teacher to make modifications to the disk to add the benefits of his or her personal experience and preferences. Using a disk these kinds of modifications can be achieved and disseminated with far less labour than using printed paper.

The book may be an ideal medium for presenting the definitive works of a master but, despite its long held central place in the teaching environment, it has never really been the ideal tool for teaching. As Jean Piaget pointed out, 'The principal goal of education is to create men who are capable of doing new things, not simply of repeating what other generations have done — men who are creative, inventive and discoverers.' The promotion of discovery of new things requires a mode of teaching which can only be offered in a very limited way by the book. This mode, as Knuth has emphasised, would teach *not just a concept in itself but how that concept could be varied.* The emphasis must be placed on making variations on themes and this can be done far more effectively through the interactive mode of exploring pre-written programs on disk.

Yet another advantage offered by the disk is in the reduction of bulk. Because non-trivial books on computer languages contain listings of sizeable programs, they necessarily become bulky and heavy-going. This is a deterrent to reading. The prescribed textbook very often remains just skimpily flicked through. By making use of the combined text/disk format the core information can be isolated and made manageable for reading during a typical twenty-hour course of lectures.

Our purposes in writing the book can now be summarised.

- To offer the student hands-on experience at the earliest opportunity.
- To minimise non-productive expenditure of tutorial time spent in

typing programs and to maximise activities which involve problem solving and learning.

- To offer material in a 'live' medium where it can grow and change to reflect personal experience and insights and where it can be used more effectively to study not just a concept in itself but how that concept can be varied.
- To reduce bulk in the text by transferring listings of computer programs and solutions to exercises to disk.

The material offered is organised into four groups: text, Quickies, Pascal laboratory and Exercises.

The **Quickies** can be answered instantly and are intended to test the basic comprehension of the material covered in the text. Solutions are provided at the end of each chapter so that the student can immediately gauge how well he or she is doing and which topics require to be read again.

The **Pascal laboratory**, which comprises pre-written programs and program shells supplied on the disk, is integrated with 50 **Activities** included in the text. The problems raised in this section have been chosen to provide a range of learning activity. Some are intended to illustrate further the topics covered in the text. Others have been chosen to bring out subtle points with which students are likely to have difficulty. A few are of a more challenging nature. The activities associated with the Pascal laboratory are central to this text. It is here that the student is offered an active role in the learning process and is encouraged to experiment and explore.

After the student has done through the Quickies and the Pascal laboratory, he or she should be well equipped to proceed to the **Exercises** that follow. These can be tackled in a class tutorial or set as homework assignments. Answers are provided on the disk to questions marked with a star.

Many of the textbooks that are on offer pose the difficulty that the reader becomes lost in technical detail by their attempting to cover too much at once without giving the reader the chance to evaluate if the material has been absorbed. The Quickies and the suggestions to go to the Pascal laboratory interspersed within the text are intended to overcome this difficulty.

It should be possible to cover the complete course in 30 contact hours: 20 hours of lectures together with 10 hours of tutorial time.

To conclude, this book sets out to exploit the potential of the book/disk combination to promote active learning. We are convinced that this combination can greatly enhance efficiency and through it students can learn more, retain more and do it faster than is achieved presently.

Jan Abas
Jaime Rangel Mondragon

Bangor, North Wales
August 1989

〉 Acknowledgments

We wish to thank our colleagues Dr Neil Rymer, Mr Dafydd Roberts and our student Mr Antony Shaw for reading and criticizing the text.

Each author would like to thank the other for the very enjoyable period of collaborative work during the writing of this book.

〉 Chapter 1

〉 Pascal and Programming: an Overview

The purpose of this chapter is to say some essential things that need to be said before we start programming. The first section of the chapter introduces some general knowledge about Pascal. The second section sets out to impart some essential preliminary awareness of the nature of problem solving and programming.

〉 1.1 About Pascal

Let us start our study of Pascal by learning something about its history.

Origins of Pascal

Languages such as FORTRAN, COBOL and BASIC which arrived before Pascal was unsuited for teaching the principles of good programming. Good programming demands that *you must first work out the method that is to be used in a program before actually proceeding to write the code for it*. There was nothing in these languages which encouraged the programmer to adopt any disciplined methodology other than simply start punching out the code. The resulting programs could be very hard to understand, debug and maintain.

Algol 60 was the first computer language designed to encourage a more thoughtful approach to programming, but it offered only a limited number of data types and was difficult to implement. In the late 1960s Professor Niklaus Wirth and his co-workers at Eidgenössische Technische Hochschule (ETH) Zürich, Switzerland set out to improve on Algol and remedy these failings. Their aim was to produce a compact and easily implemented language that would be suited to the teaching of programming as a systematic discipline.

The first version of the language was drafted in 1968, the first compiler became available in 1970 and the first authoritative document which gave the vocabulary and the grammar of the language was published by Jensen and Wirth in 1973.

The latest document to specify the language is the British Standards Institution (BSI) document BS6192: *Specification for Computer Programming Language Pascal*, which appeared in 1982. A similar document ISO 7185 published by the International Organisation for Standardisation represents the internationally agreed standard for Pascal known as ISO Pascal.

Pascal the man

The name Pascal sets out to honour a very remarkable man, the French prodigy, mathematician and philosopher Blaise Pascal (1623–62) who is credited with the invention of the first mechanical calculator at the age of 19. The calculator, called Pascaline, was a cog-and-wheel device which performed additions when linked dials were turned. Although it could only multiply via repetitions, it was an ingenious device for its time and was marketed commercially. Several specimens have survived.

Blaise Pascal did much more than design the calculator. While still a teenager he published an essay on conic sections which astounded René Descartes, the philosopher who invented coordinate geometry. The essay contained what is acknowledged to be the greatest theorem of medieval geometry. Called 'l'hexagrammê mystique' by Pascal, it states that if a hexagon is inscribed in a conic, e.g., an ellipse, the three points of intersections of pairs of opposite sides always lie in a straight line.

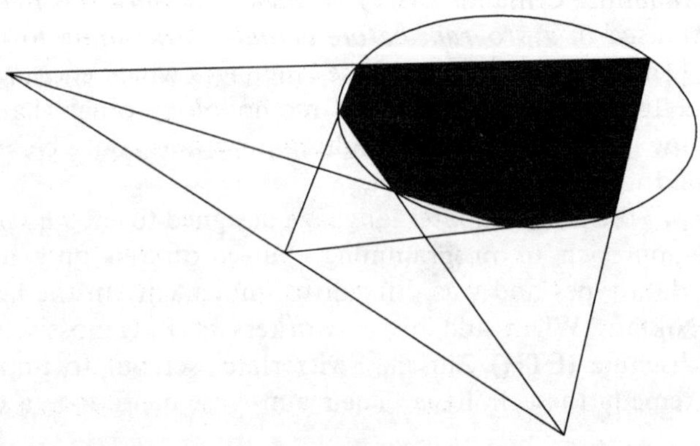

Pascal was also one of the founders of the mathematical theory of probability. The notion of probability was born from a debate on a game of chance between Pascal and another great mathematician, Pierre Fermat (1601–65), Pascal understood that the subject could be given a mathematical treatment in terms of combinations and arrangements. He used the famous Pascal's triangle (shown below) to calculate the number of combinations. Incidentally, the same triangular representation of combinations had been used earlier by the 14th century Chinese mathematician Chu Shi-kié.

```
               1
            1     1
         1     2     1
      1     3     3     1
   1     4     6     4     1
1     5    10    10     5     1
  .     .     .     .     .     .     .
.     .     .     .     .     .     .     .
```

'Let no one say that I have said nothing new', wrote Pascal, '... When we play tennis, we both play the same ball, but one of us places it better.'. Like Pascal the man, Pascal the language also said a good deal that was new and showed budding computer programmers how to place the ball of programming so much better. It soon became the *lingua franca* of computer science.

Virtues of Pascal

Pascal is an elegant language. It is designed to maximise comprehension, and to minimise ambiguities and the chances of introducing hard-to-detect bugs and errors. It is structured, which means that a large program can be organised efficiently into smaller subprograms and the handling of data, variables and subprograms can be done in a clear and well organised way.

It has a rich collection of data types which allow for easy specification of complex data structures. Unlike some other languages, Pascal allows user-defined data types so that the vocabulary used in a program can grow to satisfy the needs of the programmer. These virtues lead to efficient programming and the code produced in Pascal is easy to modify and maintain.

Finally, Pascal is a compact language. The earliest popular micro, the *APPLE*, was able to offer a Pascal compiler and many are now widely and cheaply available on today's microcomputers. The compactness of Pascal has undoubtedly contributed to its popularity and has made it highly accessible.

Having sung the praises of Pascal, it would be wrong to create the impression that Pascal offers a state of perfection. Indeed, there are major failings in all computer languages. Standard Pascal has, for example, severe limitations in input/output facilities and string handling. These and others will be commented on as we progress through the text.

Dialects of Pascal

Like any living language Pascal has many dialects. UCSD Pascal, MS Pascal, PRO Pascal and TURBO Pascal are examples of some well known versions available on micros. The non-standard dialects often offer many features that are not available in ISO Pascal. These extras can provide powerful advantages but a price has to be paid in portability. For example, the best selling TURBO Pascal, version 4 by the US firm Borland International, failed 178 out of the 500 validation tests of the British Standards Institution; nevertheless, since the language is highly popular, it has attained the status of a *de facto* standard. As a first attempt to learn the language, it is best to adhere to ISO Pascal which will be the version used in this book.

The future of Pascal

There are now several contenders for the place presently held by Pascal, the most prominent being Ada and Modula 2. Modula 2 has also been designed by Niklaus Wirth who produced Pascal and is again intended for the teaching of good programming. Ada is a more extensive language, five times larger than Pascal, and was commissioned by the US Department of Defense. It has now become the adopted official language for software in most large government systems in the USA and has also been introduced in many major industrial organisations. Both Modula 2 and Ada are slowly beginning to spread in academic departments of computer science.

Be that as it may, a widespread replacement for Pascal is still a long way away and, in fact, the use of Pascal is continuing to grow rapidly. For every computer scientist moving over to Modula 2 or Ada, there are dozens who are adopting Pascal. The language received a major impetus to its growth in 1983 through the hands of a young French mathematician and entrepreneur Philippe Kahn. In that year, the company

Borland International, founded by Kahn in the USA, placed an advertisement offering their TURBO Pascal compiler for only $49.95. The normal price for a Pascal compiler at that time ranged between 300 and 500 dollars. Not only was this an extraordinarily cheap product but it offered speeds of working which could not be matched by its competitors. In the following four months, 15 000 copies of TURBO Pascal were sold and there are now more than a million users of TURBO Pascal worldwide.

Several versions of TURBO Pascal has appeared since its launch and each has encouraged further the growth of Pascal on microcomputers. The latest version of TURBO Pascal, and also of QuickPascal from the company MicroSoft, are examples of compilers that incorporate some of the major developments in computer languages that have taken place in recent times.

There are other proposed extensions to Pascal on the way and we can be certain that Pascal will continue to remain an extensively employed high level language in the whole of the computing community in the 1990s. Anyone who wishes to become a good and proficient programmer would do well to use it as a vehicle for learning the art and science of programming.

〉1.2 About problem solving and programming

Before we start on the learning of Pascal in the next chapter, a vital point must be understood: *a language is merely a tool for problem solving and programming*. Although the text in the book will spend a great deal of time discussing the features of the language, you yourself must place the emphasis on solving the problems given as Activities for the Pascal Laboratory and as Exercises.

Programming is a multiple activity and is not the same as coding. In general, it involves a whole series of interconnected steps which will be listed below. Since the full meaning of these steps can only be grasped after an accumulation of some experience, we will not discuss the matter at great length. The theme will be picked up and developed more fully in the next two chapters after you have learnt some rudiments of Pascal. Our intention at this stage is merely to sow some very important seeds which you must make blossom if you are to truly benefit from the learning of a computer language.

Programming involves the following steps.

- *Defining the problem*
  Unless you are solving a trivial problem, some preparatory thinking must precede the action of coding. You must state clearly what needs to be done before you begin to do it. The problem must be expressed so that it is complete and unambiguous. This is the most important step in programming and, apart from the case of very simple problems, is not an easy one.

- *Producing an outline solution*
  This step involves producing a rough outline of the proposed solution. No detailed algorithm is expected at this stage. For many very straightforward problems that are solved of necessity in textbooks, this step is not always necessary. However, in more complex tasks of the kind met in the real world, it becomes an absolute necessity.

- *Developing an algorithm*
  An algorithm is a precise and ordered description of how the initial information, called data, is to be manipulated to produce the desired solution. An algorithm is expected to display the following characteristics:

  (1) It should comprise steps whose meaning is clear to the person or the machine executing the algorithm.
  (2) There should be a clearly defined starting step.
  (3) On completion of each step in the algorithm, the step to be executed next should be clearly identifiable.
  (4) There should be one or more clearly defined stopping steps which should be reached in a finite amount of time.

  How do we go about developing an algorithm? Most of the time, in real applications, we utilise algorithms that have already been developed and are available in computer libraries or in public literature. In developing new algorithms, a combination of two primary strategies is used. The first involves the use of **modularity**. This is the process of breaking down a large, complex task into a number of smaller and simpler subtasks. The second strategy is known as **top-down design** or **step-wise refinement**. This involves writing down first a very general description of the solution and then proceeding one step at a time to a more detailed description until what is proposed becomes sufficiently easy for it to be coded directly.

- *Coding and debugging*
  It is only at this stage in programming that we start coding the solution to the problem. Unlike the previous steps, this should be an easy step if the algorithm has been developed in sufficient detail using top-down design.
  Rarely will a piece of code execute without requiring some errors to be corrected. One of the major virtues of modular programming is that it facilitates debugging. Each module, as it is coded, should be debugged. You may be interested to know that in commercial environments, debugging is now the largest single cost factor in software development.

- *Testing the program*
  This step involves verifying that the program produces results that are correct and, further, that it will do so for all possible cases. Proving this is a very difficult task and, indeed, often impossible. However, the task has to be attempted very seriously in financial, military, medical and other applications where a suspected logical or coding error can lead to disastrous results.

- *Producing enhanced documentation*
  Producing documentation which explains the meaning of the code to the programmer and to the user is a continual process during the execution of the last two steps. However, when the testing is complete, the documentation should be polished up to provide all essential information for a potential user or someone who may be involved in modifying or developing the program at some future date.

- *Maintenance*
  This step is not particularly relevant in the context of a first course in programming but must be included in real applications. The kind of software that is written by professionals does not remain static. Bugs are discovered, new hardware is installed, capabilities are extended, and so on, to make it necessary for the program to be continually modified. This requires program maintenance. Modularity and good documentation are the two key factors that contribute to this step being carried out efficiently.

Having completed a brief description of the steps involved in programming, it needs to be said that these steps are not linear and we do not progress neatly from one step to another. Very often several of the steps remain active simultaneously. For example, testing a program might lead to some new insight which in turn would lead to modifications to the algorithm and so on.

Also, although it is essential for you as a student to practise the series of steps outlined above, in the kind of problems that have to be solved in a first course of programming, it would become tedious if each of the steps was discussed in great detail in every problem that is introduced. For this reason, and only for this reason, we will avoid lengthy discussions of every step after they have all been illustrated in Chapters 2 and 3.

Finally, let us conclude this chapter by saying that it would be equally wrong if you were to conclude from the above discussion of steps in programming that you must dot every i and cross every t before you dare start coding a program. As we tried to emphasise in our preface, *programming cannot be learnt by following thousands of dos and don'ts*. The steps described above should be used as a guide to good problem-solving practice rather than as means to inhibit it.

〉 References

There are dozens of good books on Pascal. The following is a selection of books that you may like to consult for extra reading.

Programming in Pascal
Peter Grogono, Addison-Wesley (1978)

This is a classic. An excellent textbook on Pascal as a first programming language.

Pascal with style. Programming Proverbs
Henry F Ledgard, Paul A Nagin and John F Hueras, Hayden Book Company Inc. (1979)

A comprehensive and beautifully written book on good programming.

Problem Solving using Pascal
Romualdas Skvarcius, PWS Publishers, Boston (1984)

An excellent and comprehensive textbook on Pascal. Very well written and contains many problems.

PASCAL User Manual and Report
Kathleen Jensen and Niklaus Wirth, Springer Verlag (1985)

The definitive reference on ISO Pascal. A tutorial and many examples are included. Three editions have been issued since its first publication in 1973.

Illustrating Pascal
Donald Alcock, Cambridge University Press (1987)

Combines a clear composition with a hand-written format, being perhaps the only such book on Pascal. Experienced programmers will find the chapter on pointers to be of unparalleled clarity and fun.

Introduction to Computers and Programming: Pascal
Peter P Smith, Wadsworth Publishing Company (1987)

A very comprehensive textbook on Pascal. The discussion of steps in problem solving and programming is covered in great detail.

Pascal Precisely (2nd edition)
Judy Bishop, Addison Wesley (1989)

This is a concise, very clearly written and well structured book. It is suitable for complete beginners and makes very little demand on mathematics.

› Chapter 2

› Writing Simple Programs

The purpose of this chapter is to get you started with Pascal and to teach you a number of good programming practices at the earliest opportunity. First you will learn about the structure of a Pascal program. Following that, you will examine an example program which will be used to introduce some basic concepts. You will then learn how to handle simple output and input operations. Finally, you will be introduced to loops and decision making. You can then proceed to your first Pascal laboratory session and start learning by doing.

› 2.1 The structure of a Pascal program

A Pascal program has the following structure:

PROGRAM *ProgramName (list of files);*
  Definitions and Declarations
BEGIN
    Executable statements
END.

The worlds **PROGRAM, BEGIN** and **END**, typed in capitals, are called **reserved words, keywords** or **delimiters**. They must appear in the places shown. There are 35 such words in Pascal (listed in Appendix 1) and they are part of Pascal's vocabulary. The meaning of the keywords is fixed by the language and they cannot be used for any purpose other than that specified by the language. By contrast, the words written in italics show those portions which vary from program to program. What exactly goes there is chosen by the programmer.

Of the italicised portions only *ProgramName* is compulsory. The other bits are optional and may be absent. The following program represents the extreme case. It has no declarations and no executable statements. It does nothing but is nevertheless perfectly legal.

```
PROGRAM Dummy;
BEGIN
END.
```

The heading and the block

The large structure of a Pascal program is made up from two substructures, namely

- A **heading** which gives the program a name and lists the **files** to be used by the program in receiving and supplying information.
- A body called a **block**. The block itself consists of two subparts: a **definition and declaration part**, which gives a description of the type of data to be operated upon by the program, and an **executable statement part**, which specifies the actions to be performed on those data. The statement part is enclosed by the keywords BEGIN and END.

Below is an example program in which you can observe the structure we have just described. Refer to this program when you are reading through the next section which will introduce you to some basic concepts in Pascal.

Example 2A: a Pascal program

```
Heading →        PROGRAM AreaOfaCircle(INPUT,OUTPUT);

                 {+-------------------------------------+
                  |                                     |
                  | Given Radius, Computes Area of a Circle |
Comment→          |       Author: Jim Blogs             |
                  |       Written: March 1989           |
                  |                                     |
                  +-------------------------------------+}
```

```
B  Definitions       CONST
L    and                    Pi=3.14159;
O  declarations      VAR
C                          Radius,Area: REAL;
K
   Executable        BEGIN
    statements              WRITE('Give Radius ');
                            READLN(Radius);
                            Area := Pi*SQR(Radius);
                            WRITELN('Radius=  ',Radius,' Area=  ',Area)
                     END.
```

〉2.2 Some basic concepts

Identifiers

To be able to refer to entities stored in a computer's memory, a high level language such as Pascal allows the programmer the facility to attach labels or names to those portions of memory. The technical term for these labels is **identifier**. In Example 2A the words 'AreaOfaCircle', 'Radius' and 'Area' are identifiers.

In Pascal an identifier can be any combination of letters and digits that conforms to the following three conditions:

Begins with a letter,
Does not contain any spaces or special symbols (most compilers do accept the understore character _),
Is not a keyword.

In recognising identifiers, Pascal makes no distinction between the upper case and the lower case letters. For example, DYBYDX, dybydx and DyByDx all refer to the same identifier.

Can you now say which of these are legal identifiers?

MYJOB23	4Y	DRAWPICTURE	X.5
X	p1×7	TWO PI	BEGIN
2+X	THIS_AND_THAT		

The following are illegal, for reasons given:

4Y	Starts with a digit.
X.5	Contains a dot.

TWO PI	Contains a space.
BEGIN	Is a keyword.
2 + X	Starts with a digit and contains a + sign.

According to ISO Pascal, the identifier THIS_AND_THAT is not a valid one. However, it will be acceptable to most compilers.

Although Pascal places no limits on the number of characters making up an identifier, particular implementations will necessarily do so. Thus, according to the rules of Pascal, PhilipAndMary is a different identifier from PhilipandMartha, but it may not be so on your machine. VAX Pascal, for example, treats the first 31 characters as significant. Any implementation of Pascal will treat at least the first eight characters as significant, but if you are going to use identifiers of longer length then you are advised to check.

Advice on good programming

Always choose self-documenting identifiers; if you are writing a program to find prime numbers then name the program PrimeNumbers, rather than Prog1. If you intend a variable to hold the value of density then choose the identifier Density, rather than D and so on.

Try to avoid introducing identifiers in the same program that are very similar in construction and can be mistyped for each other, e.g. VALUE, VALU, INITIAL, INITAL, etc. Malfunctioning of a program resulting from interchanges of such identifiers can be extremely difficult to identify.

The use of a mixture of upper and lower case letters should be utilised to make an identifier more readily intelligible, e.g. by writing SpeedOfLight rather than speedoflight.

Predefined identifiers

Pascal offers a number of identifiers (listed in Appendix 1) which are predefined. They are also called **standard identifiers**. For example, MAXINT is the name given to the largest whole number available on a particular implementation and SQR is used to compute the square of a number. Unlike a keyword, the programmer can choose to use a standard identifier for a purpose other than the standard one. For example, the identifier **SQR** could be used to produce the cube of a number. This kind of usage, however, should be avoided as it causes confusion. The standard identifiers should be treated exactly as keywords and used only for their intended purposes.

Standard scalar types

Everything in the computer is represented in terms of 0s and 1s. High level languages free the programmer from having to consider the details of this representation by associating the concept of data **type** with identifiers.

We will discuss data types more fully at a later stage. Suffice it to know initially that the simplest data types in Pascal are known as the **standard scalar types**. There are four of these, namely **INTEGER**, **REAL**, **CHAR** (character) and **BOOLEAN**. Those of type INTEGER take only a whole number value, REAL types take values which may have a fractional part, CHAR types take a character value and BOOLEAN types (which are used for logical decisions) take one of the two values **TRUE** or **FALSE**.

The diagram below is meant to show how identifiers are used to refer to memory locations. The size of the memory allocated to an identifier is determined by its type. For example, **Pi** is meant to be an identifier of type REAL. In the actual representation in a computer, everything in the diagram would be translated in terms of 0s and 1s but we have shown them in this manner to make the meaning clear.

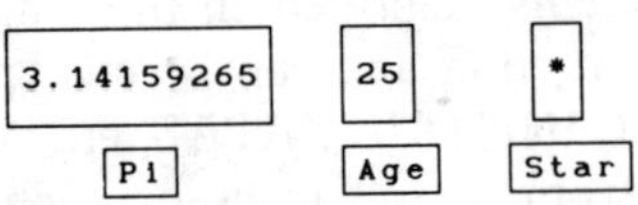

Files INPUT *and* OUTPUT

In order that a computer program can receive information and deliver the results of its operations it has to communicate with the outside world. In Pascal all communication between a program and the outside world is deemed to occur via **files**. A program receives input from some files and writes output to other files. A file is a technical term and will be discussed more fully in Chapter 6. Suffice it here to say that a file is a sequence of data of the same type. The purpose of the list of files in the heading of a program is to specify how the program is going to communicate with its environment.

We will assume at this stage that the communication between the user and the computer is going to take place via a keyboard and a screen. If a program is to do output using this standard method of communication then the keyword **OUTPUT** must appear in the heading (a program that does not do any output is not going to be of any great use). If it is to receive input then the word **INPUT** must appear. The program in Example 2A has these words in its heading because it does both input and output. It reads the value of **Radius** and prints the values of **Radius** and **Area**.

Since most of the time one uses the keyboard and the screen as the input and output devices, it is tedious that one should have to declare these. For this reason, many Pascal compilers, e.g. TURBO Pascal, do not require **INPUT**, **OUTPUT** to be so declared. Indeed, TURBO Pascal does not even require a program name. However, to comply with the ISO standard we shall continue to include the words **INPUT** and **OUTPUT** in the heading.

Comments

Comments in Pascal are written by enclosing them in braces { } or by surrounding them with (* *). For example:

```
(* This is a comment *)
{ This is also a comment }
(* This is yet another comment }
```

Whereas all other kinds of statements in a program convey information to the computer, the purpose of a comment is to explain the code to the human reader. A comment is ignored by the computer. Comments may be spread across lines as shown in Example 2A. However, comments cannot be nested. For example, the following is invalid:

```
{ This is { not a comment }}
```

Advice on good programming

Good programming requires the writing of effective comments. Your comments should be crisp and informative but should avoid stating the obvious.

Constants and variables

Constants are identifiers whose values remain fixed during program execution. Variables, on the other hand, are identifiers which may have a value assigned to them in the executable section and whose value may change as the program is executed. In Pascal all identifiers denoting constants have to be defined and all those denoting variables have to be declared. These definitions and declarations also specify the basic type of each identifier. In some other languages, such as FORTRAN and BASIC, variables can be generated at will within the body of a program. For this reason, Pascal is said to be **strongly typed**.

CONST *definition*

A constant can be of any standard scalar type. It can also be a string constant as shown in the list below and as discussed later in this chapter. Constant definitions begin with the keyword **CONST** followed by a sequence of constant names. Each name is followed by an equal sign (=) after which comes the constant's value and a semicolon. The data type of a constant is implicitly specified by its context. If the value is given as a whole number then it is assumed to be of type INTEGER; if it is given in the form of a real number then it is assumed to be of type REAL. Characters and character strings, which will be discussed later in this chapter, are specified by enclosing them in apostrophes.

The following examples illustrate a complete range of constant definitions.

```
CONST
      year = 1988;                  { INTEGER }
      n = -19;                      { INTEGER }
      pi = 3.14159;                 { REAL }
      y = 2.8e-4;                   { REAL, means 2.8 x 10^-4 }
      GRADE = 'D';                  { CHAR }
      STAR = '*';                   { CHAR }
      BLANK = ' ';                  { CHAR }
      QUESTION = 'Try Again?';      { string constant }
      PigsCanFly = FALSE;           { BOOLEAN }
```

VAR *declaration*

The **VAR** declaration associates an identifier with each variable and, unlike the CONST declaration, defines its type explicitly. Also, as many variables as need be can be declared via a single statement. Here is a typical VAR declaration:

```
VAR i, j           : INTEGER;
    Max, Min, Rate: REAL;
```

An alternative but more tedious way of making the same declaration is

```
VAR i    : INTEGER;
    j    : INTEGER;
    Max: REAL;
    Min : REAL;
    Rate: REAL;
```

In general, a **VAR** declaration has the following form:

VAR *Identifier1, Identifier2, ..., IdentifierN: TYPE;*
IdentifierX, IdentifierY, ..., IdentifierZ: TYPE;

.

.

It begins with the keyword **VAR**. Any number of identifiers are then listed naming the variables. The list terminates with a colon which is followed by the specification of type, followed by the semicolon. There may be any number of other such lists following the first one.

Assignment statement
An assignment statement, as the name suggests, assigns a value defined on the right-hand side of the **assignment operator** := to the variable named on the left-hand side. For example:

```
Age := 23;
```

The symbol := is pronounced 'becomes equal to'. The general form of the assignment statement is:

Variable := *Expression*;

where the *Expression* must reduce to a value of the same type as that of the variable, with one exception. An integer value can be assigned to a variable of type REAL. Thus it is perfectly legal to write **x** := 2; when x has been declared as REAL, but it would be illegal to write **y** := 2.5; if y is an INTEGER variable.

The semicolon
Note how frequently the semicolon appears in Example 2A. The semicolon is the basic punctuation symbol in Pascal and is used to separate consecutive items of information. Although the semicolon is seen mostly at the end of lines it does not signify the end of line. In Pascal we can write as many statements to a line as is pleasing to our eye.

A semicolon occurs between two items of code if the items need to be separated. The semicolon is optional before **END** and that is the reason why it is missing from the last but one line in Example 2A.

Program layout
You will notice that the program in Example 2A has been typed in an indented fashion. The **BEGIN** is lined up with the **END** and blank lines have been used to separate various sections and subsections. All this has nothing to do with the logic of the program. There is no relationship in a Pascal program between lines of code and its meaning. Definitions, declarations and statements may occur as many or as few to a line as is appealing to the programmer. A single statement may be spread over several lines and blank lines may be inserted freely to improve the readability of the program. The meaning of Example 2A will not be altered if we retype the heading, say, to make it look like

```
                pRoGram           aREaofaciRcle
          (inpuT,ouTput)     ;
```

It need hardly be said that a program laid out in this fashion would be very ugly and hard to decipher.

Advice on good programming

Good programming style makes use of indentations, blank lines and upper and lower case letters to make the structure and meaning of a program transparent.

INTEGER and REAL numbers
As was said earlier, Pascal has two kinds of numbers, called **INTEGER** and **REAL** numbers. Integers are whole numbers; 0, 22, −359, for example. Real numbers are numbers with fractional portions. In Pascal they are written using a decimal or an E (exponent) notation; for example,

1.23   −0.54   6.9E6   −3E−4   5.32E+6.

Note that it is illegal to write .1 and or 1. which is permitted in some languages. The notation using the letter E is known as the **scientific** or **floating-point notation**. Since real numbers are held in the computer as a fractional part and an exponent part, they are referred to as **floating-point** numbers. The scientific notation is convenient to use when writing very large or very small numbers. In this notation the integer that follows E gives the number of places the decimal point must be moved to get rid of the exponent. If the integer following E is positive then the decimal point moves to the right, if it is negative then it moves left. Thus 6.9E6 (or 6.9E + 6) is a shorthand for 6900 000 and − 3E − 4 stands for − 0.0003.

An important point for you to appreciate is that *numbers on a computer can only be represented to within a machine's range.* How large a number we can handle depends on the amount of storage we allocate to represent that number. For example, TURBO Pascal uses 2 bytes to represent an integer which allows integers to range from − 32 768 to 32 767. Standard Pascal gives a special name **MAXINT** to the largest integer and defines the range of integers to lie from − **MAXINT** to **MAXINT**. In Activity 1 you will find out the value of **MAXINT** and also the range of real numbers on your machine.

Within a machine's range, the representation of integers and any arithmetic involving them is done accurately with no rounding or approximations.

Real numbers, unlike integers, can in general only be represented to a certain accuracy of significant figures and of course to within the machine's range. This range is larger than that of integers but, unlike integers, arithmetic with reals is not always exact. It can often only be done approximately and is therefore subject to error.

One important consequence of the approximate representation of real numbers is that a real value should not be expected to be exactly equal to some particular real value. For example, if x and y are of type REAL and if we put x := 1/3 then it will be wrong to conclude that the statement y := x + x + x will make y equal to 1. Two real values should never be compared to check if they are equal but instead should be checked to see if they are very close.

Arithmetical operators

There are six **dyadic** or **binary** arithmetical operators (meaning that they act on the two values on either side of them) for doing arithmetical calculations in Pascal. These are listed below and unless otherwise stated the operand on either side of the operator can be an integer or a real.

+	Addition.
−	Subtraction.

*	Multiplication.
/	Division. The operands may be REAL or INTEGER but the result produced is REAL.
DIV	INTEGER division. Both operands must be of type INTEGER. The result produced is INTEGER.
MOD	Gives the remainder when one INTEGER is divided by another

Apart from these operators, ordinary brackets may be used in forming expressions. Also, the + and the − can act as **monadic** or **unary** operators (meaning that they act on a single value), e.g. +15, −(3 + 2), 15.5 * (−3.2).

Unlike some other programming languages, such as BASIC and FORTRAN, there is no operator for raising a number to a power. This irritation can be easily remedied using the exponential function and will be done so later.

Arithmetical expressions involving a mixture of operators and operands, e.g. 1 − 2 * 3 * (4 + 5(6/7)), are evaluated according to the rules of priority attached to the operators. These are:

Highest	( )	Bracketed expressions.
Next	:= / DIV MOD	Multiplication and division.
Lowest	+ −	Addition and Subtraction.

Operators of equal priority are applied from left to right.

Examples

Expression	Reduces to value
2 + 3 * 4	14
2 + 3 * 4.0	14.0
(2.0 + 3) * 4	20.0
10/4	2.5
10 DIV 4	2
−10 DIV 4	−2
4 DIV 10	0
11 MOD 4	3
−11 MOD 4	1
7 DIV 2 − 9 MOD 2	2
−36/6/3 * 2	−4.0

A decimal point in the last column indicates that the result produced is a real number. Note that TURBO Pascal does not obey **MOD** properly when the numbers are negative, e.g. −11 **MOD** 4 produces −3.

〉 2.3 Producing output from the computer

We can start to interact with the computer as soon as we have learnt how to get the computer to produce some output. The **WRITE** and **WRITELN** statements of Pascal provide the basic method of doing this. We shall now learn some elementary ways of using these.

WRITE *and* WRITELN *statements*

These have the forms:

WRITE(*Item1, Item2, ..., ItemN*);
WRITELN(*Item1, Item2, ..., ItemN*);
WRITELN;

where the items can be of several types. We will make a start with the simplest types of items and introduce others at suitable stages.

When executed, the first statement prints the values of the items in the list one after another. The second form does the same except that, after completing the printing, the 'printing head' is moved to the next line. Any further printing that may follow now occurs on a fresh line. The third form, which has no list of items in brackets, simply prints a blank line. The actions of the three forms are illustrated below.

Outputting string constants

A **string**, in computer jargon, is a finite sequence of characters. A variable string contains varying characters, whereas a **string constant** contains a fixed sequence of characters. In Pascal a string constant is denoted by enclosing it in apostrophes, e.g.

```
'Greetings'   '25%'   '****'   '+'   ' '   'Mother''s Day'
```

If the apostrophe character itself occurs in the sequence then it is typed twice, as done in the last example.

A string constant can be printed using the **WRITE** and **WRITELN** statements. For example, the statements

```
WRITE('Greetings. ');
WRITELN('I am having fun learning Pascal.');
```

will result in the output:

```
Greetings. I am having fun learning Pascal.
```

If we now change the first statement from **WRITE** to **WRITELN**, the output will change to

```
Greetings.
I am having fun learning Pascal
```

If now a new **WRITELN** is inserted between the two, then the statements

```
WRITELN('Greetings. ');
WRITELN;
WRITE('I am having fun learning Pascal.');
```

will produce

```
Greetings.

I am having fun learning Pascal
```

Formatting string output

In the last section we exercised no control over the position of the printing. We may wish to produce output which has some aesthetically pleasing characteristics or is in tabular form with text aligned in columns. For example, suppose that we wish to print the word Greetings so that the letter G falls in column 12. Using what we have learnt so far we could achieve this by inserting eleven blanks before G, i.e. by writing:

```
WRITELN('           Greetings');
```

There is a less laborious method of doing this.

Any string constant listed in the argument of a **WRITE** or a **WRITELN** statement can have a **field width parameter** attached to it. A field width for an item is indicated by writing a colon followed by a positive integer value after the item. It specifies the number of columns across which the item is to be printed. Within the space reserved, the item is printed in a right justified manner. For example, the statement **WRITELN('Greetings':20)** will use twenty columns for output. The last character 's' will fall in column 20. 'G' will therefore fall in column 12 and there will be eleven blank spaces before it. The statement

```
WRITE('1987','1988':8,'1989':8);
```

will use the first four columns to print 1987, the next eight columns to print 1988, and will use another eight to output 1989, giving four blank spaces in between as

```
1987    1988    1989
```

What happens if the field width specified is smaller than the number of characters in the string? For example, WRITE('Greetings':3). The answer depends on the compiler. In ISO Pascal the field width of a string constant is taken to be **exact**. If its value is N then only the first N characters will be printed. Thus in our example only 'Gre' will be printed. In some other compilers, e.g. TURBO Pascal, the field width is taken to be a **minimum**. If the string is too long to fit then it will still be printed. It will be an interesting exercise for you to find out how your version of Pascal treats the problem.

Example 2B: printing an address. We will now produce a complete program using the knowledge of output acquired so far. The program will print an address followed by a date. The printing will be right justified in column 66.

```
PROGRAM LetterHead(OUTPUT);
{Prints a letter head in which the output is right justified}
CONST
        RightMargin = 66;
BEGIN
        WRITELN('Department of Computer Science':RightMargin);
        WRITELN('University of Bognor Regis':RightMargin);
        WRITELN('Bognor Regis':RightMargin);
        WRITELN('U.K. BG11 1AT':RightMargin);
        WRITELN;
        WRITELN('11 March 1989':RightMargin);
END.
```

The output will appear as:

```
Department of Computer Science
    University of Bognor Regis
                  Bognor Regis
                 U.K. BG11 1AT

                 11 March 1989
```

The reason why we did not type 66 explicitly in the **WRITELN** statements but instead defined the name constant **RightMargin** with this value has to do with clarity and modifiability. Firstly, the name makes clear what is intended. Also, suppose we decide tomorrow that we would prefer to justify our output in column 64 rather than 66. The program as written would need only one change to cater for that, whereas if we had typed 66 explicitly then we would have to make five changes. Not only does the other method require more work in modifications but it is also more prone to error. We might fail to notice all the places needing to be changed.

Advice on good programming

Good programming uses named constant identifiers rather than explicit values of constants in literal form.

Comment We saw in the above program that it is very easy to produce right justified text. To those of you who know BASIC and are familiar with the Tab function, it may come as a surprise to learn that Pascal offers no such facility. Here is an example of an irritating limitation in Pascal.

Outputting values of arithmetical expressions

The items in a **WRITE** or a **WRITELN** statement can be arithmetical expressions containing operators and numbers. For example, we can write

```
WRITELN(2 * 3 ,15 DIV 4, 3.2 + 5.4 );
```

The exact form in which the output will be produced will vary from compiler to compiler. Two samples are shown below.

```
6 3 8.60000E + 00

63 8.6000000000E + 00
```

Neither of them are very pretty and, what is more, in the second version (produced by TURBO Pascal), there is no space between the first and the second value printed. We see that the default form of the output is tedious and open to misinterpretation.

Formatting numerical output

We can improve the style of output by supplying field width parameters. In printing numbers, the first field width specifies exactly the same thing as it does in printing string constants, namely the number of columns which are to be used for writing the value in a right justified manner. Thus **WRITE(2 + 3:4);** will use four columns and will output three blank spaces followed by the character 5. However, in the case of numbers this field width is taken to be a minimum and no truncation takes place if the field width is insufficient. For example, **WRITE(100 * 5:2)** will still print the complete answer 500, despite the fact that only two spaces are designated for the answer.

A real number or an expression whose value reduces to a real number can be output in two different styles. If no field width is specified, or if only one is specified, the value is printed in the scientific notation. If a second field width is specified, then a fixed-point representation is used for the output. The value of the second field width determines the number of digits that are printed after the decimal point. Thus, **WRITE(3.2 + 5.4:7)** will output 8.6E + 00 and **WRITE(3.2 + 5.4:7:2)** will output three blank spaces followed by 8.60. The statement **WRITE(3.14159:6:4)** will output 3.1416.

The examples below are intended to illustrate how numerical output is produced and formatted. Assume that column one is at the extreme left.

The statements

```
WRITE('Answer = ');
WRITELN( -2.34 * 1.5/( 13 DIV 4 - 15 MOD 3 ):5:2);
```

will produce

```
Answer = -1.17
```

The statements

```
WRITELN(' ':10,'The average of the numbers');
WRITELN;
WRITELN(22.3:14:1,'and':4,15.4:5:1);
WRITELN;
WRITELN('is':12,(22.3 + 15.4)/2:6:1);
```

will print:

```
          The average of the numbers

          22.3 and 15.4

          is 18.8
```

left justifying the output in column 11.

The statements

```
X:= 47;
Y:= 199;
WRITELN(X:3,' + ',Y:4,' = ',X + Y:4);
```

will output:

```
 47 +  199 =  246
```

〉2.4 Supplying input to the computer

We will now learn how to provide the computer with input. The **READ** and **READLN** statements provide the basic mechanism for this purpose.

READ *and* READLN *statements*

The **READ** and **READLN** statements are used to input data items of type INTEGER, REAL or CHAR. In this chapter we shall learn about the input of numbers, i.e. data of type INTEGER and REAL. The CHAR type will be discussed in Chapter 4. These statements have the forms:

READ(*Item1,Item2,...,ItemN*);
READLN(*Item1,Item2,...,ItemN*);
READLN;

When any of these is executed, the program pauses to recieve input. No prompt is given. For the program to continue, the first two forms require that values of the variables in the list be typed in the order of the list. After all the data has been supplied, execution resumes when the RETURN or ENTER key is pressed.

In the third form, which has no attached list of variables, execution is resumed as soon as the RETURN key is pressed. The empty **READLN** is useful when reading data from files but is very often used to pause the program to examine some output before it disappears from the screen.

In supplying numerical data, the individual items must be separated by at least one space or a new line, *but not commas*, as in some other languages. Spaces and new lines are also ignored before the reading of numerical data.

The difference between the **READ** and **READLN** statements is that, after all the required data have been typed, the **READLN** statement ignores anything else that may be typed on the same line. Any subsequent reading of data is done from the start of the next line. The **READ** statement on the other hand, continues reading whatever comes next. In the interactive input of numerical data **READ** is not of great use. It is used mainly in reading data from disk files. The empty **READLN** can also be interpreted as an instruction simply to ignore everything on the current line of input.

Example 2C: printing INTEGERs and REALs

```
PROGRAM TryInput(INPUT,OUTPUT);
{ Reads two integers and two reals. Prints their sums and
  products respectively }

VAR
    I,J: INTEGER;
    X,Y: REAL;

BEGIN
        WRITELN('Press Enter or Return key to start');
        READLN;
        WRITELN;
        WRITE('Enter two Integers ');
        READLN(I,J);
        WRITELN;
        WRITE('Enter two Reals ');
        READLN(X,Y)
        WRITELN;
        WRITE('I+J= ', I+J , ' X*Y= ', X*Y);
END.
```

Suppose that when the program above is executed, we want to give the values 2 and 3 to the integers I and J respectively. We could type our data as

```
        2 3
or      2    3
or      2
        3   The cow Jumped over the moon.
```

Remember what we said about empty spaces, new lines and any remaining junk being ignored. The first method which supplies only one separating blank space is the one that is normally used. Exactly the same applies regarding the spacing of real data, except that they can be written in the scientific notation. Also a real number with no fractional part may be supplied in integer form. For example, suppose that we want **X** to be

4.0 and **Y** to be 0.0005 in the above. We could type the data in as

```
   4.0  0.0005
or 4    5E-4
```

Quickies

1. Mark each of the following as true or false.

   (a) There is no number greater than **MAXINT** in Pascal.
   (b) The writing of two successive semicolons is invalid in Pascal.
   (c) Keywords can be redefined by the programmer by declaring them in a **VAR** declaration.
   (d) An identifier can contain a **$** sign.
   (e) A semicolon is optional before an **END**.
   (f) Keywords and predefined identifiers must be written in capital letters.
   (g) There are some names that cannot be used as identifiers.
   (h) Any feature in ISO Pascal is also present in any other dialect of Pascal.
   (i) A STRING is a standard scalar type in Pascal.
   (j) In reading REALs and INTEGERs we can separate data with as many spaces as we choose.
   (k) We can assign an INTEGER value to a variable of type REAL.
   (l) We may assign a real value to a variable of type INTEGER.

2. Let **Salary** = 350, **Address** = 1, **John** = 73.4 and **Name** = 'John'. Describe the effect of the following statements:

```
WRITELN(Address,John,Name);
WRITE(Address); WRITELN; WRITE(Name);
WRITE(John:7:3,Salary,Address:3);
WRITE(Salary); WRITELN(Address:5);
WRITE(John,' earns ',Salary:4); WRITELN(' Monthly');
```

3. Describe the output produced by the following program:

```
PROGRAM Formats(OUTPUT);
VAR
    I: INTEGER;
    J: REAL;
```

```
BEGIN
        I := 5;
        J := 3.14;
        WRITELN(I:0,I:6,' ',I:2);
        WRITELN('J = ',J:I:1);
END.
```

4. Why will the following statements produce the same output?

```
WRITE(100 + 44:1);
WRITE(100 + 44:2);
WRITE(100 + 44:3);
```

   Will the same output be produced if we write

```
WRITELN(100 + 44:4);     ?
```

5. How can the MOD operator be used to check if an integer *n* divides an integer *m* exactly?

6. What is the difference between / and DIV?

⇒ **You may now proceed to Pascal laboratory Activities 1–2.**

〉2.5 Doing repetitions

A major requirement in any computer language is the facility to perform loops, i.e. to repeat a sequence of operations a number of times. Pascal offers four different ways of doing repetitions. We shall now introduce the simplest version.

FOR *statement*
A FOR statement is used to perform a **counted loop**, i.e. a loop with a fixed number of repetitions. This fixed number is not necessarily a constant but is calculated at the start of the repetitions. The statement has two forms:

FOR *LoopCounter* := *InitialValue* TO *FinalValue* DO *action*;
FOR *LoopCounter* := *InitialValue* DOWNTO *FinalValue* DO *action*;

Here *LoopCounter* is a variable of **ordinal type**. Amongst others, INTEGERs are of ordinal type (but REALs are not) and in this chapter we shall take *LoopCounter* to be an INTEGER variable. *InitialValue* and *FinalValue* are in general expressions which must produce a value of the same type as that of *LoopCounter*.

When the **FOR** statement is executed the values of *InitialValue* and *Finalvalue* are calculated first. *LoopCounter* is first assigned the value of *InitialValue*. In the **TO** form, if the value of *LoopCounter* is found to be not greater than *FinalValue*, the loop action is performed. Following the action the value of *LoopCounter* is incremented by 1. The testing, the action and the incrementing are repeated until the value of *LoopCounter* becomes greater than the value of *FinalValue*. The control then passes to the next statement following the semicolon.

The interpretation of the **DOWNTO** form should now be obvious. In this case the loop action is only performed if the value of *LoopCounter* is found to be not less than the value of *FinalValue*. The value of *LoopCounter* is decremented by 1 at each iteration.

Comments *InitialValue* and *FinalValue* should not be altered by the loop action although any alterations would not affect the number of times the loop is executed. The values used for the loop are calculated at the start of the execution. Also, although *LoopCounter* is a variable, standard ISO Pascal does not allow the action of the statements in the loop to alter its value.

TURBO Pascal does allow *LoopCounter* to be altered. This is dangerous as it radically alters the logic of the program.

The value of *LoopCounter* becomes undefined on completion of the loop if the loop terminates normally, i.e. without a jump using a **GOTO** statement (see Chapter 4). Therefore the variable *LoopCounter* must be assigned a new value before being used elsewhere. If a jump is made using a **GOTO** then *LoopCounter* retains its value which may be utilised.

Examples 2D: FOR *loops*

(*a*)

```
FOR I := 1 TO 3 DO
WRITELN('Greetings');
```

will write Greetings three times on three lines and the result will be the same if we replace the first line with:

```
        FOR I := 0 TO 2 DO
or      FOR I := -999 to -997 DO
or      FOR I := 25 DOWNTO 23 DO
```

(*b*)

```
FOR Count := 1 TO 10 DO WRITE(Count);
```

will write the numbers

1 2 3 4 5 6 7 8 9 10

Comment The exact spacing of the numbers will depend on the compiler. For example, TURBO Pascal will leave no spaces and will write 12345678910. We can ensure proper spacing by supplying field width parameters as shown in the next example.

(*c*)

```
FOR Count := 10 DOWNTO 1 DO WRITE(Count:2);
```

will write

10 9 8 7 6 5 4 3 2 1

(*d*)

```
FOR Count := 10 DOWNTO 20 DO WRITE(Count);
```

will not get executed at all.

(*e*)

```
A := 2;
B := 3;
C := 10;
FOR Index := A * B DOWNTO C DIV B DO WRITE(Index);
```

will output the numbers 6 5 4 3. If A had been assigned the value 1 the loop would get executed only once; a value less than 1 would produce nothing.

Compound statements: BEGIN *and* END

In Examples 2D, the loops involved the repeated execution of only a single statement. We would very often wish to repeat a whole set of actions rather than just one. This is easily done using the keywords **BEGIN** and **END**. These words act exactly like brackets to group together a sequence of statements into one **compound statement**. For example, if we write:

```
FOR I := 1 to 10 DO
    BEGIN
        WRITE(I);
        WRITELN;
    END;
```

then the loop action will now include the two statements between **BEGIN** and **END**. Similarly, whenever we want to execute a whole set of statements in any other type of action we enclose them with the words **BEGIN** and **END**. The example program given below shows a typical use of a compound statement.

Example 2E: summing a series

```
PROGRAM Sum(OUTPUT);
{ Calculates the sum of 20 terms of the alternating series
        1 - 1/2 + 1/3 - 1/4 + ··· - 1/20. }

CONST Nlast = 20;
VAR
     I,Sign      : INTEGER;
     Sum,Term: REAL;

BEGIN
        SUM := 0.0;
        Sign := 1;
        FOR I := 1 to Nlast DO
             BEGIN
                    TERM := Sign/I;
                    SUM := Sum + Term;
                    Sign := -Sign;
             END;
        WRITELN('Sum =  ',Sum:6:3);
END.
```

Nested **FOR** loops

One often needs to include one **FOR** statement inside the body of another. Loops containing loops are referred to as **nested loops**. For example, the sequence of numbers

```
1 2 2 3 3 3 4 4 4 4 5 5 5 5 5
```

is produced by the statements

```
FOR Number := 1 TO 5 DO
     FOR Times := 1 TO Number DO WRITE(Number:2);
```

The pattern below

```
*
**
***
****
*****
```

will be produced by

```
FOR row := 1 to 5 DO
    BEGIN
        FOR column := 1 to row DO WRITE('*');
        WRITELN;
    END;
```

〉 2.6 Making choices

Apart from repetitions, another major requirement in a computer language has to do with being able to make choices from a set of options. Pascal offers two ways of doing this. Here we introduce the **IF** statement.

IF *statement*

The **IF** statement takes two forms:

> IF *Condition* THEN *action*;
> IF *Condition* THEN *action1* ELSE *action2*;

The first form allows for a binary choice: to do or not to do something. The second one allows for multiple choices. The interpretation is quite straightforward. The condition is evaluated and if found to be TRUE then the action following **THEN** is executed. If it is found to be FALSE then, in the first form, control passes to whatever is the next statement. In the second form, *action2* is performed before the control passes to the next statement.

In general, the condition in the **IF** statement is a **BOOLEAN expression**. These will be discussed later. In this chapter we will restrict ourselves to the condition being an expression involving arithmetical operators and one of the following **relational operators**:

<	Less than
>	Greater than
>=	Greater than or Equal to
<=	Less than or Equal to
=	Equal to
<>	Not Equal to

Example 2F: IF-THEN-ELSE

(*a*)
```
IF X<0 THEN WRITELN('X is Negative');
```

(*b*)
```
IF X<Y THEN
   BEGIN
         Temp := X;
         X := Y;
         Y := Temp;
   END;
```

(*c*)
```
IF Weight <= 10.0 THEN
   Postage := Weight * 0.75
ELSE
   Postage := Weight * 0.5;
```

(*d*)
```
IF (Number MOD 2) = 0 THEN WRITELN('Number is Even')
                      ELSE WRITELN('Number is Odd');
```

Note that there is no semicolon either preceding or following **ELSE**.

Nested IF *statements*

The statement following the **THEN** or the **ELSE** clause may be another **IF** statement. For example,

```
IF HoursWorked < 100 THEN
   IF HoursWorked > 50 THEN
      PayRate := 1.5 * StandardRate
   ELSE PayRate := StandardRate;
```

In this example the **ELSE** clause goes with the last **THEN**. In general, **ELSE** goes with the closest preceding **IF** which has no **ELSE** attached to it.

In more complicated cases the **THEN IF** construction can lead to a whole lot of 'dangling **ELSE**' as, for instance,

```
IF Condition1 THEN
   IF Condition2 THEN
      IF Condition3 THEN
         Action4
      ELSE Action3
   ELSE Action2
ELSE Action1;
```

A diagram such as the one shown below can be useful in deciphering the logic of the construction.

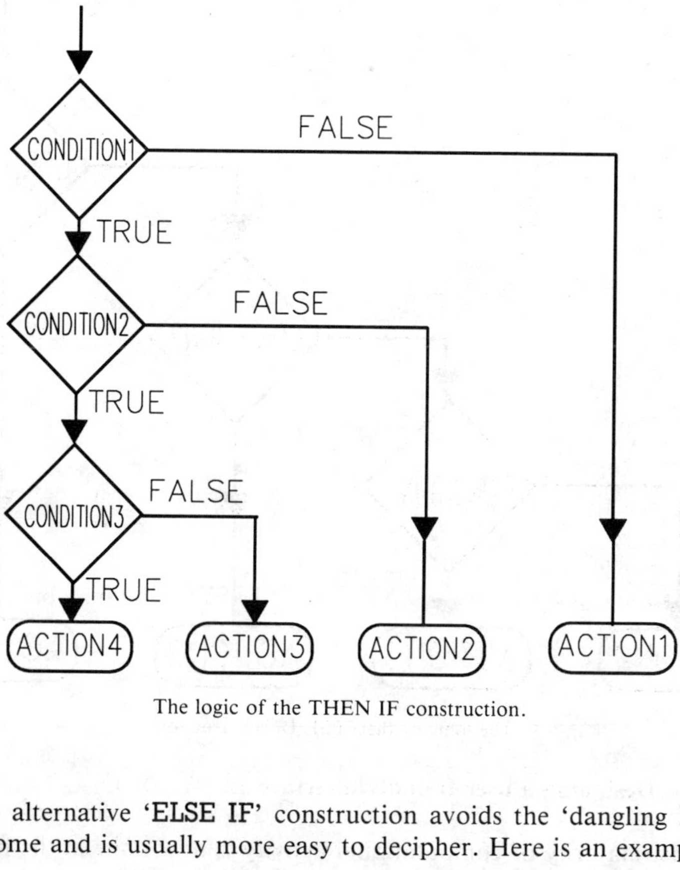

The logic of the THEN IF construction.

The alternative '**ELSE IF**' construction avoids the 'dangling **ELSE**' syndrome and is usually more easy to decipher. Here is an example:

```
If y < 0 THEN WRITELN('Y is Negative')
ELSE IF y = 0 THEN WRITELN('Can''t Divide by Zero')
ELSE WRITELN(1/y);
```

Again, in trying to understand the logic of such a construction a diagram can be useful. The logic of the statements below is displayed in the diagram that follows

If *Condition1* THEN *Action1*
ELSE IF *Condition2* THEN *Action2*
ELSE IF *Condition3* THEN *Action3*
ELSE *Action4*;

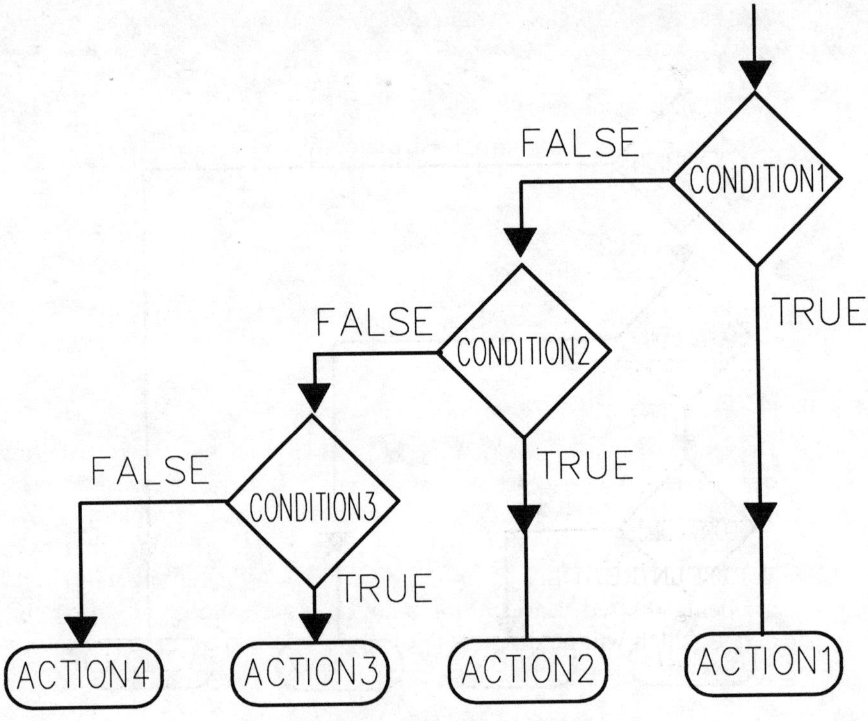

The logic of the ELSE IF construction.

〉2.7 Designing a user-friendly interface

The vast majority of computational activity is now done in the interactive mode with the user sitting in front of a screen and entering data via a keyboard. A mouse or some other interaction device is also frequently available. Knowing how to write good interactive programs is therefore of great value. This is the concern of user-interface design and is a major topic of research in computer science. Although at this stage we cannot discuss the topic in any depth, it is nevertheless important that you should begin to give thought to it at the earliest opportunity. We will make a start by offering some elementary guidelines.

1. The dialogue should be friendly but not verbose or chatty.

   Unless you are writing a one-off program for novices avoid constructions such as:

```
WRITE('Now, will you please type two numbers separated by',
      ' one or more spaces...');
READLN(X,Y);
WRITELN('Thank you, that is marvellous!');
```

For the majority of computer users this would be tiresome and boring.

2. The dialogue should be precise and attractive.

   For example, we might use:

   ```
   WRITE('Type an integer in the range 0..360 '); READLN(X);
   ```

   rather than simply:

   ```
   WRITELN('X'); READLN(X);
   ```

   Putting information about the type of a variable and any restrictions on the range of values in the prompt improves precision. The **WRITE/READLN** combination displays the prompt and the data on the same line and gives a neater layout than the **WRITELN/READLN** combination when only a few items of data are being entered. Large amounts of data are usually only read into arrays which will be discussed in Chapter 5. When this is the case, a count should be displayed for each item and the completion of data entry should be announced. For example, in entering five integers, the dialogue might take the form:

   Type 5 integers:

   1: *32*   2: *17*   3: *24*   4: *−32*   5: *147*

   That completes the data.

3. The quantity of output produced should be controlled and the user given sufficient time to absorb the contents before they disappear from the top.

4. The dialogue should keep the user informed.

   A program of reasonable size should start by introducing itself. At no time during the executions should the user be left wondering as to what is going on. Computational activities that leave the user unoccupied should be announced. For example:

   ```
   *** PROGRAM SortNumbers : Version 1.2 ***
       *** Now reading data from file ***
      *** Sort successfully completed ***
   ```

The dialogue should use special means such as blinking characters, beep sounds and colour to attract attention when necessary, for example when printing an error message. If there are any options available, e.g. in a program which requires some special input from the user to bring it to an end, then clear information should be provided. For instance:

```
Type
  0     for help information
  1     to repeat
  2     to quit
```

5. The dialogue should anticipate problems.

   It is unreasonable to assume that a human user will always type exactly what is expected. All data that is input should ideally be validated for correctness. We will return to this topic in Chapter 4.

〉2.8 A problem

We shall close this chapter by tackling a problem. The object will be to illustrate the steps involved in problem definition and in the preparation of an outline solution. More steps involved in problem solving will be discussed at the end of the next chapter.

PROBLEM. Write a computer program to produce a pattern of the type displayed below.

Before you look at our solution, you are invited to work out your own strategy for solving the problem.

Defining the problem
In this problem, it is clear that the output involves only the character *. We only need to decide what type of data will be necessary to specify such a pattern. Let us think how we might produce it by hand. We might draw two sets of equally spaced parallel lines, one set horizontal and another one sloping. We could then place the stars at the intersection points of the two sets. The pattern will be fixed if we were to provide the following information.

How wide it should be?
How long it should be?
What should be the gap between the horizontal lines?
What should be the gap between the sloping lines?

This leads us to think that four pieces of data would be required to define the task.

Now, whereas the above method is very easy to implement by hand, it is not so easy to program on a computer. Let us see if we can work out a smarter strategy.

If we look at the pattern, we notice that each horizontal line is repeated at every fourth output. This allow us to think of the pattern in terms of groups of four adjacent lines. Also, every line in a group is produced merely by shifting the previous line by a constant distance so that the number of stars in each line is a constant.

Producing an outline solution
Bearing the above in mind, we can now produce an outline solution:

Set the number of lines of output.
Set the number of stars per line.
Set the gap between stars.
For each line of output do the following:
    Produce the right offset.
    Print the row of stars.

Before implementing the above in a program, we will make one important observation. Whenever there is a structure that repeats itself we should consider whether the **MOD** function would prove useful. Several illustrations of this are given in the activities contained in the

Pascal laboratory. In the program given below the **MOD** function is utilised to work out the offset of each line.

```
PROGRAM STARS(INPUT,OUTPUT);
{ This program prints sloping parallel lines of stars.
  By varying the parameters StarsPerLine and Gap, a series of
  interesting patterns can be produced. Try, for example
                              StarsPerLine    Gap
                                   1          10
                                   2          10
                                  12           5          }

CONST
        NumLines = 30;

VAR
      Line,StarsPerLine,column,Gap: INTEGER;

BEGIN
       WRITE('Stars per Line: ');
       READLN(StarsPerLine);
       WRITE('Gap: ');
       READLN(Gap);
       FOR line := 0 TO NumLines DO
            BEGIN
                 WRITE(' ':1 + (line MOD gap));
                 For column := 1 TO StarsPerLine DO WRITE('*':gap);
                 WRITELN;
            END;
END.
```

Quickies

7. What would the following produce?

```
FOR I := 1 TO 4 DO
    FOR J := I DOWNTO 1 DO
        WRITE(I * J);
```

8. Why is the following incorrect?

```
IF Number := 1 THEN X := X + 1;
               ELSE X := X - 1;
```

9. Find the mistakes in the following:

```
FOR index := 1 TO 100 DO;
    READLN(Term);
    SUM := SUM + Term;
```

10. Which of the following are valid in Pascal? Give reasons for finding any of them invalid.

(a)
```
VAR L1,L2,Second : REAL;
            First : INTEGER;
                X : REAL;
```

(b)
```
FOR J := 0 DOWNTO -1 DO
    BEGIN
        J := J - 1
    END;
```

(c) `VAR i,j,k = INTEGER;`

(d) `CONST PositiveInteger = -2.5;`

(e) `CONST Name: 'C3PO';`

(f) `x2 + 1 := 1;`

(g) `READLN(X:10:3);`

(h) `WRITE('Life's uncertainties');`

(i) `WRITE;`

(j)
```
WRITELN('Any programmer who fails to comply
    with the standard naming, formatting
    or commenting conventions ought to be shot')
```

(k) `Answer := (N/M) MOD 5;`

(l) `Root := SQRT(-(X*X + 20));`

(m) `Area := Pi*R**2`

⇒ **You may now proceed to Pascal laboratory Activities 5–12.**

〉 Pascal laboratory

Activity 1. Run TUTOR01. What does it do?. Change the first **WRITELN** statement to **WRITE** and run the program. Explain. Change it to write two sentences on different lines. Change it to write two sentences separated by an empty line. Change it to print the value of **MAXINT**.

Activity 2. Run TUTOR02. What does it do?. Change it to write also the perimeter of the given rectangle. Change the word **Height** to **Height:7:3** in the **WRITELN** statement and run the program. Explain. Change the area to be displayed to two decimal places.

Activity 3. Run TUTOR03. What does it do?. Change it to ask for the product **17 * 4** instead. Change it to ask for both the sum and the product of 17 and 4 and print the answers.

Activity 4. Run TUTOR04. Use it to find the greatest power of 10 available on your machine. What happens if the variable **Power** is declared as an INTEGER. Interpret.

Activity 5. Run TUTOR05. Improve the format of its output. Change it to write the odd numbers from 1 to 11. Change it to provide a table (with headings) of the squares and square roots (rounded to 4 decimal places) of the integers from 1 to 20 as follows:

INTEGER	SQUARE	SQUARE ROOT
1	1	1
2	4	1.4142
3	9	1.7320
.	.	.

Activity 6. The method to obtain a printout of your program and results will depend on the operating system. Find out how this is done at your installation and test it on the program you developed in Activity 5.

Activity 7. Run TUTOR06. Modify it to let i run from 0 to 5.8 and run again. What happens? Explain. Change it to generate the original sequence in decreasing order. Change the argument of the **WRITE** statement to i **MOD 5** and run the program. Explain the pattern obtained if instead of computing i **MOD 5** we compute i **MOD 2**, i **MOD 7** or i **MOD (−5)**.

Activity 8. Run TUTOR07. Modify it to display the addition table for integers from −3 to 4 in the form

```
      -3  -2  ..
 -3   -6  -5  ..
 -2   -5  -4  ..
  .    .   .
  .    .   .
```

Activity 9. Run TUTOR08. What does it do? Modify it to compute the sum

$$a + (a + 1) + (a + 2) + \cdots + (a + n)$$

where a is a real number and given another real number b ($b > a$), n satisfies

$$a + n < b < a + (n + 1).$$

Modify it to compute the factorial of a given number.

Activity 10. Run TUTOR09 for several values of the parameter step. Modify the program to tabulate the values of **SIN(X)** in the range 0 to $\pi/2$ in steps of $\pi/10$.

Activity 11. Run TUTOR10 and explain its function. By modifying it, test if 6679 and 5757 are prime numbers.

Activity 12. Run TUTOR11 and study how it works. The same result can be achieved using only two **FOR** statements and a single **IF**. Modify the program to achieve this before looking at the solution in program SOL11.PAS.

〉 Exercises

1. Evaluate the expression

   ```
   -5*(781 MOD 3)+4*(1.6+2.9/2)-((19 DIV 5) MOD 2)
   ```

2. What computer output might be expected when the following program is run?

   ```
   PROGRAM Calculation(OUTPUT);
   BEGIN
           WRITELN(123 + 4/5/6 * 7);
   END.
   ```

Insert parentheses in the **WRITELN** statement in a way that does not change the value printed, but makes it easier to understand.

3*. Mark each of the following as true or false.

(a) I = J * (I DIV J) + (I MOD J) for any two integers I and J.
(b) The statement

```
IF 1234 * 5678 > 10 THEN
  WRITELN('Obviously')
ELSE
  WRITELN('Oops!');
```

may produce the output

```
Oops!
```

4. Criticize and improve the following syntactically correct statements.

(a)
```
IF TestFlag = 1 THEN ELSE WRITELN('End of program');
```

(b)
```
N := 10; M := 5; Sum := 0;
For J := N DOWNTO M DO Sum := Sum + 1;
```

(c)
```
Y := 1; Z := 1;
FOR I := - 10 TO 10 DO
    BEGIN
        X := Y;
        Y := Z;
        Z :=X + Y;
    END;
```

5*. What do each of the following segments of code accomplish?. Variables A, B, D, S, I are INTEGER, R1 and R2 are REAL.

(a)
```
S := A + B;
IF B > A THEN D := B - A ELSE D := A - B;
FOR i := (S - D) DIV 2 to (S + D) DIV 2 DO WRITE(i:3);
```

(b)
```
READLN(R1,R2);
R1 := R1 + R2;
R2 := R1 - R2
R1 := R1 - R2;
WRITELN(R1,R2);
```

6. Draw diagrams to clarify the relationships between the conditions and the actions in the following:

   (a)
   ```
   IF Age>40 THEN WRITE('Sorry GranDad') ELSE
   IF Age < 30 THEN IF Income > 1E4 THEN WRITE('You,
   Yuppi')
   ELSE WRITE('You don''t count!');
   ```

   (b)
   ```
   IF Mark > 7 THEN BEGIN
     IF Mark <> 10 THEN WRITELN('Very good')
   ELSE WRITELN('Excellent')
   END
   ELSE WRITELN('Not good enough');
   ```

7. List good programming practices with regard to the following:

   Choosing identifiers
   Writing comments
   Indentation

   Rewrite the following program using good layout, indentation and comments. This program is included in the disk as program UGLY1.PAS.

```
                proGraM
                uglY1(
                                    OutPut); var one:            REAL;
                                                               I: intEGer
        ;two:                                                   real; Begin
                              onE : =3.1416;
                            ;tWo : =8.7

                                         ;writeLn(one,' plus',
        two,'                   is Equal To       ',
        one+Two); { then we make a loop }
                                    fOr
                                    i:
                                    =1
                                    to 10 DO
        wrIteLn(i:          i{pyramid of numbers}
    )enD. { end of program UGly1 }
```

8. Alter the program below using meaningful identifiers, sensible comments and improved indentation. This program is included in the disk as program UGLY2.PAS.

```
PROGRAM AnExampleOfDifferentVariableTypes(OUTPUT);
{ The variables in this program are: }
VAR     Z48: INTEGER; ALFA,X,H3: REAL; PUPPY: INTEGER;

BEGIN { Our program begins here }
          H3 := 5; Z48 := 3;
          ALFA := 3.141592; { VALUE of PI }
          X := 8.3; { radius of the circle whose area we want to
          compute }

          IF x>1 THEN puppy := 1 ELSE puppy := 0;
          { puppy is 1 if x is greater than one }
          h3 := (alfa*x)*x;
          WRITELN('AREA OF THE CIRCLE=',H3);
          WRITELN('END OF PROGRAM');
END.
```

9*. Write a program to raise real numbers to positive integral powers.

10. Write a program that will read a three-digit integer, add the number 11 to this integer, and print out the result (possibly a four-digit integer) with one asterisk between each digit. For example, for 519 the program should produce 5*3*0 and for 992 the program should produce 1*0*0*3.

11. Write a program to find the sum of the first M positive integers

$$s = 1 + 2 + 3 + \cdots + (M - 1) + M$$

for different values of M and compare the result with the closed-form expression

$$S = M(M + 1)/2$$

12. Write a program that sums the geometric series

$$S = 1 + a + a^2 + a^3 + \cdots + a^M$$

for different values of a and M and compare the result with the closed-form expression

$$S = \frac{1 - a^{M+1}}{1 - a}.$$

13. Write a program that sums the series for $\exp(x)$ for a given value

of x:

$$\exp(x) = \frac{1}{0!} + \frac{x}{1!} + \frac{x^2}{2!} + \frac{x^3}{3!} + \cdots$$

within the accuracy of your computer and compare the value obtained by using the Pascal function **EXP(x)**. Write the running values of the sum and the increment to the sum for each term.

14. Modify program TUTOR10 to display all the divisors of a given positive integer. Alter your program again to generate the first 50 integers having only two prime divisors.

15*. Find all integer solutions to the equation $5x + 3y - 4z = 11$ for values of x, y and z in the range 0 to 10 and such that $x \leqslant y \leqslant z$.

16. In her autobiography, Queen Rhiannon tells of an occasion during her childhood when she decided to write down all the integer numbers from one to one million. It was a noble undertaking, but her arm gave out after she had written only 47 876 digits. Write a program a find out what was the last digit she wrote before her arm grew numb.

Answers to quickies

1. (a) F, (b) F, (c) F, (d) F, (e) T, (f) F, (g) T, (h) F, (i) F, (j) T, (k) T, (l) F.
2.
```
1  73.4  John
1
John  73.400  350  1  350  1
73.4 earns 350 Monthly
```
3.
```
5     5 5
J= 3.1
```
4. In the case of numbers, the field width is taken to be a minimum and no truncation takes place if the field width is insufficient. The last statement will produce a blank before writing 144.
5. m MOD n = 0.
6. **DIV** is integer division.
7. 1 2 1 3 2 1 4 3 2 1 (the actual spacing will be compiler dependent).
8. No colon after **Number** and no semicolon at the end of the first line.

9. No semicolon after **DO** and the following two statements should be enclosed with a **BEGIN** and **END**.

10. (a) Valid.
    (b) Invalid. J must not be changed in the loop
    (c) Invalid. : instead of =
    (d) Valid.
    (e) Invalid. = instead of :
    (f) Invalid. No operations on the left-hand side of the assignment operator.
    (g) Invalid. No formatting allowed in reading.
    (h) Invalid. **Life's** should be written with a double apostrophe, i.e. **Life''s**.
    (i) Invalid.
    (j) Invalid, cannot spread character strings over several lines. The intended effect could be achieved by writing

```
WRITELN('Any programmer who fails to comply ',
                'with the standard naming, formatting ',
                'or commenting conventions ought to be shot');
```

    or by using separate **WRITE**s or **WRITELN**s.
    (k) Invalid, **N/M** is always REAL and **MOD** operates on INTEGERs only.
    (l) This is syntactically correct but it will produce a run-time error since it will always attempt to extract the square root of a negative number.
    (m) Invalid.

〉 Chapter 3

〉 A First Look at FUNCTIONs and PROCEDUREs

Pascal was designed to teach programmers how to write elegant, clear, concise and error-free programs. The main tool for achieving these purposes is the structuring of a program into modules or subprograms — called **FUNCTION**s and **PROCEDURE**s. The purpose of this chapter is to introduce you to these building blocks of a good Pascal program.

〉 3.1 The importance of modularisation

A principle of great importance which must be grasped and put into practice by a novice programmer is that *complex tasks are accomplished by breaking them down into a number of fairly independent sub-tasks or modules.* This principle applies not only to programming tasks but to tasks in all spheres of human activity.

Consider, for example, the task of flying air travellers. The whole task is divided into sub-tasks for pilots, air traffic controllers, engineers, stewards and hostesses, caterers, refuelling crews, baggage handlers, customs and immigration staff, travel agents and a host of others. Only in this way can the complexity be handled. Each of these tasks has its sphere of independence but interacts with others in varying degrees to meet the needs of the whole.

Non-trivial programming tasks demand to be tackled in exactly the same way. They require the identification and isolation of individual tasks into separate modules and can have more or less an independent identity. In Pascal, **PROCEDURE**s and **FUNCTION**s provide the mechanism for accomplishing this.

PROCEDUREs and **FUNCTION**s offer the following advantages:

Ability to handle complex tasks
Clarity
Compactness
Improved productivity
Modifiability
Reliability.

A complex task becomes more manageable when it is divided up into smaller subtasks, each of which can be coded as a **FUNCTION** or a **PROCEDURE**. The names of these modules can be chosen to reflect their purposes leading to clarity. For example, a program that draws an airplane might have the following structure:

```
PROGRAM Airplane(INPUT,OUTPUT);
        .
        .
PROCEDURE DrawWings;
        .
        .
PROCEDURE DrawBody;
        .
        .
PROCEDURE DrawTail;
        .
        .
PROCEDURE DrawWheels;
        .
        .
{ Main Program }
BEGIN
        DrawWings;
        DrawBody;
        DrawTail;
        DrawWheels;
END.
```

PROCEDUREs and **FUNCTION**s, which together are referred to as modules, reduce the size of code thereby offering compactness. The parts that are repeated need only be written and tested once, which improves productivity. Self-contained modules can be developed and tested separately and possibly simultaneously by different programmers. This leads to easily modifiable and more reliable programs.

Advice on good programming

Always organise your program to break down the main task into subtasks which should be coded into separate modules. Ideally, your main program should comprise only a set of calls to these subprograms.

〉 3.2 Structure of a Pascal module

All modules in Pascal, including the main program which can be thought of as the largest module, have a similar structure. They all comprise a **heading** and a body called the **block** as we saw in the case of the main program in the last chapter.

The exact form of the heading depends on the type of the module but the block always comprises a Definitions and Declarations section and an Executable section as we explained in the last chapter and summarised again in the diagram below.

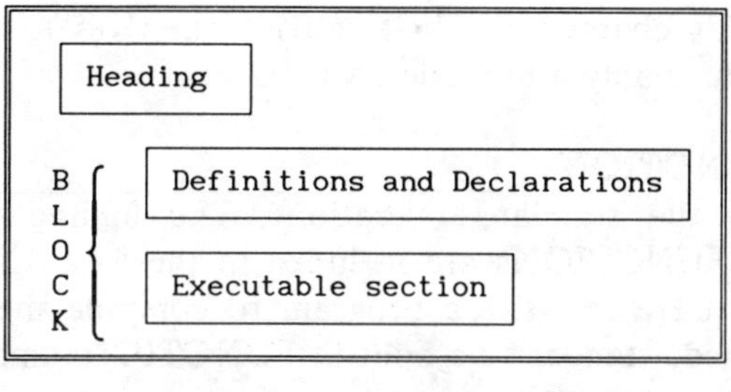

The general structure of a Pascal module.

In the last chapter we only introduced the **CONST** and the **VAR** declarations that may appear in the Definitions and Declarations section. The Definitions and Declarations section can contain up to five subsections show in the diagram below. The first four in the list must appear in that order zero or one times, but there is no restriction on the number of **FUNCTION** and **PROCEDURE** declarations. Also, the declarations of **FUNCTION**s and **PROCEDURE**s can occur in any order after the **VAR** declaration except that if a module A calls a module B than module B must be declared before module A (this latter restriction can be removed by the **FORWARD** declaration which will be discussed in Chapter 8).

```
LABEL declaration.
CONST definitions.
TYPE definitions.
VAR  declarations.
FUNCTION and PROCEDURE declarations.
```

The structure of the Definitions and Declarations section.

〉3.3 FUNCTIONs

In mathematics a function is a rule for producing one and only one value, given the values of one or more variables. For example, the expression x^3 defines a function. Given $x = 2$, it produces 8. Given $x = -1$, it produces -1 and so on.

In Pascal a **FUNCTION** is a subprogram for doing exactly the same thing, i.e. for producing a single value when supplied with the values of one or more variables. The type of values, however, that can be produced by **FUNCTION**s in Pascal is not confined to numbers, although in this chapter we shall restrict ourselves to **FUNCTION**s which do produce only a numerical value.

Predefined FUNCTION*s*

For many of the standard operations, like finding square roots, the necessary **FUNCTION**s are included in the Pascal language. The user does not have to write a program to compute them. These are called **predefined**, **standard** or **built-in** **FUNCTION**s and are listed in Appendix 2.

Typically, to compute the square root of 13.7 and assign the result to the variable **x**, we need only write:

```
x:= SQRT(13.7);
```

The value 13.7 is called the **argument** or the **actual parameter** of the **FUNCTION**. Note that some of the standard **FUNCTION**s can take a REAL as well as an INTEGER argument (Appendix 2), but the result produced is not necessarily of the same type. For example, **ABS(x)** can take an INTEGER or REAL argument and the result produced is of the same type as the argument, e.g. **ABS(2) = 2** and **ABS(−5.8) = 5.8**. On the other hand, **SQRT(x)** also takes INTEGER or REAL arguments but the result produced is always REAL, e.g. **SQRT(4) = 2.0**.

Here are two further examples of statements involving **FUNCTION**s:

```
S:= SIN(3.14159*Angle/180);
```

(The argument of a trigonometric function is assumed to be given in radians. Here, if **Angle** is given in degrees, then it will be converted into radians.)

```
WRITELN('Hypotenuse = ', SQRT( SQR(Side1) + SQR(Side2)));
```

The above line is meant to emphasize that the the argument does not have to be a literal like 13.7; it can be an arithmetical expression which may itself involve functions.

Recall that Pascal does not supply an operator for raising to a power. However, it does supply the exponential function **EXP** and the logarithmic function **LN** (Appendix 2) and these can be used to raise a positive real value to a real power using

$$a^x = EXP(x*LN(a))$$

TRUNC*ating and* ROUND*ing*

One sometimes needs to convert a real number into an integer, for example, to be able to use a **FUNCTION** which takes an integer argument. Pascal supplies two standard **FUNCTION**s to convert a REAL value to an INTEGER. The **FUNCTION TRUNC** chops off the digits to the right of the decimal point to produce an integer. The **FUNCTION ROUND**, as the name suggests, rounds a real value to the closest integer. Both of these **FUNCTION**s take a REAL argument and produce an INTEGER result.

Examples:

```
TRUNC(9.52) = 9          ROUND(9.52) = 10
TRUNC(-2.75) = -2        ROUND(-2.75) = -3
TRUNC(-0.87) = 0         ROUND(-0.87) = -1.
```

User-defined FUNCTION*s*

If the list of standard **FUNCTION**s does not include the **FUNCTION** that one needs for a calculation then one has to write it. A user-defined **FUNCTION**, unlike a predefined **FUNCTION**, must be declared in a declaration section before it can be used. The declaration has the following form

FUNCTION *FunctionName(List of formal parameters and their type): Function Type;*
Local Definitions and Declarations;
BEGIN
Executable statements with at least one assignment in which FunctionName appears on the left
END;

The **FUNCTION** is invoked by writing its name and supplying the actual parameters (or expressions from which the values of the actual parameters are to be calculated).

The meanings of the terms used to describe the above structure will be discussed in detail after we have looked at the two examples that follow.

Example 3A: an INTEGER **FUNCTION**. This example is intended to show how a **FUNCTION** may be used in a complete program. The program **PrintCubes** uses the **FUNCTION XCube** to print a table of cubes from 1 to NMax:

```
PROGRAM PrintCubes(OUTPUT);
CONST NMax = 10;
VAR I:INTEGER;

FUNCTION XCube(X: INTEGER): INTEGER;
{Computes the cube of X}
BEGIN
        XCube := X*X*X;
END;{XCube}

{ ------- Main Program ------- }
BEGIN
        WRITELN('TABLE OF CUBES');
        WRITELN;
        FOR I := 1 TO NMax DO WRITELN(I:8,XCube(I):5);
END.
```

Example 3B: a REAL **FUNCTION**. Here is another example of a user-defined **FUNCTION**:

```
FUNCTION Answer(X,Y:REAL; N:INTEGER):REAL;
{  Finds the answer to the sum of two real numbers X and Y
   divided by an integer N. If N = 0 then the answer is set
   to MAXINT.   }
VAR
   Sum: INTEGER;
```

```
BEGIN
        Sum := X + Y;
        IF N = 0 THEN Answer := MAXINT
                 ELSE Answer := Sum/N;
END; {Answer}
```

Some typical calls to this **FUNCTION** could be

```
X := Answer(1.2,5.3,2);
Y := Answer(2*X + 1,Y*SIN(X),N1);
R2D2 := 3*Answer(x,2,3) + Answer(5,SQRT(2),7);
```

Refer to this example when you are reading through what follows where we examine the structure of a **FUNCTION** in greater detail.

Function heading

The first line in a **FUNCTION** declaration, analogously to a program, is the **function heading.** It starts with the keyword **FUNCTION**, followed by an identifier which is the name of the **FUNCTION**. This is followed, in parentheses, by a list of so-called **formal parameters** and their associated types. In the **FUNCTION Answer** above, **X**, **Y** and **N** are the formal parameters; **X** and **Y** are of type REAL and **N** is of type INTEGER. The structure of this list is analogous to the structure of the **VAR** declaration except that the list does not end with a semicolon. For example, we could have written

```
FUNCTION Answer(X:REAL; Y:REAL; N:INTEGER):REAL;
```

After the parameter list, enclosed in parentheses, comes a type declaration for the **FUNCTION** itself. In the **FUNCTION Answer**, this is the purpose of the keyword **REAL** following the colon, specifying that this **FUNCTION** produces a real value.

In this chapter we shall only look at **FUNCTION**s of types REAL and INTEGER. A **FUNCTION** can be of any scalar type (see Chapter 4) or pointer type (see Chapter 9).

Local and global identifiers

As we have said, the definitions and declarations section of a **FUNCTION** has an identical structure in every respect to the corresponding section of a main program. The programmer is free to define any identifiers so long as they do not appear in the list of parameters. However, the identifiers defined in a **FUNCTION** can only be used within the **FUNCTION**. For this reason they are said to be **local**. Any attempt to reference them outside the **FUNCTION** will cause an error. In the **FUNCTION Answer, Sum** is a local variable.

We can also declare a **FUNCTION** within a **FUNCTION**. This gives rise to a nested structure such as

```
PROGRAM Nested(INPUT,OUTPUT);
VAR
    I,J: INTEGER;
      FUNCTION A(..);
      VAR
          A1,A2: REAL;
            FUNCTION B(..);
            VAR
                B1,B2: INTEGER;
                A1: REAL;
            BEGIN
                Body of function B
            END; {B}
      BEGIN
            Body of function A
      END; {A}
BEGIN
      Body of main program
END.
```

In the above structure, the variables I and J declared in the main program can be utilised anywhere and are called **global**.

The variables A1 and A2 declared in **FUNCTION A** are local in the body of **FUNCTION A** and are global in the body of **FUNCTION B**. They cannot be referenced in the body of the main program.

The variables B1 and B2 declared in **FUNCTION B** are local to **FUNCTION B** and are only available in the body of **FUNCTION B**. The same applies to the local variable A1 but its name clashes with the global variable A1 declared in **FUNCTION A**. In such a case, *when the name of a local variable happens to be the same as that of a global variable, Pascal specifies that the reference will always be to the local variable.*

In general, if a subprogram refers to a variable A, it means the local variable A. If no such local variable exists then it searches one level higher in the nesting structure.

Going back now to the **FOR** loop, which was introduced in section 2.5, ISO Pascal requires that *LoopCounter* in a **FOR** loop should be a local variable.

Side effects
When a subprogram modifies a global identifier, i.e. an identifier declared outside the subprogram, it is said to produce a **side effect**. For example, the **FUNCTION** below produces a side effect in the global variable **X**.

```
FUNCTION SideEffect(i:INTEGER);
BEGIN
      X:= X + 1;
      SideEffect:= i*X;
END; {SideEffect}
```

Such side effects are usually produced by accident, typically through making frequent use of identifiers such as **X**, **Y**, **Z** whilst forgetting to declare them locally.

Advice on good programming

Although the use of a global variable in a subprogram is sometimes necessary, e.g. in a **PROCEDURE** which reads data and assigns initial values to global variables, it should be avoided as far as possible. It can give rise to errors that may be very hard to locate.

〉 3.4 PROCEDUREs

A **PROCEDURE** is more general than a **FUNCTION**. It may produce more than one value, or it may produce no value at all but be invoked to do some action, e.g. to produce a beep sound to draw you attention. There are a number of predefined **PROCEDURE**s available in Pascal which are listed in Appendix 2. User-defined **PROCEDURE**s must be declared in the main program in exactly the same way as **FUNCTION**s.

A **PROCEDURE** declaration has the following form:

PROCEDURE *ProcedureName (List of formal parameters and their types);*
Local Definitions and Declarations;
BEGIN
    Executable statements
END; {*Name*}

A **PROCEDURE** has no type associated with it and, not surprisingly, its name is not assigned a value inside its body as is the case for

FUNCTIONs. Also, unlike a **FUNCTION**, a **PROCEDURE**'s name cannot appear in an expression. To invoke a **PROCEDURE** we simply write the name of the **PROCEDURE** and supply appropriate actual parameters.

Here is a **PROCEDURE** that produces *n* blank lines:

```
PROCEDURE BlankLines(N: INTEGER);
{Produces N blank lines}
VAR
    I: INTEGER;
BEGIN
      FOR I := 1 TO N DO WRITELN;
END; {BlankLines}
```

The statement

```
BlankLines(5);
```

will cause the **PROCEDURE BlankLines** to output five blank lines.

A **PROCEDURE** may have no parameters at all. For example, the **PROCEDURE**

```
PROCEDURE Prompt;
BEGIN
      WRITELN('It is time to go home.');
End;  {Prompt}
```

when invoked, will produce the intended prompt.

Value and **VAR** *parameters*

The formal parameters that go into the parameter list of the heading can be of four different kinds, of which two are used most frequently (the other two will be discussed in Chapter 8). **Value parameters** are parameters which cannot pass back any results. Any attempt to change a value parameter does not affect the corresponding argument. Consider for example

```
PROCEDURE addOne(X: INTEGER);
BEGIN
      X := X + 1;
      WRITELN('The value of X inside the procedure is ',X);
END;  {addOne}
```

In the above **PROCEDURE**, **X** is a value parameter. Suppose now that from the main program the above **PROCEDURE** is invoked using the following statements:

```
X:= 4;
addOne(X);
WRITELN('The value of X in the main program is ', i);
```

The output produced will be

```
The value of X inside the procedure is 5
The value of X in the main program is 4
```

The fact that **X** was changed inside the **PROCEDURE** has not affected **X** in the main program. This is so because the **X** in the main program refers to a different memory location to the **X** in the **PROCEDURE**. Value parameters passed to a **PROCEDURE** are treated as local parameters and storage is allocated to them separately. Such parameters are used to **supply values** to a **PROCEDURE**. For example, in the following **PROCEDURE**, the value parameter **n** supplies the value of the number of blank lines to be printed:

```
PROCEDURE nBlankLines(n: INTEGER);
VAR
    i: INTEGER;
BEGIN
        FOR i:= 1 TO n DO WRITELN;
END; {nBlankLines}
```

The second type of parameters are known as **VAR** (variable) **parameters**. Any changes in these parameters affect the corresponding argument from the calling program. Such parameters are specified using the keyword **VAR** as shown in the modified version of **PROCEDURE addOne** that we met above:

```
PROCEDURE addOne(VAR X: INTEGER);
BEGIN
        X:= X + 1;
        WRITELN('The value of X inside the procedure is ',X);
END;  {addOne}
```

Here **X** is a **VAR** parameter. If we now invoke our modified **PROCEDURE** using exactly the same statements from the main program as before then the output will change to

```
The value of X inside the procedure is 5
The value of X in the main program is 5
```

The value of **X** in the main program has now been altered by the **PROCEDURE**. **VAR** parameters are treated as global variables and provide a mechanism for **returning results** from the **PROCEDURE** to the calling program. The following example should make this clear:

```
PROCEDURE Inverse(X,Y: REAL; VAR Z: REAL);
{Calculates X/Y and puts the result in Z}
BEGIN
        IF Y <> 0 THEN Z := X/Y
        ELSE
                WRITELN('Attempt to divide by zero in ',
                        'procedure Inverse');
END; {Inverse}
```

Here **X** and **Y** are value parameters and **Z** is a **VAR** parameter. In supplying the actual parameters we must give a variable of the right type for **Z**. Unlike **X** and **Y**, **Z** cannot be substituted for by a number or an expression. We may write, for example,

```
X := 1.5;
Inverse(2.3*4.5, SQRT(X), Result);
WRITELN(Result);
```

where **Result** would have been declared of type REAL. After the **PROCEDURE** call, **Result** will take the value of **2.3*4.5** divided by the square root of 1.5.

Several example programs containing **PROCEDURE**s and **FUNCTION**s are given in the Pascal laboratory. We shall also look at one such example in the problem discussed at the end of this chapter.

The diagram below shows the difference in treatment when an argument P, whose value happens to be 17, is substituted for a formal parameter Q for the two cases when Q is a value and **VAR** parameter.

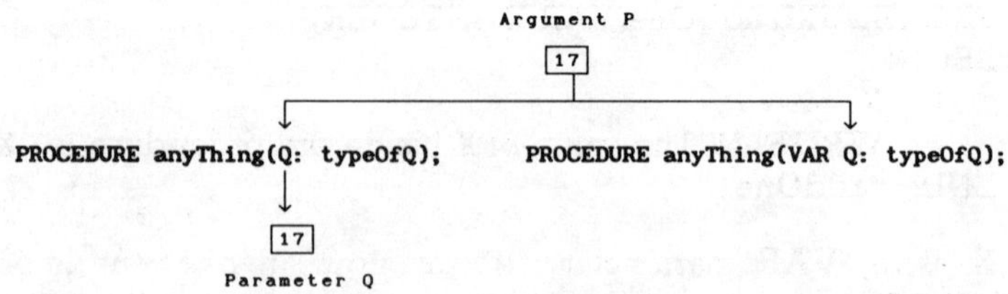

A copy of P is produced in a temporary location and labeled Q. Computations involving Q refer to this temporary storage. No changes are made into the storage location P. Q is lost on exit from the PROCEDURE.

The parameter Q now refers to the same location as P. The changes made to Q remain in P on exit from the PROCEDURE.

〉3.5 Scope of identifiers

We discussed the concept of local and global variables in the context of **FUNCTION**s and what was said there applies also to **PROCEDURE**s. Related to these is the concept of the **scope of identifiers**. By the scope of an identifier we mean the region in which the identifier is known. This region comprises the block in which the identifier is declared.

For instance, consider the diagram which shows a main program named **M** with five modules A, B, C, D and E in a nested structure:

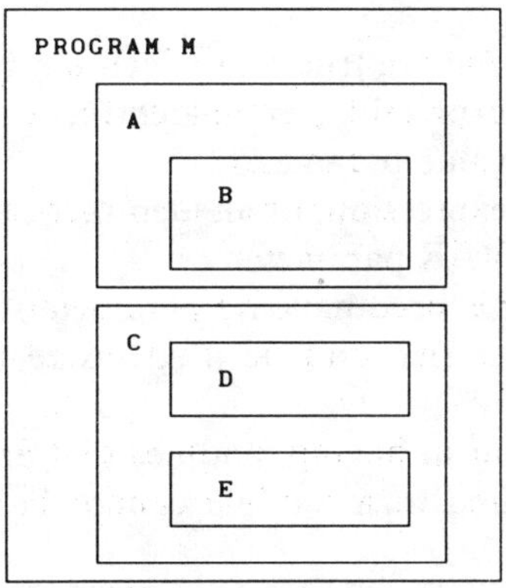

The table below shows the accessibility of modules within **M** and the identifiers available to each of them.

Module	May be called by	Can call	Can use identifiers declared in
A	M	B	M and A
B	A	None	M, A and B
C	M	A, D and E	M and C
D	C	None	M, C and D
E	C	D	M, C and E

The table below shows the scope of identifiers, i.e. the region in which the identifiers declared in each module are available.

Identifiers declared in	Are available in (scope)
M	Everywhere
A	A and B
B	B
C	C, D and E
D	D
E	E

Quickies

1. Which of the following are true and which are false?
   (a) A constant, an expression, or an identifier can be supplied as an argument to a value parameter.
   (b) A constant, an expression, or an identifier can be supplied as an argument to a **VAR** parameter.
   (c) A **PROCEDURE** need have no parameters.
   (d) All the variables that can be used inside a module must be declared in it.
   (e) There is no point in having modules that are used only once.
   (f) Variables declared in a module cannot be used by the main program.
   (g) I DIV J = TRUC(I/J) if I and J are INTEGERS.
   (h) ROUND(R) = TRUNC(R + 0.5)
   (i) SIN(90) will produce the answer 1.

2. Which of the following headings are valid?
   (a) PROCEDURE Game(VAR I: INTEGER): REAL;
   (b) FUNCTION Answer(I: REAL; VAR X: INTEGER;
       Ans: INTEGER): REAL;
   (c) PROCEDURE Play;
   (d) FUNCTION DoNothing:INTEGER;
   (e) PROCEDURE Alpha(VAR I,J: REAL);
   (f) PROCEDURE Choose(X: REAL; VAR J: INTEGER;
       VAR X: REAL);

3. What is wrong with the following statement?

```
IF Ask(Answer) > 16 THEN WRITELN('Adult')
                    ELSE WRITELN('Child');
```

where **Ask** has been declared as

```
PROCEDURE Ask(VAR Age: INTEGER);
BEGIN
      WRITE('Age? ');
      READLN(Age);
END; {Ask}
```

4. Consider the **PROCEDURE**

```
PROCEDURE Swap(First,Second: INTEGER);
VAR
    Copy: INTEGER;
BEGIN
      Copy := First;
      First := Second;
      Second := Copy;
END; {Swap}
```

The **PROCEDURE** is invoked from the main program thus:

```
P := 5;
Q := 6;
Swap(P,Q);
WRITELN(P,Q);
```

What will be the output?

5. Given two INTEGERs **X** and **Y**, it is required to produce the value of the largest. The following declarations could all be used. Which of them is the most appropriate? Criticize the others.

   (a) PROCEDURE Max(X,Y: INTEGER; VAR M: INTEGER);
   (b) FUNCTION Max(X,Y: INTEGER): INTEGER;
   (c) PROCEDURE Max(VAR X,Y,M: INTEGER);
   (d) FUNCTION Max(VAR X,Y: INTEGER): INTEGER;

⇒ **You may now proceed to Pascal laboratory Activities 13–14.**

〉3.6 Top-down programming

In this chapter we have emphasized the importance of modularisation.

This is important in the organisation of a complex task. There is another related concept which is of great value in problem solving.

Given a problem to solve, we should start by first producing a very general description of the solution. We should then proceed, one step at a time, to fill in more details until all the steps required to solve the problem emerge. This method of problem solving is called **top-down** design or **step-wise** refinement.

In the problem that follows we shall illustrate the organisation of tasks into modules as well as the method of top-down programming. The steps involved in testing and documenting a program will also be examined.

Problem Write a computer program to produce a graphical representation of an arbitrary function $y = f(x)$ of a real argument.

Defining the problem

To fix ideas, let us begin by writing down some examples of FUNCTIONs:

$$f(x) = x^2 - x + 3,$$
$$f(x) = \sin(x)*\cos(2x),$$
$$f(x) = \cos(x)^2 - \sin(x^3 + 1).$$

Typical graphical representations might appear as

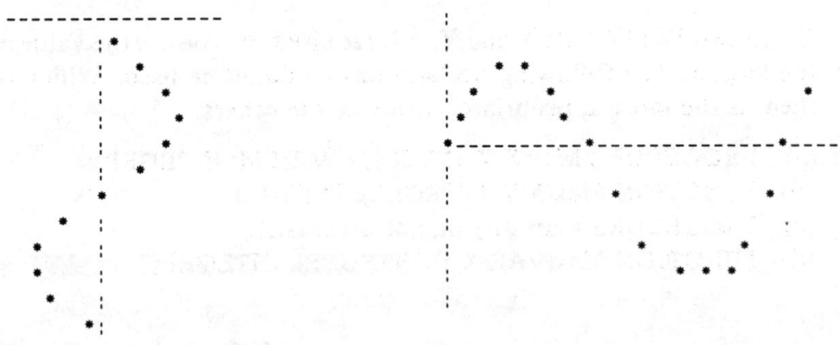

Some reflection will show that apart from the function itself we need to provide answers to the following:

1. What will be the range of x values?
2. What will be the range of values produced by the function?
3. What are the dimensions of the region available for the graph?
4. How will the axes be chosen?

5. What characters will be used for the axes and for the graph?
6. Will the axes be labelled?

To define the problem we will proceed as follows. We will specify the range of x values by reading in two real numbers **XMin** and **XMax**.

We could calculate the range of values produced by the function and scale the graph appropriately but to keep the program to a reasonable size we will specify the range of $f(x)$ by supplying two real numbers **YMin** and **YMax**.

To fix the dimensions of the graph, the number of lines and the number of columns will be specified by the integer variables **NumLines** and **NumColumns**.

We will choose the X axis to be drawn vertically and the Y axis horizontally. Again, to simplify matters, we shall choose not to attempt to label the axes.

The character '–' will be used for the Y axis, the character '|' for the X axis and the values of $f(x)$ will be displayed using the character '**I**'.

For instance, the following values will specify the data for a plot for values of x between 0.0 and 3.141 592 6 and values of y between –1.0 and 1.0. The graphical output will span 20 lines and 75 columns.

```
XMin = 0.0
YMin = -1.0
XMax = 3.14159265
YMax = 1.0
numLines = 20
numColumns = 75
```

Producing an outline solution

Here is an outline solution to our problem. It is written in a form that is suitable for top-down design and that leads easily to modularisation.

Step 1. Define $f(x)$.
Step 2. Set the values of the variables **XMin**, **XMax**, **YMin**, **YMax**, **NumLines** and **NumColumns**.
Step 3. Plot the Y axis.
Step 4. From line number 1 to line number **NumLines** do the following:

Calculate the value of x corresponding to this line.
Evaluate $f(x)$.
Calculate the column number corresponding to this value of $f(x)$.
Plot the chosen character on this column.
Process next line.

Developing an algorithm

We can now proceed to refine the steps above to develop a more detailed algorithm.

Step 1. We can define $f(x)$ by declaring a **FUNCTION** as follows:

```
FUNCTION f(x:REAL): REAL;
BEGIN
        { Define f(x) here }
END; {f}
```

Step 2. The data for step 2 can be read in or set via a **PROCEDURE** such as

```
PROCEDURE SetData(VAR MinX,MinY,MaxX,MaxY: REAL;
                  VAR Lines,Columns: INTEGER);
BEGIN
      { Read or set required data here }
END; {SetData}
```

Step 3. This step can also be implemented in a **PROCEDURE** which will use a **FOR** loop to do the task:

```
PROCEDURE PlotYAxis;
BEGIN
      For i := 1 TO NumColumns DO
            { Write out the chosen character for the axes }
END; {PlotYAxis}
```

Step 4. In this step we have to calculate the value of x corresponding to a particular line and also the column number corresponding to a value of $f(x)$. At this stage we will assume that the answers to these will be provided by two **FUNCTION**s, **getX** and **getColumn**. The details of these **FUNCTION**s could be provided later.

```
PROCEDURE DrawGraph;
BEGIN
        FOR line := 1 TO NumLines DO
            { Use getX and getColumn to work out
              where a bar should be placed to
              mark a point on the graph }
END; {DrawGraph}
```

Expanding step 4

All the steps, except step 4, can now be coded quite easily in Pascal. Step 4, however, requires further refinement to work out the details relating to FUNCTIONs getX and getColumn.

Given a line, the FUNCTION getX will compute the real number corresponding to that line. This can be achieved by scaling. The range of lines 1...NumLines must correspond to the range of x values XMin...XMax, producing getX(1) = XMin and getX(NumLines) = XMax. The FUNCTION will have the following form:

```
getX(line) = (XMax – XMin)*(line – 1)/(NumLines – 1) + XMin
```

Similarly, the FUNCTION getColumn that we require must map the range of values YMin...YMax into the range 1...NumColumns, giving getColumn(yMin) = 1 and getColumn(yMax) = NumColumns. Also whereas getX maps a set of integers into a set of real numbers, getColumn does the opposite. A real number has to be turned into an integer before it can be assigned to an integer variable. This is achieved using the standard FUNCTIONs ROUND or TRUNC described earlier in this chapter. You can verify that the required FUNCTION has the following form:

```
getColumn(y) = 1 + ROUND((y – YMin)*(NumColumns – 1)/
                                            (YMax – YMin))
```

Coding the solution

We can now proceed to code the algorithm developed above into a complete program. The problem tackled here is a relatively simple one but it demonstrates the method that should be followed in solving complex problems.

Advice on good programming

Always break down a complex task into separate subtasks and attack complex problems using the method of step-wise refinement.

In studying the program below note how readable the main program becomes when we use modularisation. The program is included on the disk under the name GRAPHICS.PAS.

```
PROGRAM GRAPH(OUTPUT);
CONST
        Pi = 3.14159265;
        Dash = '–';
        ThickBar = 'I';   {These symbols may not be available in your machine}
        ThinBar = '|';    {Replace them with suitable characters of your choice}
```

```
VAR
    NumLines,NumColumns,posXaxis: INTEGER;     { posXAxis is used to calculate
                                                 the midpoint of the Y axis. The
                                                 X axis passes through this point }
    YMin,XMin,XMax,YMax             : REAL;

    FUNCTION f(x:REAL): REAL;
BEGIN
      f := sin(3*x)*cos(2*x);
END; {f}

PROCEDURE SetData(VAR MinX,MinY,MaxX,MaxY: REAL;
                      VAR Lines,Columns,pos: INTEGER);
BEGIN
      Lines := 70;
      Columns := 79;
      MinY := -1;
      MaxY := 1;
      MinX := 0;
      MaxX := 2*Pi;
      pos := 1 + (Columns DIV 2);
END; {SetData}
PROCEDURE PlotYAxis;
VAR
   i: INTEGER;
BEGIN
      FOR i := 1 TO NumColumns DO WRITE(Dash);
      WRITELN;
END  {PlotYAxis}
FUNCTION getX(line: INTEGER): REAL;
BEGIN
       getX := (XMax - XMin)*(line - 1)/(NumLines - 1) + XMin;
END; {getX}
FUNCTION getColumn(y:REAL): INTEGER;
BEGIN
      getColumn := 1 + ROUND((y - YMin)*(NumColumns - 1)/(YMax - YMin));
END; {getColumn}
PROCEDURE DrawGraph;
VAR
   x           : REAL;
   column,line: INTEGER;
BEGIN
      PlotYAxis;
      FOR line := 1 TO NumLines DO
        BEGIN
           x := getX(line);
           column := getColumn(f(x));
           IF column < posXaxis THEN
             WRITELN(ThickBar:Column,ThinBar:posXaxis - column);
           IF column = posXaxis THEN
             WRITELN(ThickBar:column);
           IF column > posXaxis THEN
             WRITELN(ThinBar:posXaxis,ThickBar:column - posXaxis);
```

```
        END;
END; {DrawGraph}

BEGIN {main program }
        SetData(XMin,YMin,XMax,YMax,NumLines,NumColumns,posXAxis);
        DrawGraph;
END.
```

A sample output from the program is shown below. It shows a graph of the function $f(x) = \sin(3x)\cos(2x)$ in the range $0 \leqslant x \leqslant 2\pi$.

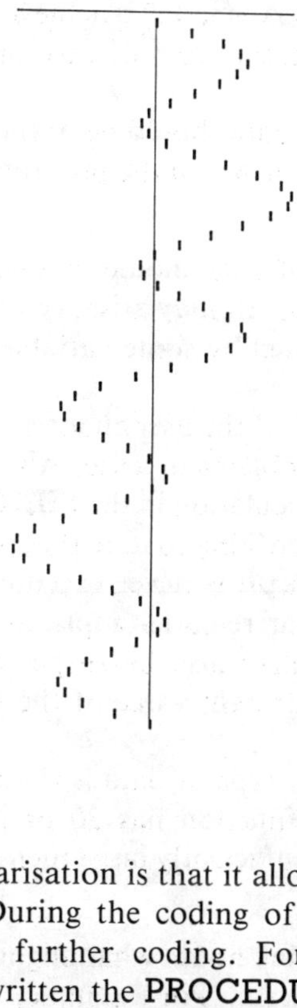

Testing the program

A major virtue of modularisation is that it allows for the testing of each module independently. During the coding of a program each module should be tested before further coding. For example, in the above program, after we have written the **PROCEDURE SetData** it should be tested to see if it performs as expected by writing out the data. Similarly, after we have coded the **PROCEDURE PlotYAxis** it should be tested to see if it plots the y axis and so on.

After a program has been completed all the modules should be tested together to check their performance in the complete environment. In this second phase of testing the object should be to demonstrate that the program will produce correct results for all possible data.

One major area of research in computer science is the search for formal methods that will prove the correctness of computer programs. These methods use the same techniques as the ones employed in mathematics to prove theorems. At present this work, however, is largely of theoretical interest. Except for very small programs and special cases, it is generally impossible to prove that a program is 'correct', i.e. that it will function as intended for *all possible* input data.

In practice all we can do is to convince ourselves that the chances that our program will fail are very small. To achieve this goal we must try out the program on three different types of carefully chosen data sets.

Type 1. Our first choice of data should be of the type where we expect no problems of any sort and for which the program should function exactly as intended.

Type 2. The second type of data should involve a range of special cases where we suspect that problems may arise, typically, when a very large or a very small value is attained by some variable in the program.

In the program **GRAPH**, if the user chooses a function which becomes infinite, then we expect problems to arise. Also, if **NumLines** is chosen to be equal to 1 then the calculation in the **FUNCTION getX** will involve a division by zero. It is interesting to note that if **NumLines** is set to zero then the loop in **DrawGraph** is never executed and no call is made to **FUNCTION getX**. Similar remarks apply to the case **YMax** = **YMin**. The case **XMax** = **XMin** may also be suspected as being problematic. However, in this case a constant value of the function is plotted giving the correct result.

Another example of this type of data is the choice $f(x) = \sin(20x)$ in the range 0 to 2π. This function has 20 oscillations in this range. If **NumLines** is not chosen sufficiently large then what is produced appears meaningless.

Type 3. We should also think about what might happen if a user supplies invalid data to our program. For example, suppose that a negative integer is supplied for a variable when the program was designed to expect a positive value only. The program may produce a run-time error or it may produce erroneous results. Ideally, a program should have tests to check the validity of data built into it but of course this is very hard to implement in general. Data validation will be discussed in the next chapter.

In the program **GRAPH** some examples of invalid data are

1 NumLines $\leqslant 0$
2 NumColumns $\leqslant 0$
3 XMin > XMax
4 YMin > YMax.

In case 1, only the *y* axis is drawn. The loop in the **PROCEDURE DrawGraph** never gets executed. Case 2 produces nonsense. In cases 3 and 4, a graph is plotted but the ranges are reversed producing in case 3 a reflection in a line parallel to the *y* axis passing through the middle of the *x* range, and in case 4 a reflection in the *x* axis.

Producing enhanced documentation

Like the testing, the writing of comments in a program is a two-phased affair. Of course, comments should be written to explain the coding as each module is produced. However, after the complete program has been tested in the manner described above, enhanced documentation should be added to give the user the benefit of the experience. This documentation should also include the date when the program was completed and a version number. For the program **GRAPH**, the enhanced documentation might be:

```
{ WRITTEN BY Jim Blogs
  DATE PRODUCED March 1989
  VERSION NUMBER 1.2
  DESCRIPTION:
  Draws a graph of f(x) in the range XMin <= x <= XMax. User must
  supply values of YMin and YMax which are the minimum and the
  maximum values of f(x) in the chosen range. NumLines and
  NumColumns set the number of lines and number of columns over
  which the graphical representation is produced. All data is set in
  procedure SetData.
  WARNING: The program will fail to perform satisfactorily if

  — f(x) becomes infinite in the chosen range.
  — NumLines = 1 or YMax = YMin.
  — If NumLines is chosen too small in the case of a rapidly varying
  function.
  — XMin > XMax or YMin > YMax. }
```

⇒ **You may now proceed to Pascal laboratory Activities 15–19.**

〉 Pascal laboratory

Activity 13. Run TUTOR12. Produce patterns of various sizes. Change **MOD 2 = 0** to **MOD 3 = 0**. Compare the output. Predict what will happen if you use **MOD 20 = 0** and verify. Modify the code so that it uses instead a **PROCEDURE Pattern(NumLines,NumColumns)** and use it to produce a 25 × 50 checkerboard pattern.

Activity 14. TUTOR13, which is meant to calculate the real roots of a quadratic equation, is incomplete. Complete the **PROCEDURE**s **ReadData** and **WriteAnswer** and test the program. Extend the program to handle complex roots.

Activity 15. Read TUTOR14. Predict what the output will be. Verify. Change the program to produce sensible output.

Activity 16. Study TUTOR15. Run it. Produce a modular version in which the objectives of the **FOR** loops are achieved by invoking a **PROCEDURE**.

Activity 17. TUTOR16 contains the identifiers amount and index declared repeatedly. The object of the program is to show what happens when the name of a local variable is the same as that of a global one. Run the program and explain the output.

Activity 18. Read TUTOR17. Predict the output. Verify.

Activity 19. Examine TUTOR18. Identify its local and global variables. Run the program and explore. How is the **FUNCTION** f utilised despite the fact that it has no parameters?

〉 Exercises

1*. Suppose that in the following program the statement

```
c := Side(b) + Side(b);
```

is replaced by the statement

```
c := 2*Side(b);
```

Will the program produce the same output? If not, why not?

```
PROGRAM First(OUTPUT);
VAR
    a,b,c: INTEGER;

FUNCTION Side(I: INTEGER): INTEGER;
BEGIN
        a := a + 1;
        Side := a*i;
END;  {Side}
BEGIN
        a := 8;
        b := 17;
        c := Side(b) + Side(b);
        WRITELN(c)
END.
```

2. As done in section 4.5 of the text, draw two tables to show the scope of variables for the structure shown below.

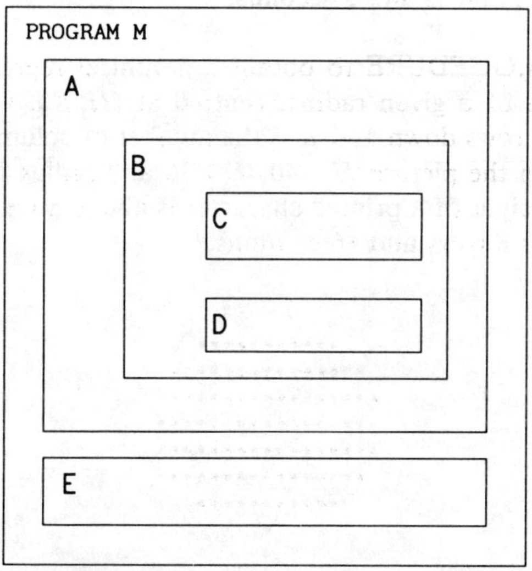

3*. Write a **FUNCTION** to calculate the number of spaces needed to print an integer. For example, to print 1234 we need four spaces and to print −5678 we need five spaces. Hint: use the predefined **FUNCTION LN**.

4*. Write two **FUNCTION**s, one to calculate $n!$ for integer n and another to calculate x^n for real x. Write another **FUNCTION** **Sine(x)** which uses the two **FUNCTION**s to calculate the sine of x from its power series:

$$\sin(x) = x - \frac{x^3}{3!} + \frac{x^5}{5!} - \cdots .$$

Write a complete program to print the approximations for $\sin(x)$ as more and more terms are chosen. Explore the behaviour of your program as the magnitude of x and the number of terms are varied and comment.

5*. Write a **PROCEDURE** which makes use of the **FUNCTION** f in TUTOR18 to print a calendar for a given month and year.

6. As in the last exercise, write a **FUNCTION** which reads two dates and computes the elapsed time between them. For example, the time elapsed between 12:00:07, 4 May 1989 and 15:35:10, 4 May 1989 is 3 hours 35 minutes and 3 seconds.

7*. Write a **PROCEDURE** to obtain a graphical representation of a filled circle of a given radius, centred at (H, K), where H is the number of rows down and K is the number of columns across. For example, in the picture $H = 40$, $K = 10$ and radius $= 8$. Note that, since the height of a printed character is about twice the width, the circle spans 8 rows and 16 columns.

```
        *
   ***********
 ***************
*****************
*****************
*****************
 ***************
   ***********
        *
```

Answers to quickies

1. (a)T, (b)F, (c)T, (d)F, (e)F, (f)T, (g)T, (h)F but T if R > 0, (i)F.
2. (a)Invalid, (b)valid, (c)valid, (d)valid, (e)valid, (f)invalid.
3. Ask is not a **FUNCTION**. Cannot be used in an expression.

4. The output will be 5 6. Procedure **Swap** should use **VAR** parameters to produce the intended result.
5. (b) is the most appropriate. For a single-valued answer, a **FUNCTION** is most appropriate because it can be used in an expression, hence (a) is less appropriate. (c) and (d) could produce side effects and are to be avoided.

〉 Chapter 4

〉 More on Syntax, Types, Decision Making and Loops

The purpose of the last chapters has been to introduce enough Pascal at a fairly rapid pace so that you can start writing some non-trivial programs. In this chapter we shall expand on some of the concepts that have been only partially discussed previously. We will also introduce some new TYPEs, and ways of making decisions and performing repetitions other than the IF-THEN-ELSE construction and the FOR loop.

〉 4.1 Pascal's grammar

All languages possess a grammar which determines the 'correctness' of phrases and sentences in them. The **syntactical** rules of grammar dictate the order in which various classes of words (nouns, verbs, etc) may be combined and the manner in which various constructions may be punctuated. The **semantic** rules decide which combinations are meaningful. For example, in English it would be syntactically incorrect to say 'A cat white climbed a tree'; and though the sentence 'A tree climbed a white cat' is syntactically correct, it is incorrect semantically.

The major difference between an ordinary language and a computer language is that whereas in the former gross violations of grammar may still succeed in conveying the intended meaning — 'It is a a rayning a not in Tokyo tonite' — in the latter the rules must be obeyed exactly. The **syntax rules** of Pascal define permissible ways to combine keywords, reserved symbols (e.g. arithmetical operators; see Appendix 1) and identifiers into meaningful units such as declarations, statements and complete modules.

Because a computer language must obey its grammar exactly, the rules of grammar must be defined unambiguously. Two notations are commonly employed in Pascal for this purpose. One of them is the pictorial method of **syntax diagrams**. The other is the **Backus–Naur form** (BNF) which uses a set of special symbols. The BNF notation describes the syntax rules very rigorously and concisely but has to be mastered. By contrast, syntax diagrams are easy to interpret but lack conciseness. Although the use of these methods becomes essential when trying to resolve subtleties or when attempting such tasks as writing compilers, they are not utilised to any great extent in ordinary circumstances. For these reasons, we will not discuss the BNF notation in this book. Because syntax diagrams are met very frequently, we shall briefly look at some examples in the next section.

Syntax diagrams
A syntax diagram is drawn by joining labelled rectangular boxes, reserved words and reserved symbols with arrows. The rectangular boxes stand for elements which themselves require definition and are defined elsewhere in their own syntax diagram.

To interpret a diagram we simply follow any of the paths along the arrows. The idea is very simple to grasp and the two examples below should make the meaning quite clear.

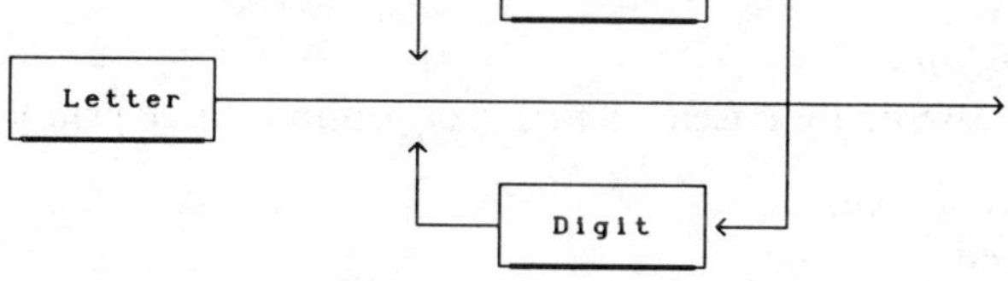

Syntax diagram for an IDENTIFIER.

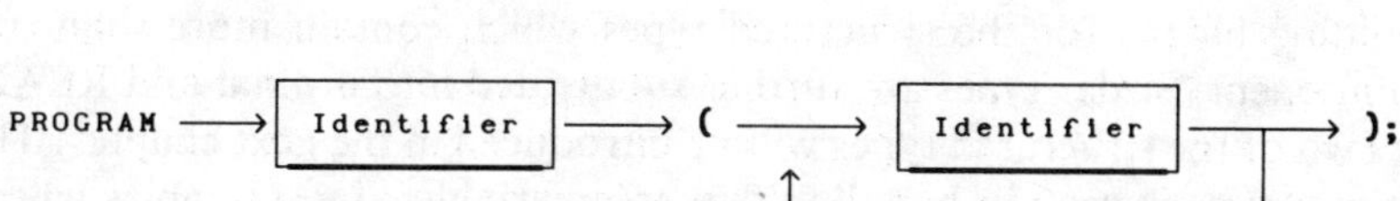

Syntax diagram for a PROGRAM HEADING.

The first diagram gives the syntax rule for an identifier, i.e. that an identifier begins with a letter and is followed by any number of letters or digits. The second one defines the rule for a program heading. By following the arrows we deduce that a program heading must begin with the word **PROGRAM** followed by an identifier (defined by its own syntax diagram) followed by an open bracket, followed by at least one but optionally many identifiers separated by commas, followed by a close bracket, followed finally by a semi-colon.

〉4.2 Pascal's types

The standard scalar types of Pascal were mentioned in Chapter 2 and, of these, the INTEGER and the REAL types were met in greater detail. In this section we shall develop the concept further. Every data item in Pascal is associated with a data type. The type of an item determines:

the internal representation of the item in a computer,
the storage space needed for the item,
the range of values the item can span,
the operations that can be performed on it,
the manner in which the item can be input and output, and
the accuracy of the results obtained from operations performed on data of that type.

From the point of view of the programmer, the first two in the above list are not usually of much concern and are handled by the compiler.

Type categories
The types offered by Pascal can be grouped into three prime categories:

scalar or simple,
structured,
pointer.

The scalar types are the fundamental types of Pascal and serve as the building blocks for the structured types which contain more than one component. Scalar types are further subdivided into **ordinal** and REAL.

Two of the structured types will be introduced in the next chapter. The pointer type is used in handling dynamic variables, i.e. variables whose storage requirements are not fixed in advance at compile time. We will meet it in the last chapter.

The diagram below summarises the various data types of Pascal.

It is worth mentioning that the diagram depicts only the types offered by ISO Pascal. Some dialects of Pascal offer many other types. For example, TURBO Pascal offers five types of integers, namely BYTE, SHORTINT, INTEGER, WORD and LONGINT.

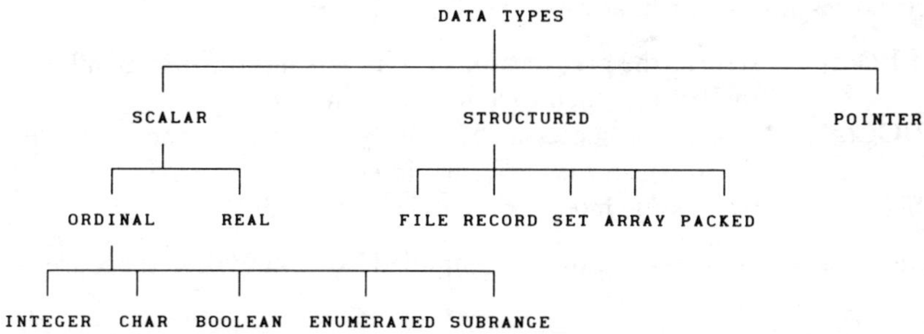

Ordinal types

We can see from the above diagram that five of the scalar types are together referred to as being of ordinal type. We have met the INTEGER type before. All of the others will be introduced in this chapter but first we describe the properties that are common to all of them and form the basis for the categorisation.

Ordinal types are characterised by two properties: they are **discrete** and they are **ordered**. Discrete implies that between any two permissible values of an ordinal type there are only a finite number of other available values. For example between the integers 1 and 5 there are only three other integers, between the characters P and R there is only one other character, and so on. This is in contrast with the REAL type where between any two there are an infinite number of others.

Ordinal types are also either naturally ordered or can be put into order by choice. For instance, with the integers or the letters of the alphabet the ordering is quite natural, but given a finite set of arbitrary characters we can order them by choice. Thus the ASCII code (Appendix 3) chooses to place the digits before the upper case letters and the upper case letters before the lower case ones. In this code the digit 1 is the 49th character in the list, the upper case A is 65th and the lower case a is 97th. The question mark character (?) is 63rd and so on.

Every ordinal type of data has an **ordinal value**. For the INTEGER type, the ordinal value is the value of the integer itself; for other types the first element in the list has the ordinal value zero, the second has the ordinal value one, and so on. We shall look at these as we examine the new types to be introduced in this chapter.

Predefined functions for ordinals

Pascal supplies three predefined functions for ordinals whose arguments are expressions of ordinal type.

PRED(*a*) returns the predecessor of *a*, unless *a* is the first member of the list in which case it results in error.

SUCC(*a*) returns the successor of *a* unless *a* is the last member in the list in which case it results in error.

ORD(*a*) returns the integer which gives the ordinal value of *a*.

Examples of the above functions applied to INTEGER type are as follows:

```
PRED(45) = 44
PRED(-45) = -46
SUCC(20 MOD 3) = 3
ORD(45) = 45
ORD(-45) = -45
```

BOOLEANSs

To facilitate logical decision making, Pascal provides us with the standard data type that takes only one of two values: **FALSE** or **TRUE**. This type is known as the BOOLEAN type, named after the 19th century British mathematician George Boole who invented the algebra of logic.

BOOLEAN constants and variables are declared in the following way:

```
CONST Yes = TRUE;
VAR Found,Condition: BOOLEAN;
```

A BOOLEAN variable can be assigned one of the values TRUE or FALSE. For example,

```
Found := TRUE;
IF Found THEN WRITELN('I"ve found it!');
```

In practice, BOOLEAN values arise from comparisons, e.g..

```
Y := X < 20;
```

In the case of BOOLEANs there are only two possible values and Pascal chooses to arrange them in the order FALSE, TRUE. For this reason the following relationships hold:

```
FALSE < TRUE
ORD(FALSE) = 0
ORD(TRUE) = 1
SUCC(FALSE) = TRUE
PRED(TRUE) = FALSE
```

SUCC(TRUE) will produce an error message because **TRUE** has no successor in the list of BOOLEAN values and so will **PRED(FALSE)**.

Boolean variables can be printed using the **WRITE** and **WRITELN** statements. For example, the statements

```
a := FALSE;
WRITELN(a);
```

will produce the output **FALSE**.

Boolean variables, however, cannot be entered in the parameter list of a **READ** or **READLN** statement. We will shortly see how to overcome this limitation.

There are three BOOLEAN operators: **AND**, **OR** and **NOT**. Their meaning is explained in the following tables where it is assumed that **X** and **Y** are of type BOOLEAN and **F** and **T** stand for FALSE and TRUE respectively.

X	Y	X AND Y
F	F	F
F	T	F
T	F	F
T	T	T

X	Y	X OR Y
F	F	F
F	T	T
T	F	T
T	T	T

X	NOT X
F	T
T	F

BOOLEAN operators, together with arithmetical and relational operators, are used to construct BOOLEAN expressions. Such expressions can be evaluated to give the values TRUE or FALSE. Examples of BOOLEAN expressions are

0 > X
(0 > X) OR (X > 1) AND (X + Y < >1)

A BOOLEAN expression may be assigned to a BOOLEAN variable. For example, the statements

```
a := 20;
b := 5;
c := a - 3 < = b;
WRITELN(c);
```

will produce the output **FALSE**.

The evaluation of BOOLEAN expressions requires rules of precedence. The rules given earlier in Chapter 2 are now extended as follows:

Highest	( )	Bracketed expression
Next	- NOT	Negation operators
Next	* DIV MOD AND	Multiplication and Division operators
Next	+ - OR	Addition and subtraction operators
Lowest	< <= => >>= <>	Relational operators

Once again, operators of equal priority are evaluated from left to right.

Example. Suppose that X = 5 and Y = 6; then in evaluating the expression

NOT(X + Y > 12) OR (Y - X < 2)

first we reduce the terms in brackets. Since X + Y = 11, the first bracket yields **FALSE** and the second bracket yields **TRUE**. Next, the operator **NOT** is applied, i.e. we evaluate **(NOT FALSE) OR TRUE** which gives **TRUE OR TRUE**. Thus the whole finally reduces to the value **TRUE**.

It is important to remember that BOOLEAN operators can only act upon BOOLEAN expressions. A common form of error is to write something like

Number = 1 OR 2

It has to be written as **(Number = 1) OR (Number = 2)**. In general, Pascal requires brackets to be used when combining comparisons. For example, it is invalid to write **A = B = C** even if **A**, **B**, **C** are all BOOLEAN variables. It has to be written as **(A = B) AND (B = C)**.

There are three predefined BOOLEAN functions in Pascal:

ODD(*x*)	TRUE if the INTEGER expression *x* yields an odd value.
EOLN	Short for End Of LiNe. TRUE when all the characters on a line have been read. Its usage is explained towards the end of this chapter.
EOF	Short for End of File. TRUE when the last character in the final line in a file has been read. Its usage is explained in Chapter 6.

Example 4A: BOOLEAN expressions. The program below reads three real numbers a, b, c and decides whether they can form a triangle.

```
PROGRAM CheckForTriangle(INPUT,OUTPUT);
VAR
    a,b,c: REAL;
    Positive, Condition1,Condition2,Condition3: BOOLEAN;
BEGIN
      WRITE('Give a,b and c: ');
      READLN(a,b,c);
      Positive := (a > 0) AND (b > 0) AND (c > 0);
      IF NOT Positive THEN WRITELN('Side of triangles have to be positive')
        ELSE
          BEGIN
               Condition1 := a + b > c;
               Condition2 := b + c > a;
               Condition3 := a + c > b;
               IF Condition1 AND Condition2 AND Condition3 THEN
                 WRITELN('Can form a triangle')
               ELSE WRITELN('Cannot form a triangle');
          END;
END.
```

Short-circuit evaluation of BOOLEAN expressions

On some compilers, for example in TURBO Pascal, a complex BOOLEAN expression may not always be fully evaluated by default. The user has to choose this option. Consider for example the expression

IF (X = A) OR (Y = 1/X) THEN Z := Y;

If **X** happens to be **A**, then it would seem more efficient not to bother to check if **Y** = 1/**X** and indeed in general this is true. This partial evaluation of a BOOLEAN expression is what is meant by short-circuit evaluation (SCE). However, consider the case when A = 0; then in SCE the program will still run without producing an error despite the fact the condition **Y** = 1/**X** now becomes undefined. If instead we write

IF (Y = 1/X) OR (X = A) THEN Z := Y;

then logically the statement is unaltered, but now an error will be reported. In the case when the conditions contain function calls, SCE can cause serious alterations in the behaviour of a program. This arises from bad programming and is not the fault of SCE which is designed to reduce running times. So be warned. See problem 2 in the Exercises.

Quickies

1. Interpret in words the syntax diagram below

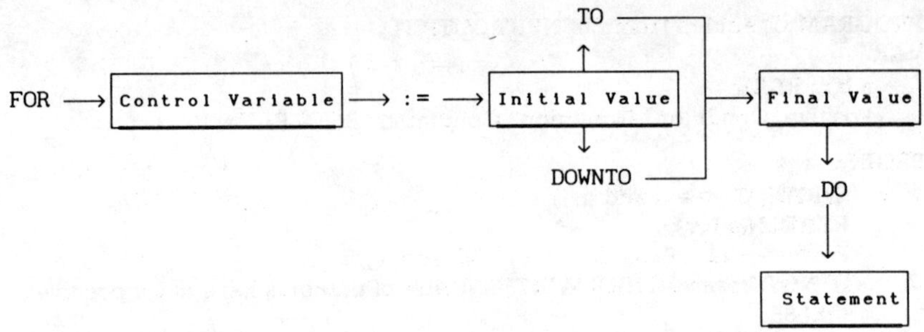

2. Name the two properties that categorise the type ordinal.

3. Mark each of the following as true or false.
   (a) The statement NonSense := 1 + 1 = 3; is syntactically incorrect.
   (b) NOT(A AND B) is the same as (NOT A) AND (NOT B).
   (c) NOT(A OR B) is the same as (NOT A) AND (NOT B).
   (d) NOT(A = B) is the same as A <>B.
   (e) All Pascal numbers can be used for counting in a loop.

4. Write Boolean expressions which are true if
   (a) $X < 0$ and $(X + 1)(X + 2)(X + 3) > 0$.
   (b) Any two or all three of X, Y, Z are equal.
   (c) X is even and divides Y exactly.
   (d) X does not lie between -1 and 0 or between 4 and 5.

⇒ **You may now proceed to Pascal laboratory Activity 20.**

CHAR *type*

The processing of characters is fundamental to computing. Indeed, before a Pascal program can be executed, it has to be compiled, which involves precisely this. In Chapter 2 we met the concept of a string constant which contains a fixed sequence of characters. We now look at character variables.

In Pascal the CHAR data types take single character values and are declared in the following way:

```
CONST Star = '*';
VAR Digit: CHAR;
```

The actual characters that can be handled on a machine can vary. The two sets of characters that are most commonly available are those coded in **ASCII** (American Standard Code for Information Interchange) and **EBCDIC** (Extended Binary Coded Decimal Interchange Code). Of these, ASCII (Appendix 3) is by far the most popular.

To assign a value to a CHAR type variable, we enclose the value in single quotes exactly as for string constants; for example

```
VAR
      CH1,CH2,Digit: CHAR;

CH1 := 'P';
CH2 := '/';
Digit := '1';
```

Another way to give values to CHAR type variables is by reading them in, e.g.,

```
READLN(CH1,CH2,Digit);
```

However, the input of character data differs from that of numerical data in two ways. The notation used in supplying items of data is not identical to that used inside a program. Items of data are not written enclosed in apostrophes. The other important distinction is that, unlike numerical values, blank spaces and new lines are treated as being significant.

For example, if we want CH1 to take the value 'P', CH2 the value '/' and Digit to take the value '1' then in response to the statement READLN(CH1,CH2,Digit) we must type the data as

```
P/1
```

Consider another example. Suppose we need to supply data to the statement READ(Number,CH) where Number is of type INTEGER and CH is of type CHAR. Suppose we type the data as

```
150 A
```

It might be mistakenly assumed that CH will take the value 'A' but this is not the case. CH will be assigned the value ' ', i.e. the character blank. The correct data format is

```
150A
```

Suppose now that we want CH to become the character '1'. This poses a problem because if we now type 1501 then this value will be assigned to Number. One way to get round this is to introduce a dummy character variable which can be used to read the blank space, e.g.

READ(Number,CHDummy,CH). The data can now be typed more sensibly as

150 1

The output of CHAR type data using **WRITE** and **WRITELN** is treated in exactly the same way as a string constant of length one which was discussed in Chapter 2.

The only operators that apply to CHAR type data are the six relational operators:

```
<   <=   >   >=   =   <>
```

The ordering of the complete character set is not prescribed by Pascal and may differ from computer to computer. Pascal only defines ordering relations for three subsets of character values, namely the upper and lower case alphabetic characters and the numeric characters. The following is true for all Pascal implementations:

```
'A' < 'B' < ... < 'Z'
'a' < 'b' < ... < 'z'
'0' < '1' < ... < '9'
```

However, the ASCII set (Appendix 3) with 128 characters which have ordinal values from 0 to 127 is the one that is most commonly used.

Apart from the ordinal functions **SUCC**, **PRED** and **ORD**, the function **CHR** is defined for characters. Its argument is an integer expression.

CHR(a) returns the character whose ordinal value is a.

The function given below shows an example of the use of **CHR**. It converts upper case letters to lower case and will work for any choice of character set.

```
FUNCTION LowCase(CH: CHAR): CHAR;
BEGIN
        IF ('A' < = CH) AND (CH < 'Z') THEN
          LowCase := CHR(ORD(CH) - ORD('A') + ORD('a'))
        ELSE LowCase := CH
END; {Lowcase}
```

Quickies

5. Look up the ASCII table in Appendix 3 to find out:

(a) ORD('8')
(b) PRED(':')
(c) CHR(ORD(SUCC('f'))–3)

6. Write the following in simpler form assuming **X** is of type CHAR and **I** is INTEGER:

(a) CHR(ORD(X))
(b) ORD(CHR(I))
(c) CHR(ORD(X) – 1)
(d) CHR(ORD(X) + 1)

7. Explain why the expression PRED(CHR(3 DIV 5)) is invalid.

⇒ **You may now proceed to Pascal laboratory Activity 21.**

Subrange types

The types INTEGER, REAL, BOOLEAN and CHAR are the predefined scalar types of Pascal. Two other scalar types may be defined by the programmer in the following ways:

by restricting the range of values of an existing type,
by enumerating, i.e. by specifying in order, all the values that variables of the type can assume.

These types are used essentially to minimise errors in data and to make the program more readable.

The subrange type is used when it is expected that a variable of ordinal type will only assume a specific range of values of that type. For any ordinal type it is possible to create a subrange type which caters for this possibility. The declaration of a subrange type has the form:

VAR
    Identifier: LowerBound...UpperBound;

For example, in marking an examination paper we may be awarding grades between A and E. We can declare:

```
VAR
    Grade: 'A'..'E';
```

This indicates to the compiler that the variable **Grade** will be restricted to take the subrange of values **A, B, C, D, E** from the complete range of type CHAR. We say that **Grade** is a subrange type whose **base** or **host**

type is CHAR. It will be invalid to write Grade := PRED('A') or Grade := SUCC('E') because these would assign values outside the subrange. The function ORD when supplied with an argument from a subrange returns the same value as set in the base type. For example, in the above ORD('A') will give 65, assuming ASCII.

Here are some examples of subrange types whose base type is INTEGER:

```
VAR
    Marks: 0..100;
    Date: 1..31;
    BirthDay: 1900..1988;
```

Example 4B: using subranges. In the program below the object is to find what percentage of students from a total of 20 students obtained each of the grades A to E. There are three points you should note. The program becomes more readable through the use of subranges. The input of data is automatically validated to lie between 1 to 20; if a number is typed outside this range the compiler will issue an error message indicating that the variable is out of range. Finally, note how the use of ordinals instead of integers in a loop statement makes the meaning more clear.

```
PROGRAM PercenGrade(INPUT,OUTPUT);
CONST TotalStudents = 20;
VAR
    Students: 1..TotalStudents;
    Grades: 'A'..'E';
    Percentage: 0..100;
BEGIN
      FOR Grades := 'A' TO 'E' DO
      BEGIN
            WRITELN('How many grade',Grades:2,' students? ');
            READLN(Students);
            Percentage := ROUND(Students/TotalStudents*100);
            WRITELN('Percentage of grade',Grades:2,' students = ',Per-
            centage:3);
      END;
END.
```

Comment. In TURBO Pascal range checking is not performed automatically but is an option. It can either be set in the environment or can be switched on using the $R+ directive.

Enumerated types

This type is created by listing each of the possible values. For instance, the following declaration will create **Profession** as a variable of enumerated type.

```
VAR
    Profession: (Scientist, Artist, Dancer, Actor, Musician, Other);
```

Profession can now take one of the values in the list. Any other enumerated type declared in the same way must not contain any of the values listed previously. For example, a further declaration

```
Thinker: (Philosopher, Scientist, Mathematician);
```

would be invalid because it contains the value **Scientist**. The assignment statement takes the usual form, e.g.,

```
Profession := Dancer;
```

The order in which the values are listed establishes the ordering for the type. In our example,

```
Scientist < Artist < Dancer < Actor < Musician < Other
```

Also, the ordinal value of **Scientist** is 0, the ordinal value of **Artist** is 1, and so on.

Exactly as for the CHAR type, only the relational operators are available to enumerated type.

Enumerated types can neither be read nor written using the usual **READ**, **READLN**, **WRITE** and **WRITELN** statements. To read and write enumerated type values some decoding has to be performed. For example,

```
READLN(I); IF I = 1 THEN Profession := Artist;
IF ORD(Profession) = 3 THEN WRITELN('He is an Actor');
```

Also, see Example 4D below.

In applying the ordinal functions **PRED** and **SUCC** it must be remembered that the first value in the list of enumerations has no predecessor and the last one has no successor. Thus, in our example, the statements

```
Profession := PRED(Scientist);
Profession := SUCC(Other);
```

will result in error.

〉 4.3 TYPE definition

A TYPE definition is used to create a new, distinct type and associate with it a **TYPE identifier**. It has the general form:

```
TYPE
        TypeIdentifier = Type;
```

The following are examples of TYPE definitions:

```
Type
    Byte = 0..255;
    WeekDay = (Monday,Tuesday,Wednesday,Thursday,Friday,Saturday,Sunday);
    WeekEnd = Saturday..Sunday;
    Letter = 'A'..'Z';
    OneToSeven = 1..7;
```

We can use the type identifiers defined in this way to declare variables of that type in exactly the way it is done for predefined types. For example,

```
VAR
    i,j,k       : Byte;
    Day1,Day2   : WeekDay;
    Holiday     : WeekEnd;
    CH1,Ch2     : Letter;
```

An important point to appreciate is that the type identifier in a TYPE definition is not a variable and cannot be assigned a value. For instance, the statement

```
WeekDay := Thursday;
```

is invalid exactly as would be the statement

```
INTEGER := 5;
```

The role played by a user-defined type identifier corresponds exactly to the role played by predefined type identifiers such as INTEGER, REAL, BOOLEAN and CHAR.

TYPE definitions make the program more readable and help to identify meaningless statements. For example, if X is of type WeekDay and Y is of type Letter, then it is easy to identify X + Y as being a nonsensical statement.

TYPE definitions become essential when we have to specify the type of a FUNCTION or the type of formal parameters in a PROCEDURE or a FUNCTION when any of them are other than standard scalar. For example, suppose we want to declare a function which, given an integer between 1 and 7, will name the corresponding day. A declaration such as

```
FUNCTION WhichDay(DayNumber:1..7): (Monday,Tuesday,Wednesday,
                                    Thursday,Friday,Saturday,Sunday);
```

would be invalid. Using the **TYPE** definitions given at the beginning of this section, a valid declaration can take the form

```
FUNCTION WhichDay(DayNumber: OneToSeven): WeekDay;
```

Advice on good programming

To make the meaning clear, to help identify meaningless statements and to allow for automatic validation of data, use TYPE definitions and subrange and enumerated type variables. Also remember that the counting in a loop does not have to be done using integers. Use other ordinal types where appropriate.

Example 4C: using enumerated TYPE*s*. This program produces a skew line of characters as shown after the listing.

```
PROGRAM SkewChars(INPUT,OUTPUT);
TYPE
      Hours = (Zero,One,Two,Three,Four,Five,Six,
               Seven,Eight,Nine,Ten,Eleven,Twelve);
VAR
     Time: Hours;
     I   : INTEGER;

BEGIN
       FOR Time := Zero to Twelve DO
            BEGIN
                   I := ORD(Time);
                   WRITELN(CHR(I + 33):I + 1);
            END;
END.
```

```
!
 "
  #
   $
    %
     &
      '
       (
        )
         *
          +
           ,
            -
```

Quickies

8. Which of the following type definitions are legal? If a definition is illegal, state why.

   (a) Negative = 0.. – 10;
   (b) Positive = – 100..0;
   (c) Colours = (Red,Blue,White);
       TrafficLights = (Red,Green,Yellow);
   (d) OneToFive = (1,2,3,4,5);
   (e) Range = 1.5..3.5;

9. Find all the mistakes in the following:

```
TYPE
      Pet: (Cat,Dog,Rabbit);
VAR
     Pet1,Pet2: Pet;
BEGIN
       Pet := Cat;
       Pet1 := Dog;
       READLN(Pet2);
       WRITELN(Pet,Pet1,Pet2);
END;
```

〉4.4 CASE statement

Making multiple choices via the **IF** statement becomes cumbersome if the number of options is large. In situations where conditions to be tested involve ordinal values, we can use the **CASE** statement to do the task more elegantly. The statement takes the general form:

```
CASE CaseSelector OF
        list1 of constants: Statement1;
        list2 of constants: Statement2;
        .....................
        listN of constants: StatementN;
END;
```

Note that there is no **BEGIN** corresponding to the **END** in a **CASE** statement. For example,

```
CASE X OF
    1,3: WRITE(X);
      4: ;
      2: Y := X;
END;
```

Here, **X** is *CaseSelector*. When **X** has value 1 or 3 its value will be written. When **X** is 4 nothing is done and when **X** is 2, **Y** is set equal to **X**. Note that the order in which values of *CaseSelector* are listed inside the **CASE** statement is not of significance.

In general the statement is executed in the following way. The *CaseSelector* following the keyword **CASE**, which is an expression of ordinal type, is evaluated. The value returned should lie in one and only one of the lists of constants. The statement corresponding to the list in which this value occurs is then executed.

Standard Pascal does not lay down the course of action if the value of the *CaseSelector* does not match any of the constants in the lists. In some implementations a run-time error occurs. In some others the control merely passes on to the statement following **END**. Some non-standard dialects of Pascal provide the extra keyword **OTHERWISE** to allow for this eventuality.

Example 4D: writing enumerated **TYPE***s*. Earlier on it was stated that the reading and writing of enumerated types requires some decoding. A **CASE** statement is often useful for this purpose and the function **Colour** in this example gives an illustration. Here integers are converted to enumerated values which may then be assigned to variables of that type.

```
   TYPE Colours = (Black,Blue,Green,Cyan,Red,Magenta,Brown);
        ColourRange = 0..6;

   FUNCTION Colour(C:ColourRange): Colours;
BEGIN
     CASE C OF
          0: Colour := Black;
          1: Colour := Blue;
          2: Colour := Green;
          3: Colour := Cyan;
          4: Colour := Red;
          5: Colour := Magenta;
          6: Colour := Brown;
     END;
   END; {Colour}
```

〉 4.5 GOTO statement

Like the **CASE** and the **IF** statements, the **GOTO** statement may be used to skip over a portion of code. The difference is that the **GOTO** statement has no condition attached to it, and may be used to transfer execution to a statement which occurs before it in the listing. It has the form:

GOTO *Label*;

where *Label* is an integer in the range 0–9999. The execution of the statement will cause the labelled statement to be executed next.

Labels have to be declared, their declaration preceding all others in the definitions and declarations section of a block. Their declaration consists of the keyword **LABEL** followed by a list of labels separated by commas. A statement is labelled by placing a label number and a colon before it. The order in which label numbers occur is immaterial. For example,

```
LABEL 10,100;
.
.
BEGIN
.
. 100: READLN(X);
.
.
IF X > Xmax THEN GOTO 10;
.
.
10: FOR I := 1 TO 10 DO
.
.
GOTO 100;
.
.
END;
```

There are a number of restrictions as to where a jump may be made using the **GOTO**. A **GOTO** statement may only cause a jump within the scope (see Chapter 2) of the label that it jumps to. Also, a **GOTO** statement may not be used to jump inside a structured statement, e.g. in the middle of a compound statement, a conditional statement or a **FOR** loop.

The use of **GOTO** is generally discouraged in Pascal because it goes against one of the fundamental requirements of good programming, namely that the structure of a piece of code should be easy for the reader to discover. Its frequent use can produce code involving a tangled set of jumps to arbitrary locations. As an illustration of what is known as **spaghetti** code, examine the following program which calculates the highest common factor of two integers. A much clearer structure for doing the same will be given in the next section when we have learnt about unconditional loops.

```
PROGRAM Spaghetti(INPUT,OUTPUT);
LABEL 1,2,3;
VAR
    Num1,Num2: INTEGER;

BEGIN
      WRITE('Enter two integers: ');
      READLN(Num1,Num2);
      WRITE('HCF(',Num1,',',Num2,') = ');
1:    IF Num1 > Num2 THEN Num1 := Num1 - Num2
                 ELSE GOTO 2;
      GOTO 1;
2:    IF Num2 > Num1 THEN Num2 := Num2 - Num1
                 ELSE GOTO 3;
      GOTO 2;
3:    IF Num1 <> Num2 THEN GOTO 1;
      WRITELN(Num1);
END.
```

It would be wrong to conclude from the above that the use of **GOTO** leads to confusion under all circumstances. There are some situations where its judicious use is quite acceptable. In particular, **GOTO** can be useful in making a neat exit from a procedure when an error condition of some sort makes it unnecessary to execute a large part of the procedure body.

Suppose, for example, that we are trying to handle the following situation:

READ(X);
IF X > 100 THEN *print X is too large and exit from the procedure*
          ELSE *carry out the procedure*

If *carry out the procedure* involves a very large piece of code then the use of **IF-THEN-ELSE** will make the procedure body into a one long **ELSE**.

The structure will be clearer if instead we use:

> READ(X);
> IF X > 100 THEN *print X is too large and* GOTO 10
> *carry out the procedure*
> 10: . .
> END; *of procedure*

Some dialects of Pascal, e.g. TURBO Pascal, provide an exit procedure which can be used in the same way as this construction.

Advice on good programming

Try to avoid using GOTO. If you must, use it sparingly and write clear comments to explain what you are doing.

〉4.6 Conditional loops

A FOR loop can only be used when the number of iterations is known or can be calculated at the start of the loop. Very often we do not know how many iterations will be needed to complete a task. For example, if the task involves reading data we may not know the number of items to be read. There are two conditional loops provided in Pascal. In these the number of iterations is not fixed.

REPEAT *statement*
This has the general form:

> REPEAT
> *Statement list*
> UNTIL *BOOLEAN expression*;

The statement list is repeatedly executed until the value of the BOOLEAN expression becomes true. Since the BOOLEAN expression is evaluated at the end, *the statements in a* REPEAT *loop are always executed at least once.*

For example, the following construction could be used to compute the sum of a sequence of numbers when the length of the sequence is not known. The end is signalled by the number 999. Typical data could be

−10 54 33 123 999

```
Sum := 0;
READ(Number);
REPEAT
        Sum := Sum + Number;
        READ(Number);
UNTIL   Number = 999;
```

Note that there is no **BEGIN** and **END** to enclose the list of statements. The keywords **REPEAT** and **UNTIL** serve this purpose.

Also, note that if there are no data and we simply type 999 then Sum will take the value 999 when the first statement inside the **REPEAT** loop is executed and the program will hang expecting to read another number. This is a consequence of the fact that a **REPEAT** loop, as we said earlier, is always executed at least once. This difficulty is overcome by the **WHILE** statement.

WHILE *statement*

This executes one or more statements while a specified condition remains true. Unlike the **REPEAT** statement, if the controlling condition is not true then nothing is done. It has the form

WHILE *BOOLEAN expression* DO *Statement*;

BOOLEAN expression is evaluated before *Statement* (which may be a compound statement) is executed. If *BOOLEAN expression* returns the value FALSE then the loop body is not executed and the control passes to the statement following the semicolon. If it returns TRUE then *Statement* is executed and *BOOLEAN expression* is evaluated again.

Alternatively, the task in the last example can be done using:

```
Sum := 0;
READ(Number);
WHILE Number <> 999 DO
    BEGIN
            Sum := Sum + Number;
            READ(Number);
    END;
```

Unlike the **REPEAT** construction given previously, this works even when there are no data. The Sum now takes the correct value 0.

In the **FOR** loop the increment in the loop counter varies in steps of unity. The **WHILE** and **REPEAT** statements can be used when fractional steps are involved. For example, to do something starting at **X1**, finishing at **X2** and increasing in steps of **DX**, we can use the following basic construction:

```
X := X1;
WHILE X <= X2 DO
   BEGIN
      Do whatever has to be done
      X := X + DX;
   END;
```

In the final example in this section we return to the HCF problem. A bad solution was presented earlier through the program **Spaghetti** when we discussed the **GOTO** statement. The example also illustrates the nesting of unconditional loops.

```
FUNCTION HCF(Num1,Num2: INTEGER): INTEGER;
BEGIN
      REPEAT
            WHILE Num1 > Num2 DO Num1 := Num1 - Num2;
            WHILE Num2 > Num1 DO Num2 := Num2 - Num1;
      UNTIL Num1 = Num2;
      HCF := Num1;
END; {HCF}
```

In calculating the HCF of the integers **Num1** and **Num2** (the largest integer that will divide **Num1** and **Num2** exactly), use is made of the fact that the HCF of two numbers also divides their difference.

EOLN

The predefined Boolean function **EOLN** is supplied in Pascal for detecting the end of a line of data during input. The function returns TRUE if *the next character to be read* is the end-of-line character. The end-of-line character is either produced by pressing carriage return while working interactively, or by the use of **WRITELN** when writing data to **TEXT** files (discussed in Chapter 6). Constructions involving **EOLN** usually occur in a **WHILE** or a **REPEAT** loop, for example,

```
VAR nextNumber: INTEGER;
.
.
WHILE NOT EOLN DO
   BEGIN
      READ(nextNumber);
      WRITE(nextNumber:3);
   END;
```

A typical input and output from this fragment is shown below.

INPUT: −1 25 0 8 < CARRIAGE-RETURN >

OUTPUT −1 25 0 8

Comments: Clearly, there is a logical flaw in **EOLN** when it comes to interactive work. How, you may ask, can Pascal read your mind and predict that you are going to press carriage return to generate the next character? This flaw is a reflection of the fact that Pascal was not designed for interactive work from the start. The implementation of **EOLN** for input from the keyboard varies and you may find that you do not get the output in the way indicated above. Your computer may write each number as soon as it has been read. Most implementations these days rely on a line buffer. As data are typed at the keyboard, they are temporarily stored in this buffer and only made available for reading by the program when the carriange return is pressed. This means that a complete line including the end-of-line character is presented at a time and Pascal does not have to rely on fortune-telling.

Data validation

In Chapter 2, in discussing interactive programming we mentioned that we cannot expect a human user to type everything correctly. We also stated that ideally all data should be validated for correctness. In general this is a difficult problem. We now consider two examples to illustrate how validation can be incorporated in the input of data.

Very often we want to check if an input is in range. The use of subrange type can detect errors of this kind but suffers from the disadvantage that the program stops. The user is not given the opportunity to correct any typing errors. The following statements check to see if a number lies between 0 and 100 and, if not, the number is entered again.

```
REPEAT
        WRITE('How many numbers you want to sort (0..100)? ');
        READLN(Number);
        InRange := (0 <= Number) AND (Number <= 100);
        IF NOT InRange THEN
          WRITELN('Number out of range. Please enter again.');
UNTIL   InRange;
```

Consider now the following problem. We want to enter a stream of three-digit numbers which are expected to lie between 213 and 455. The following set of statements first verify that what is entered is indeed a number. This is done by reading the number as three characters and verifying that each character is a digit. Next, the **ORD** function is used to calculate the magnitude of the number and to check if this is in the required range.

```
FUNCTION valid(CH: CHAR): BOOLEAN;
BEGIN
    valid := ('0' < = CH) AND (CH < = '9');
END; {valid}

REPEAT
    WRITE('Type a 3-digit number. ');
    READLN(D1,D2,D3);
    ok := FALSE;
    numbers := valid(D1) AND valid(D2) AND valid(D3);
    IF NOT numbers THEN WRITELN('Error in data. Enter again.')
    ELSE
      BEGIN
        n := (ORD(D1)-ORD('0'))*100 + (ORD(D2) - ORD('0'))*10 + ORD(D3) - ORD('0');
        ok := (213 < = n) AND (n < = 455);
        IF NOT ok THEN WRITELN('Error in data. Enter again.');
      END;
UNTIL numbers AND ok;
```

Example 4E: the Mandelbrot set. We shall close this chapter with an example which illustrates how a conditional loop may be employed to generate the Mandelbrot set (MS). MS constitutes one of the most fascinating mathematical discoveries of recent times and has been described as 'the most complicated object in mathematics'. The explorations of various regions of MS give rise to pictures of extraordinary beauty and complexity. These pictures are examples of **fractals**. The

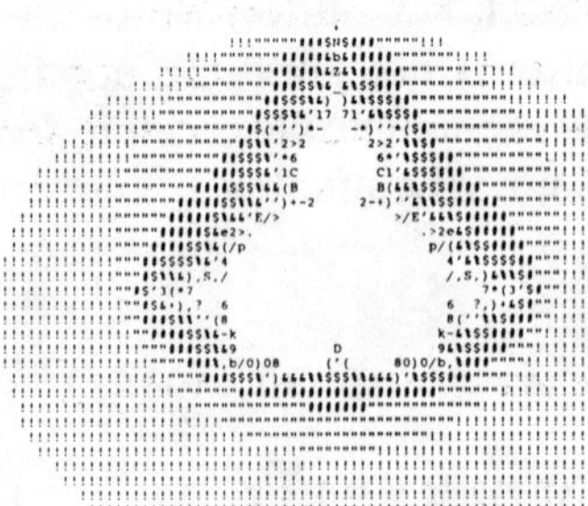

(*a*) −2, 2, −2, 2

(*b*) −0.7, 0.5, −1.2, 0

(*c*) −0.4, 0.2, −1.2, −0.6

(*d*) −0.3, 0.1, −1.1, −0.7

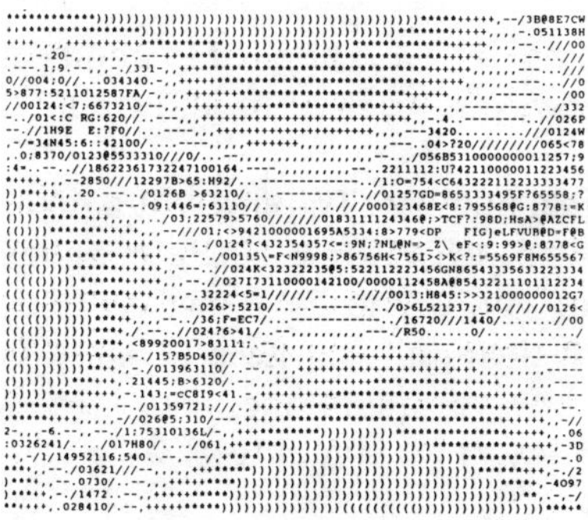

(*e*) −0.15, −0.05, −1, −0.9

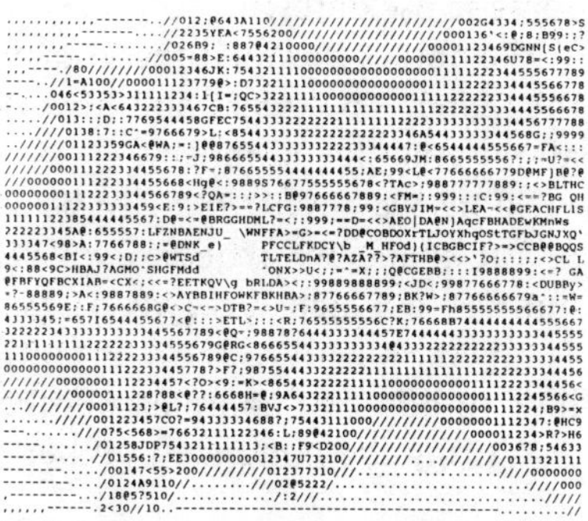

(*f*) −0.125, −0.085, −0.99, −0.9

Explorations of six regions surrounding the Mandelbrot set. The values shown refer to the choices of xMin, xMax, yMin and yMax, respectively.

fascinating thing about fractals is that no matter how small a region we explore, we find no diminution in complexity. In the accompanying figure we show a zoom sequence exploring six fractal regions.

After explaining the theory behind MS, we will examine the program **MANDEL**. You may use program **MANDEL** to indulge in a limitless number of intriguing explorations. Be warned though: such activity is potentially highly addictive.

Consider the infinite process described by the following Pascal statements:

```
z := 0;
REPEAT
        z := SQR(z) + c;
UNTIL FALSE;
```

in which z is a variable of type REAL and c is a REAL constant.

Let us examine what happens to z as we choose different values for the constant c. For example, setting $c = 1$ produces the sequence of z values 0, 1, 2, 5, 26, ... The values of z grow without limit. We say that z diverges.

The choice $c = 0.1$ produces the sequence 0, 0.1, 0.11, 0.1121, 0.1125, ... We now have a sequence of values which seems to be settling down. In fact, if we carry on repeating we will find that z gets nearer and nearer to the value 0.112 7016. In this case we say that the sequence converges.

A third type of behaviour occurs if we choose $c = -1$. We now obtain the oscillating sequence 0, -1, 0, -1, ... Thus we discover that for some choices of c the sequence z diverges, for others it converges and for some it oscillates.

We obtain the MS if the same iteration $z := z^2 + c$ is applied to points in the plane. To understand how this can be done we need to know a little about complex numbers.

So far we have taken z to be a single real number. To represent a point in the plane we require two real numbers (x, y) or a single complex number z which has two parts. Most of you would have met complex numbers, but if you are unfamiliar with them, all you need to know is how to add two complex numbers and how to square one.

Writing the complex number z as $z = (x, y)$ we compute z^2 as

$$z^2 = (x^2 - y^2, 2xy).$$

The sum of two such numbers $A = (x_1, y_1)$ and $B = (x_2, y_2)$ is

$$A + B = (x_1 + x_2, y_1 + y_2).$$

For instance, the square of the complex number $(2, 0)$ is $(4, 0)$, the square of $(0.1, 2.1)$ is $(-4.4, 0.42)$ and the sum of the two latter numbers is $(-4.3, 2.52)$.

Knowing how to square and add complex numbers, we can now allow z to be complex in the iteration we studied above. For instance, choosing $c = (1, 2)$ gives rise to the sequence $(0, 0)$, $(1, 2)$, $(-3, 4)$, $(-7, -24)$, $(-527, 336)$.... As for real numbers, different choices of c lead to different types of behaviour. MS consists of those complex numbers c for which this complex sequence does not diverge, i.e. neither of the two parts become infinitely large.

How can we decide whether a sequence will converge or diverge eventually? It can be proved that if, for a particular choice of c, the number $z = (x, y)$ produced by the iteration reaches a value such that $x^2 + y^2 \geqslant 4$, then the sequence will diverge. In that case c does not belong to the MS. This provides us with a bound for the number of terms that need to be generated in deciding on c. For example, $c = (1, 2)$ does not belong to MS because $z = (1, 2)$ produced by this choice is such that $x^2 + y^2 = 1 + 4 = 5 > 4$.

The algorithm given below is implemented in program **MANDEL** which follows after the discussion.

ALGORITHM FOR GENERATING THE MANDELBROT SET

- Set the coordinates of the region to be explored (**xMin, xMax, yMin, yMax**), the number of rows (**numRows**), columns (**numColumns**) and maximum number of iterations (**maxIterations**).
- For each of the grid points (**XRow, YColumn**) do the following:

  Get its corresponding complex number **c = (cReal,cImag)**.

  Set **z = (x,y) = (0,0), Counter = 0**.

  Repeat the next instruction until $x^2 + y^2 > 4$ or **Counter > maxIterations.**

    Set **z = z²+ c**, i.e. **z = (x² − y² + cReal, 2xy + cImag)** and increment **Counter** by one.

  Print a symbol at (**XRow, YColumn**) corresponding to the value of **Counter**.

In the above algorithm, the symbol to correspond to **Counter** can be chosen as a printable character or a coloured dot on the screen. The correspondence is entirely arbitrary and the choice of the ASCII character associated with **Counter**, as done in program **MANDEL**, is purely for convenience.

In the program **MANDEL** (also included on the disk), c is chosen in the rectangular region xMin ⩽ x ⩽ xMax, yMin ⩽ y ⩽ yMax. Of course this region contains an infinite number of points. To select a finite number of points we consider this region to be covered with a discrete grid. For graphical output in **MANDEL** this grid is defined by the choice of **NumRows** and **NumColumns** as was done in program **GRAPHICS** given at the end of Chapter 3.

In **MANDEL** the nature of c is decided by exploring whether or not the sequence produced by c diverges. If it does then c does not belong to MS. We need to set some limit on the number of iterations before concluding whether or not the sequence will diverge. In **MANDEL**, at most 127 iterations are performed. If it is true that at the 127th iteration the value $z = (x, y)$ is such that $x^2 + y^2 < 4$ then we conclude that c is a member of MS.

The pictorial interest is achieved through depicting the behaviour of points not belonging to MS. To do this, we associate the character CHR(j + 31) with each point c, where j is the number of iterations needed to decide whether or not c belongs to MS. The number 31 is added to avoid the first 32 characters which are control characters in ASCII. Since 127 is the largest ordinal value in the standard ASCII set, it provides a convenient place to stop. If the iteration reaches the value 127 then we print the character blank to depict all those points which lie in MS. The blank is chosen purely for convenience.

```
PROGRAM Mandel(INPUT,OUTPUT);
CONST
        numRows = 39;
        numColumns = 78;
        maxIterations = 96;     { number of printable characters in standard ASCII }
TYPE
      row     = 0..numRows;
      column  = 0..numColumns;
VAR
     xMin,xMax,yMin,yMax,cReal,cImag : REAL;
     x,y,XSq,YSq,XSqPlusYSq           : REAL;
     XRow                             : row;
     YColumn                          : column;
     counter                          : 0..maxIterations;

PROCEDURE transf(r: row; c: column; VAR x,y:REAL);
{ This produces the x,y coordinates of a grid point }
BEGIN
     x := (xMax - xMin)*r/numRows + xMin;
     y := (yMax - yMin)*c/numColumns + yMin;
END; {transf}

BEGIN
        WRITELN('*********** PROGRAM MANDEL ***********' :60);
        WRITELN; WRITELN;
        WRITELN('Give coordinates of the region to be explored');
        WRITELN('xMin,xMax,yMin,yMax: ');
        READLN(xMin,xMax,yMin,yMax);

        FOR Xrow := 0 TO numRows DO
            BEGIN
                  FOR YColumn := 0 TO numColumns DO
                      BEGIN
                            transf(XRow,YColumn,cReal,cImag);
                            counter := 0;
                            x := 0;
                            y := 0;
```

```
                    REPEAT
                        XSq := x*x;
                        YSq := y*y;
                        y := 2*x*y + cImag;
                        x := XSq - YSq + cReal;
                        XSqPlusYSq := XSq + YSq;
                        counter := counter + 1;
                    UNTIL (XSqPlusYSq > 4) OR (counter = maxIteration);
                    IF counter = maxIteration THEN counter := 1;
                    WRITE(CHR(31 + counter));
                END;
            WRITELN;
        END;
END.
```

The output from **MANDEL** for the choice **xMin** = −2, **Max** = 2, **yMin** = −2, **yMax** = 2, **numRows** = 39 and **numColumns** = 78 is as shown in the first of the figures in the above sequence. Program **MANDEL** needs to be explored. Included on the disk (files MANDEL1.TXT...MANDEL11.TXT) are pictures produced from explorations of MS at increasing magnifications. These are ASCII files and can be viewed in exactly the same way as your program listings.

For the benefit of TURBO Pascal users we include program T_MANDEL which produces graphical output in colour using the highest possible resolution.

Quickies

10. Find all the mistakes in the following:

(a)

```
X := A/B;
Y := 0;
CASE X OF
  BEGIN
     x < 1: Action1;
         Y: Action2;
     1,2,5: X := x + 1;
     X > 5: Action3;
     END;
```

(b)

```
CASE Number OF
  -10..-1: x := x - 1;
        0: ;
    1..10: x := x + 1;
END;
```

11. Given the declaration:

    VAR Colour: (Red, White, Blue);

    write a CASE statement to output values of Colour.

12. Under what circumstances are the WHILE and the REPEAT loops more appropriate than the FOR loop?

13. What is the minimum number of times a WHILE and a REPEAT loop is executed?

14. Explain what is wrong with the following:

```
a := 1;
REPEAT
        a := a/2;
UNTIL  a = 0.001;
```

⇒ **Your may now proceed to Pascal laboratory Activities 22–27.**

〉 Pascal laboratory

Activity 20. Program TUTOR19 is supposed to read an integer and check to see if it satisfies the following conditions: it is positive, odd, divisible by 7 and not greater than 1000. The program contains several errors; correct the errors and test it. Modify the program so that it tests for REALs which are negative and lie in the range -2 to -1.

Activity 21. Study program TUTOR20 and run it. The reason why the output is not very pretty is that many of the characters are not printable and are used for special purposes. For example, in the ASCII code, character number 10 is for line feed, character number 6 rings a bell, etc. From character number 32 onwards all the characters are printable. Find out all the printable characters on you machine. Try printing characters whose ordinal values are in the range 128–255. What happens? Modify the program so that it reads a character and prints its ordinal value, its predecessor and its successor. For example, given P, it should print 80 O Q (assuming ASCII).

Activitiy 22. Study TUTOR21 and try to predict its output. Run and verify. Modify it to compute the number of digits contained in the binary representation of a positive integer (e.g. there are five digits in the binary representation of 26).

Activity 23. Extend TUTOR22 to generate a sequence of integers i from a given positive integer N according to the following algorithm:

(1) Set $i = N$;
(2) If $i = 1$ stop.
(3) If i is even then set $i = i/2$, print i and go to step 2.
(4) Set $i = 3i + 1$ and go to step 2.

Make a conjecture as to whether the program will stop for any value of N.

Activity 24. Study TUTOR23 and predict its output for two positive integers. Verify. Try to make the program work for negative values of a and b.

Activity 25. Explore TUTOR24. Modify the program to produce Fibonacci numbers in decreasing order from 987 to -987.

Activity 26. Study TUTOR25. Predict its output. Run and verify.

Activity 27. This activity is intended for mathematically inclined students. Run TUTOR26. Study the logic behind the first section of the program. The second section utilises a mathematical result to produce the same output. Observe how the range of output is extended when n is changed from 3 to 4 in the second section. Rewrite the first section to generate the same output. Why would the second method be vastly more efficient for $n = 10$?

〉 Exercises

1*. Let A, B be Boolean variables and S_1, S_2 and S_3 be statements which are executed depending on the values of A and B according to the following table.

A	B	Execute
true	true	S_3
true	false	S_2
false	true	S_3
false	false	S_1

Write down a statement (as short as possible) to achieve this behaviour.

2*. Work out the output produced by this program when a full evaluation and when a short-circuit evaluation is performed:

```
PROGRAM ShortCircuit(OUTPUT);
VAR
    Max,Min: REAL;
    A      : INTEGER;
FUNCTION Init:BOOLEAN;
BEGIN
        Max := 100;
        Min := 0;
        Init := TRUE;
END; {Init}
BEGIN
        A := 0;
        Max := 7;
        Min := 1;
        IF (A = 0) OR Init THEN WRITELN(Max,Min);
END.
```

3*. Under what circumstances is the statement

```
B := (i = 0)  OR  ((j MOD i) = 0);
```

equivalent to the statement

```
IF i = 0 THEN B := TRUE ELSE B := (j MOD i) = 0;
```

4*. Modify TUTOR10 to replace the inner **FOR** loop with a **REPEAT-UNTIL** loop and write the code so that the variable **PRIME** is no longer needed.

5*. Modify TUTOR18 so that the main program uses a **CASE** statement and the following declarations are utilised.

```
TYPE
      Days = (Sunday,Monday,Tuesday,Wednesday,Thursday,Friday,Saturday);
VAR
     Year  : 1900..1999;
     Month: 1..12;
     Day   : 1..31;
FUNCTION f: Days;
```

6*. Write a set of statements which make use of the **WHILE** statement to execute a loop starting at **X1**, finishing at **X2** and changing in steps of **DX**. If **X1** > **X2** then the construction should automatically set **DX** decreasing so that the loop works correctly.

7. Given that two numbers are suspected of being consecutive in the Fibonacci sequence, write a program that could be used to test this conjecture.

8. Consider the sequence of pairs

$$(78, 35),\ (43, 35),\ (8, 35),\ (8, 3),\ (2, 3),\ (2, 1),\ (0, 1).$$

Each pair is obtained from the preceding one by subtracting some positive integral multiple of one of its elements from the other. Write a program that, given two positive numbers a and b, will print the shortest sequence starting with (a, b) and ending with (0, 1) or (1 0).

9. If we wanted to include the value 1234567 in a Fibonacci sequence, then what would be the two smallest positive numbers that could be used to start the sequence?

10. Suppose that in a language called RASCAL the **LOOP** statement has the following form:

$$\textbf{LOOP}\ (\mathscr{L}_1),\ \mathscr{B},\ (\mathscr{L}_2);$$

where $\mathscr{L}_1$ and $\mathscr{L}_2$ are sequences of Pascal-like statements and $\mathscr{B}$ is a Boolean expression. Examples of the **LOOP** statement are

```
LOOP (i := 1), i < 10 ,(i := i + 1;);

LOOP (i := H; H := H – 1), (i > = H) OR (j < i) ,(i := i + 1; j := j – 1;);

LOOP (i := 0; FOR N := 1 TO M DO
              BEGIN
                    i := i + N*i;
                    j := 2*j – i;
              END;),
     (i > j) AND (j > 30),
     (M := M + 1; WHILE j < SQRT(M) DO j := 2*j;);
```

Draw the syntax diagram corresponding to the **LOOP** statement.

11. Assign a Boolean expression to the variable **LeapYear** which will give TRUE if the INTEGER variable **Year** takes a value corresponding to a leap year (a leap year is divisible by four and not divisible by 100 unless it is also divisible by 400). Assuming that in a program the values of the variables **Year** and **Month: (JAN, FEB, MAR, JUN, JUL, AUG, SEP, OCT, NOV, DEC)** have been set properly, write a **CASE** statement which will check that the INTEGER variable **DayNumber** has a suitable value. For example, **DayNumber = 29** is unsuitable if **Year = 1945** and **Month = FEB**.

Answers to quickies

2. Discrete and ordered.
3. (a) F if **NonSense** is of type BOOLEAN, T otherwise
   (b) F, it equals (NOT A) or (NOT B)
   (c) T
   (d) T
   (e) F, only ordinals.
4. (a) (X < 0) AND ((X + 1)*(X + 2)*(X + 3) > 0)
   (b) (X = Y) OR (X = Z) OR (Y = Z)
   (c) NOT ODD(X) AND (Y MOD X = 0)
   (d) NOT(((– 1 < X) AND (X < 0)) OR ((4 < X) AND (X < 5))).
5. (a) 56
   (b) 9
   (c) d.
6. (a) **X**
   (b) I

(c) **PRED(X)**
(d) **SUCC(X)**.

7. **PRED(CHR(0))** is not defined.
8. (a) Illegal. The range must be increasing.
   (b) Silly but legal.
   (c) Illegal. Red has been introduced twice.
   (d) Illegal. The values in the list must be identifiers.
   (e) Illegal. Only ordinals can be used in subranges.
9. **Pet = (Cat,Dog,Rabbit)**
   Pet := Cat; is nonsense. **Pet** is not a variable.
   The **READLN** and **WRITELN** statements are invalid. Enumerated types cannot be read or written.
10. (a) **CASE** selector must be of ordinal type. **X** here is clearly REAL. No **BEGIN**. The selection list can only contain constants, hence **X < 1**, **X > 5** and **Y** are invalid.
    (b) No subranges allowed in the selection list.
11.
```
CASE Colour OF
  Red: WRITELN('Red');
 White: WRITELN('White');
  Blue: WRITELN('Blue');
END;
```
12. When the condition that terminates the loop is not known at the start of the execution.
13. 0, 1.
14. It may never stop. Real numbers should not be compared in an equality. It has to be written something like:
    UNTIL abs(a – 0.0001) < 1E – 6.

〉 Chapter 5

〉 Manipulating Structured Data: SETs and ARRAYs

In the previous chapters, the variables we met had only one component. By contrast, a variable of a structured type comprises many components. In this chapter we shall look at SETSs and ARRAYs which are the simplest structured types.

〉 5.1 SETs

In mathematics, a set is defined as an **unordered** collection of objects. No restriction is placed as to what kind of objects may form a set. Pascal offers a restricted version of this concept.

In Pascal, a SET is an unordered collection of objects of *the same TYPE* which is called the **base TYPE** of the SET. The base TYPE is restricted to be an ordinal TYPE. A number of other restrictions are imposed by the way SETs are implemented. These will be explained later.

A SET TYPE is defined via a TYPE statement or directly via a VAR statement. The TYPE statement has the form:

```
TYPE
    SetTypeIdentifier = SET OF BaseType;
```

where, as we said earlier, *BaseType* can be any ordinal TYPE. Once the SET TYPE has been defined, SET variables are defined via the VAR statement in the usual way. For instance,

```
TYPE
    Alphabet = SET OF CHAR;
    Subjects = (Mathematics, Physics, Chemistry);
```

```
VAR
    Letters  : Alphabet;
    Syllabus: SET OF Subjects;
    Digits   : SET OF 0..9;
    Grades  : SET OF 'A'..'F';
    Capitals: SET OF 'A'..'Z';
    Smalls   : SET OF 'a'..'z';
```

SETs are written by enclosing them between square brackets and by enumerating their elements. For example,

```
Letters := [];      { This denotes the empty set which has no elements }
Syllabus := [Mathematics,Chemistry];
Digits := [0..3,6,9];
Grades := ['C','D','A'];
Capitals := ['P','A','S','C','A','L'];
Smalls := ['p','a','s'];
Digits := [2,i,j + k];   { The element can be expressions of the base type }
```

Note that the order in which the elements are enumerated is immaterial; for example, the assignment

Grades := ['D','A','C'];

defines exactly the same set as before.

The relational operators defined on **SET**s have the following meaning:

A = B	SETs A and B contain the same elements.
A < > B	SETs A and B do not contain the same elements.
A < = B	SET A is contained in SET B.
A > = B	SET A contains SET B.

For example, consider X = [1 ... 10], Y = [2, 4, 6, 8, 10], Z = [6, 8, 4, 10, 2]. Then

Y = Z	TRUE
X = Y	FALSE
X < > Y	TRUE
Y < = X	TRUE
Y < = Z	TRUE
Y > = Z	TRUE

The fundamental way in which **SET**s are used involves deciding whether or not various items are included in some **SET**. A special operator, denoted by the keyword **IN**, is available to test set membership. The syntax of its usage is

Expression IN *Set*

where *Expression* must yield a value of the base **TYPE** of *Set*. For example, to test whether **O** is contained in the set **S** we can write

IF O IN S THEN *SomeAction*;

The **IN** operator is particularly useful in simplifying Boolean conditions. For example,

IF (CH = 'A') OR (CH = 'E') OR (CH = 'I') OR (CH = 'O') OR (CH = 'U') THEN ...

can be written more compactly as

IF CH IN ['A','E','I','O','U'] THEN ...

The operators +, * and − are used in manipulating **SET**s. Their meanings for **SET**s **A** and **B** are

A + B Union. The SET containing the elements which are in either A or B or both.

A * B Intersection. The SET containing the elements that are common to both A and B.

A − B Difference or Complement. The SET containing the elements of A that are not included in B.

For example, assuming X = [1..5,26..29], Y = [25..30]:

```
X + Y = [1..5,25..30];
X * Y = [26..29];
X − Y = [1..5];
Y − X = [25,30];
```

The four relational operators =, <>, <= and >=, and the operators +, * and − when applied to sets have exactly the same precedence as the corresponding arithmetical operators. For example, in evaluating the expression

[7..15] − [3..25] >= [1..100] * [50..200] + [120..210]

the intersection * will be evaluated first, then the difference − followed by the union +. The relational operator >= will be applied last.

SETs cannot be read or written directly. To output a set we have to loop over the complete range of the base **TYPE** and use the **IN** operator to check whether or not an element is in the set; if it is, it can be printed. The input requires some special treatment depending on the base **TYPE** but it can be achieved by reading an element and adding it to the set using the union operator, as shown in Example 5A.

Comment. As we remarked at the beginning of this section, the way **SET**s are implemented in Pascal limits the number of elements that can belong to a **SET**, a typical limit being 256 (TURBO Pascal and VAX Pascal). Furthermore, the maximum ordinal value is restricted which limits the INTEGERs that can belong to a **SET**. For example, assuming a restriction of 256, the integers in the subrange 0 ... 100 can be included in a **SET** but the integers in the subrange 200 ... 300 cannot, since **ORD**(300) = 300 > 256. Because the **SET** data type is restricted by the implementation, there can be many situations where it cannot be used in practice despite the fact that logically it would be the most appropriate data structure.

Example 5A: computer dating. The problem tackled in this example is this: a computer dating service wants to decide if an applicant is a suitable match for another. A suitable individual in this instance is one whose interests include *at least one* from the list: books, opera and drinking and who dislikes *all* in the list: dancing, TV and fashion.

Program **ComputerDating**, which is given below, solves this problem. In it **PROCEDURE Choose** is used to input the sets **YesSet** and **NoSet** which reflect the interests and dislikes of an applicant. **FUNCTION Suitable** is used to decide whether the applicant satisfies the requirements.

Let **A** denote the set of interests of an applicant. The algorithm used in the **FUNCTION Suitable** is based on the fact that the intersection of the **YesSet** with the set [**Books,Opera,Drinking**] must have at least one element and the set [**Dancing, TV, Fashion**] must be contained in **NoSet**.

Typical data for the program might be

```
0689  { giving YesSet = [Eating, Books, Religion, Jogging] }
2457  { giving NoSet = [Dancing, TV, Fashion, Opera] }
```

With these data the applicant will be judged as being suitable.

Program **ComputerDating** is included in the disk under the name TUTOR27.

```
PROGRAM ComputerDating(INPUT,OUTPUT);
TYPE
    Pursuits     = (Eating,Drinking,Dancing,Travel,TV,
                    Fashion,Books,Opera,Religion,Jogging);
    Interests    = SET OF Pursuits;
    numPursuits = 1..10;
```

```
VAR
    YS,NS : Interests;
    choice: numpursuits;

FUNCTION Suitable(YS,NS: Interests): BOOLEAN;
VAR
    s: Interests;
    Intellectual,Common: Interests;
BEGIN
      Intellectual:= [Books,Opera,Drinking];
      Common:= [Dancing,TV,Fashion];
      s:= YS*Intellectual;
      Suitable:= (s <> []) AND (s <= Intellectual) AND (Common <= NS);
END; {Suitable}

PROCEDURE Choose(VAR YesSet,NoSet: Interests);
VAR
    ch : CHAR;
BEGIN
      WRITELN('                    --- PURSUITS ---'); WRITELN;
      WRITELN('     0: Eating           5: Fashion');
      WRITELN('     1: Drinking         6: Books');
      WRITELN('     2: Dancing          7: Opera');
      WRITELN('     3: Travel           8: Religion');
      WRITELN('     4: TV               9: Jogging');
      WRITELN; WRITELN;
      WRITE(' List all the numbers corresponding to your likes: ');
      YesSet:= [];
      WHILE NOT EOLN DO
          BEGIN
              READ(ch);
              CASE ch OF
                  '0': YesSet:= YesSet + [Eating];
                  '1': YesSet:= YesSet + [Drinking];
                  '2': YesSet:= YesSet + [Dancing];
                  '3': YesSet:= YesSet + [Travel];
                  '4': YesSet:= YesSet + [TV];
                  '5': YesSet:= YesSet + [Fashion];
                  '6': YesSet:= YesSet + [Books];
                  '7': YesSet:= YesSet + [Opera];
                  '8': YesSet:= YesSet + [Religion];
                  '9': YesSet:= YesSet + [Jogging];
              END;
          END;
      READLN; { This gets rid of the EOLN }
      WRITE(' List all the numbers corresponding to your dislikes: ');
      NoSet:= [];
      WHILE NOT EOLN DO
```

```
        BEGIN
                READ(ch);
                CASE ch OF
                        '0': NoSet := NoSet + [Eating];
                        '1': NoSet := NoSet + [Drinking];
                        '2': NoSet := NoSet + [Dancing];
                        '3': NoSet := NoSet + [Travel];
                        '4': NoSet := NoSet + [TV];
                        '5': NoSet := NoSet + [Fashion];
                        '6': NoSet := NoSet + [Books];
                        '7': NoSet := NoSet + [Opera];
                        '8': NoSet := NoSet + [Religion];
                        '9': NoSet := NoSet + [Jogging];
                END;
        END;
    READLN;
END; {Choose}

BEGIN
    REPEAT
            Choose(YS,NS);
            IF YS * NS <> [] THEN
              BEGIN
                    WRITELN; WRITELN;
                    WRITELN(' Incorrect data. Type again');
                    WRITELN;
              END;
    UNTIL YS * NS = [];
    WRITELN; WRITELN;
    IF Suitable(YS,NS) THEN WRITELN('This person is ok!')
                       ELSE WRITELN('Sorry. Reject this one');
END.
```

Quickies

1. List all possible values of the following sets:

   (a) SET OF (1..2)
   (b) SET OF (cat, dog, bird)

   In general, how many distinct **SET** values are defined if the base **TYPE** has *n* values?

2. Which of the following are valid? If invalid explain.

   (a) VAR Grades: SET OF ['A'..'F'];
   (b) VAR Grades: SET OF 'A'..'F';

(c) TYPE Grades = ('A','B','C','D','E','F');
Results = SET OF Grades;
(d) CONST Fruits = ['Apple','Banana'];
(e) TYPE Jobs = (Baker,Tinker,Tailor,Postman);
Employees = SET OF Jobs;
Staff = SET OF Employees;
(f) x NOT IN [0..10]
(g) IF 'a' IN [1,2] THEN

3. Given X = [1 .. 3,20 .. 30], Y = [2 .. 10], Z = [7 ..17], evaluate

(a) X*Z
(b) (X + Y)*Z
(c) X + Y − X*Y
(d) NOT(5 IN X)
(e) X*Y > = Z

4. Given that p, q, r, s are all variables of the same ordinal TYPE, use SETs to simplify

(a) (p > = '0') AND (p < = '9')
(b) (p = s) OR (q = s) OR (r = s)
(c) (p = s) AND (q = s) AND (r = s)

⇒ **You may now proceed to Pascal laboratory Activity 28.**

〉 5.2 One-dimensional ARRAYs

The **SET** is a primitive data structure. The elements of a set are unordered and cannot be accessed directly. A structure in which the elements can be accessed directly is provided by the data **TYPE ARRAY**.

The **ARRAY** is the simplest structured **TYPE** that is suitable for manipulating and organising large collections of similar data. Since such tasks are fundamental to computing, the **ARRAY** is one of the most widely used data structures. Also, the **ARRAY** is the counterpart of vectors and matrices which are basic mathematical tools. For this reason **ARRAY**s are heavily used in scientific calculations.

Pascal offers one-dimensional as well as multi-dimensional arrays (arrays of arrays). Also, **ARRAY**s may optionally be **packed** to make more efficient use of memory. Let us examine one-dimensional **ARRAY**s.

A one-dimensional **ARRAY** is an ordered structure with a fixed number of elements, all of the same **TYPE**. Here is a simple example to show how we can declare such an array:

VAR x: ARRAY [1..5] OF INTEGER;

This declaration makes **x** an **ARRAY** variable having five elements of **TYPE** INTEGER. The elements of **x** are referenced as **x** [1], **x** [2], **x** [3], **x** [4] and **x** [5] and can be pictured as pigeonholes:

X[1]	X[2]	X[3]	X[4]	X[5]
1	2	3	4	5

The value used inside the square bracket to refer to an element is called its **index** or **subscript**. In general the index can be an expression of the appropriate **TYPE**, e.g. **x** [2 * I + 15 DIV J], but the expression must produce a value in the range defined by the declaration. For example, here it would be illegal to write **x** [I + J] if I = 4 and J = 2.

Each element of an **ARRAY** is a variable in its own right and all the operations that are available to its **TYPE** can be performed in the usual way. For example, the statement

x [3] := 7;

assigns the value of 7 to the third element of **x**.

The reading and writing of **ARRAY**s has to be done via individual elements and the manner depends on their **TYPE**. The statements below show how, with the above declaration, we could read five integer values into the array **x** and find and print the smallest element and its position.

```
WRITE('Enter 5 integers: ');
FOR index := 1 TO 5 DO READ(x [index]);
READLN;
position := 1;
FOR index := 2 TO 5 DO
    IF x [position] > x [index] THEN position := index;
WRITELN('The smallest element is x [',position,'] = ',x [position]);
```

In general, the **TYPE** statement for an **ARRAY** has the form

```
TYPE
    ArrayTypeIdentifier = ARRAY [IndexMin..IndexMax] OF ElementType;
```

where *IndexMin..IndexMax* is a subrange of an ordinal **TYPE** and

ElementType is any data **TYPE** except a **FILE TYPE** (to be introduced in the next chapter).

Some examples of **ARRAY** declaration are

```
CONST
      min = – 10;   max = 10;   classSize = 30;
TYPE
    Range = 1..20;
    Colours = (Red,White,Black,Green,Blue,Yellow,Cyan);
    Marks = ARRAY [1..classSize] OF INTEGER;
VAR
    X: ARRAY [min..max] OF REAL;
    Name: ARRAY [Range] OF CHAR;
    colourCode: ARRAY [Red..Cyan] OF 1..7;
    firstYear,secondYear,thirdYear: Marks:
    bitPatterns: ARRAY [1..8] of BOOLEAN;
    pattern: ARRAY [1..10] OF Colours;
```

Each of these declarations, apart from giving a name to an **ARRAY**, establishes the **TYPE** and range of the index and the **TYPE** of its elements.

The only operation defined on **ARRAYS** is that of assignment. Care has to be taken, however, since the assignment may only be performed on **ARRAY**s of identical **TYPE**. For example, given the declarations

```
TYPE
      list = ARRAY [1..100] OF INTEGER;
VAR
      list1,list2: list;
      x: ARRAY [1..10] OF REAL;
      y: ARRAY [1..10] OF REAL;
```

it is valid to write

```
list1 := list2;
```

However, the statement

```
x := y;
```

is illegal. This may come as a great surprise, being an example of overzealous use of **TYPE** in Pascal. To make two **ARRAY**s of identical **TYPE** it is necessary to use either a **TYPE** definition as done for **list1** and list2 or to include them in the same **VAR** declaration, i.e.

```
X,Y: ARRAY[1..10] OF REAL;
```

〉5.3 Searching and sorting

One of the major uses of **ARRAY**s is in searching and sorting. Searching is the process of looking for a particular element in a list and sorting involves the rearranging of items in a list into ascending or descending order. There are a multitude of searching and sorting algorithms and their suitability depends on factors such as: how many elements are there, are the elements expected to be almost ordered or are they in entirely random order, etc? What constitutes the *best* search or sort algorithm depends on the particular task and usually involves a compromise between various conflicting demands such as execution times and storage space. Below we look at some examples.

Sequential search
This is the simplest method and involves examining each item in the list in turn to determine if it is the one we are searching for. Assuming that the list comprises n items and is stored in the **ARRAY** List with the index in the range 1 ... n, the Pascal code for the algorithm is

```
i:= 1;
WHILE (List[i] <> needed) AND (i<n) DO i:= i + 1;
found:= List[i] = needed;
IF found THEN WRITE('The needed element exists at position ',i)
         ELSE WRITE('Element not found.');
```

Binary search
If the list to be searched is in order then a far more efficient method, called a binary search, can be used. Let us assume that we have a list in ascending order. The algorithm employs a divide-and-conquer strategy. It starts by examining the middle element, or one near the middle if the list contains an even number of elements. If this element is found to be larger than the test item, then the algorithm repeats the same process for the first half of the list; otherwise, it repeats it for the second half.

For example, to search for ‘f’ in the list

'b','e','f','g','h','r','z'

the algorithm will first find ‘g’. It will then consider the portion of the list 'b', 'e', 'f' to find 'e'. In the next step, it will discover 'f'. Here is a fragment of Pascal code for the algorithm:

```
left := 1;
right := n;
found := FALSE;
WHILE (left < = right) AND NOT(found) DO
    BEGIN
        mid := (left + right) DIV 2;
        IF needed < List[mid] THEN right := mid - 1
        IF needed > List[mid] THEN left := mid + 1;
        IF needed = List[mid] THEN found := TRUE;
    END;
IF found THEN WRITE ('The needed element exists at position ',mid)
    ELSE WRITE('Element not found.');
```

Bubble sort

The simplest method of sorting is perhaps the bubble sort. It is not an efficient method for sorting a truly disorganised list, but a list in which only a few items are out of place is sorted quickly. The method has attracted a lot of notoriety and has been described as being 'unbeatable in its inefficiency' but, because the algorithm is a natural one, it is worth studying.

In this method, the first two items are compared and interchanged if necessary; then the same is done to the second and third and so on until the $(n-1)$th and the nth. Now the whole process is repeated again with the first $n-1$ items in the rearranged list, then with $n-2$ items and so on until there are only two items left to compare. This is demonstrated below for the list 68, 13, 56, 3:

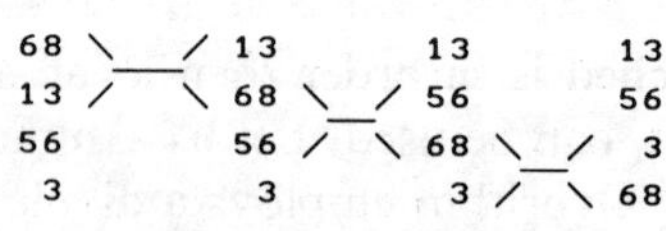

In the first pass shown above, the 'heaviest' number 68 'sinks' to the bottom. The second pass considers the list 13, 56, 3 and the final one considers the list 13, 3 to achieve the sorted result.

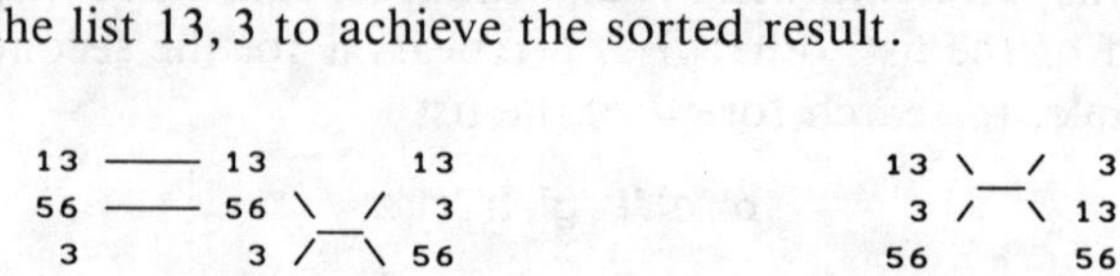

Note how the 'lightest' element 3 has 'bubbled up' to the top. This is the origin of the name of the method.

The method can be coded quite easily using two loops:

```
FOR i := 1 to n – 1 DO
    FOR j :=i + 1 to n DO
        IF List [i] < List [j] THEN
          BEGIN
                temp := List [i];
                List [i] := List [j];
                List [j] := temp;
          END;
```

Insertion sort

Insertion sort is another simple method of sorting. In it, one test value at a time is inserted in that part of the list of elements which is already in order. For example, consider the following list of integers:

5 –3 18 3 0 5

To sort them in ascending order we proceed as follows.

Start by choosing the second element. On comparing it with the first element we find that it is smaller and so we place the second element in the first position in the list and rearrange the list as

–3 5 18 3 0 5

Part of the list comprising the first two elements is now in order.

We now pick on the third element 18 and we try to insert it in the correct position in the ordered part of the list. As it happens, it is occupying the correct position so the list does not change.

We now repeat the same process with 3 0 5 and the list changes as

–3 3 5 18 0 5
–3 0 3 5 18 5
–3 0 3 5 5 18

In general, the insertion sort algorithm to sort n elements which have been placed in an **ARRAY List** is

Do from $j = 2$ to $j = n$ the following:

(1) Find the correct position k of List $[j]$ in the range $1 \ldots j$.

(2) If $k \neq j$ then shift all the elements from List $[k]$ to List $[j-1]$ one position to the right. Make List $[k]$ = List $[j]$.

PROCEDURE InsertSort given below implements this algorithm. Step 1 is achieved by the **FUNCTION findWhere**. It returns the position where the *j*th element should be inserted. Step 2 is achieved by the **PROCEDURE shiftRight**.

```
CONST
        nMax = 100; {Maximum number of elements}
TYPE
      listSize = 0..nMax;
      list = ARRAY [listSize] OF INTEGER;

PROCEDURE InsertSort(VAR L:list; size:listSize);
TYPE
      testPosition = 1..nMax;
      insertPosition = 1..nMax;
VAR
     position: testPosition;
     where: insertPosition;

     FUNCTION findWhere(j:testPosition): insertPosition;
     VAR
          k: 0..nMax;
     BEGIN
            k := j;
            REPEAT k := k - 1;
            UNTIL (k = 0) OR (L[k] < = L[j]);
            findWhere := k + 1;
     END; {findWhere}

     PROCEDURE shiftRIGHT(j1: insertPosition; j2: testPosition);
     VAR
          t: INTEGER; k: 1..nMax;
     BEGIN
            t := L[j2];
            FOR k := j2 DOWNTO j1 + 1 DO L[k] := L[k - 1];
            L[j1]:= t;
     END; {shiftRight}

BEGIN
       FOR position := 2 TO size DO
            BEGIN
                   where := findWhere(position);
                   IF where < > position THEN shiftRight(where,position);
            END;
END; {InsertSort}
```

⟩ 5.4 Passing ARRAY parameters to PROCEDUREs and FUNCTIONs

Note that, in the **PROCEDURE InsertSort**, the **TYPE** of the **ARRAY L** has been defined via a **TYPE** declaration. This was not done merely to improve the appearance of the program. In Pascal there are two ways of declaring **ARRAY**s as formal parameters.

The first method used here requires the declaration of a *type name* in a **TYPE** declaration and it is the *type name* which must be given in the parameter list. Since a **TYPE** declaration fixes the size of an **ARRAY**, this method only allows the passing of **ARRAY**s of exactly the same size to a **PROCEDURE** or a **FUNCTION**. Ideally, one would like to be able to write something such as

```
PROCEDURE InsertSort(size: INTEGER; VAR L: ARRAY[1..size] OF INTEGER);
```

so that one need not reserve space for more than is necessary. This is not allowed in Pascal and is a limitation.

Another method, called **conformant array parameters**, which does allow some liberty in passing **ARRAY**s of variable sizes, will be discussed towards the end of this chapter.

There is another point about passing **ARRAY** parameters which has to do with efficiency. When an **ARRAY** value parameter is supplied to a **PROCEDURE** or a **FUNCTION**, a copy of the **ARRAY** has to be made to perform the computations involving the elements. For a sizeable **ARRAY** this copying process increases the execution time. For this reason, it is normal practice to supply **ARRAY**s as **VAR** parameters even when we do not require any values to be returned. Of course, care must be taken that no unintentional corruption takes place.

Advice on good programming

Always pass **ARRAY**s to **PROCEDURE**s and **FUNCTION**s as **VAR** parameters, otherwise execution time as well as memory is wasted.

Quickies

5. Which of the following are valid? If invalid, explain.

   (a) VAR X: ARRAY[10] OF REAL;

(b)
```
TYPE
      cardSuits = (club,diamond,heart,spade);
VAR
      hand: ARRAY [cardSuits] OF cardSuits;
```
(c) `VAR Y: ARRAY [-10..10] OF 10..100;`
(d) `FUNCTION F(X: INTEGER): ARRAY [1..10] OF INTEGER;`
(e) `PROCEDURE X(N: INTEGER: A: ARRAY [1..N] OF REAL);`
(f) `VAR X: ARRAY [10..10] OF SET OF 1..10;`

6. Describe the effect of the following statements:

(a)
```
FOR Student := 1 TO 100 DO
    Mark [Student] :=
        ROUND((ExamMark [Student] + ProjectMark [Student])/2);
```
(b)
```
FOR Letter := 'A' TO 'Z' DO
    Position [Letter] := ORD(Letter) - ORD('A') + 1;
```
(c)
```
Sum := 0;
FOR i := 1 TO size DO
    IF A [i] > 0 THEN Sum := Sum + A [i];
```

⇒ **You may now proceed to Pascal laboratory Activities 29–30.**

〉5.5 Strings

A string, as you recall, is a sequence of characters. Such sequences have to be manipulated frequently in the processing of textual information. Standard Pascal offers only limited facilities for manipulating strings. Most implementations of Pascal offer many extensions but of course the use of these restricts portability.

String constants were introduced early in Chapter 2. In the next section we shall learn how to handle variable strings.

PACKED ARRAY*s* OF CHAR

In Pascal, a string variable has to be declared as a PACKED ARRAY OF CHAR. The TYPE declaration takes the form

```
TYPE
      String = PACKED ARRAY [1..IndexMax] OF CHAR;
```

where *IndexMax* is an integer greater than one. For example,

```
Type
        Address: PACKED ARRAY[1..30] OF CHAR;
```

The word PACKED needs to be explained. Normally, the unit of storage in a computer is a **word**, which may typically comprise 16 or 32 bits. This usage, however, can be extremely inefficient; for example, to represent a Boolean value only one bit is needed. To make more efficient use of computer memory, an obvious move is to pack as many items into a word as possible. In Pascal, the word PACKED in the definition of an ARRAY (or RECORD, to be introduced in the next chapter) is a directive to the compiler to squeeze the elements into as little space as possible. Although PACKED can be specified in any ARRAY declaration, it is most relevant in the case of strings. Such ARRAYs have extra facilities which are not available to other ARRAY TYPEs. We shall now describe them making use of the following declaration:

```
VAR
    Name,HisName,MyName: PACKED ARRAY[1..10] OF CHAR;
```

The assignment of values to string variables is done using single quotes. For instance,

```
Name := 'John Smith';
```

In standard Pascal, the assignment is only valid if the value on the right-hand side has exactly the number of characters declared in the PACKED ARRAY. Thus, it will be invalid to write

```
Name := 'John'; or
Name := 'Sherlock Holmes';
```

In the case where the number of characters is fewer than the size of the ARRAY we can pad the string with blanks; thus we could write

```
Name := 'John      ';
```

In standard Pascal, the reading of string variables has to be done via single characters, e.g.

```
FOR i := 1 TO 10 DO READ(Name[i]);
```

although many implementations of Pascal will also allow the reading in one go, e.g.

```
READ(Name);
```

A string variable can be output by referring to its name, e.g.

```
WRITE(Name);
```

Strings *of equal length* may be compared using the relational operators. The criteria for comparison are based naturally on ordinal values. When testing two strings, corresponding characters in each are compared. When two characters are found to be different, then their ordinal values decide which string has the greater value. For instance, 'BLAST' < 'BLAZE'. Some typical examples of statements involving string comparisons are

```
If MyName < = HisName THEN WRITE('Names are in alphabetical order');
IF Name = 'John Jones' THEN WRITELN('He is a Welshman');
```

Example 5B: word wrap. As an example on PACKED ARRAY OF CHAR we consider the following problem: write a program that will accept a line of text and will output a set of wrapped lines, as shown below for the input CONCISE PASCAL:

```
CONCISE PASCAL
ONCISE PASCAL C
NCISE PASCAL CO
CISE PASCAL CON
ISE PASCAL CONC
SE PASCAL CONCI
E PASCAL CONCIS
 PASCAL CONCISE
PASCAL CONCISE
ASCAL CONCISE P
SCAL CONCISE PA
CAL CONCISE PAS
AL CONCISE PASC
L CONCISE PASCA
 CONCISE PASCAL
CONCISE PASCAL
```

The algorithm used is as follows:

Read the line into a PACKED ARRAY OF CHAR
Repeat
  Save the first character in the array
  Shift the remaining characters one position to the left
  Put the saved first character at the last position
  Write out the array
until we have gone through all the characters.

```
PROGRAM Wrap(INPUT,OUTPUT);
TYPE
    range = 1..50;
VAR
   sentence      :PACKED ARRAY[range] OF CHAR;
   i,length,row  :range;
   aux:          :CHAR;

BEGIN
     WRITE('Input text (less than 50 characters long): ');
     i := 1;
     WHILE NOT EOLN DO
          BEGIN
                READ(sentence[i]);
                i := i + 1;
          END;
     length := i - 1;
     FOR row := 1 TO length DO
          BEGIN
                FOR i := 1 TO length DO WRITE(sentence[i]);
                WRITELN;
                aux := sentence[1];
                FOR i := 1 TO length - 1 DO sentence[i] := sentence[i + 1];
                sentence[length] := aux;
          END;
END.
```

Quickies

7. Name two additional properties that are available to a **PACKED ARRAY OF CHAR** which are not available to other **TYPE**s of **ARRAY**s.

8. In comparing strings, what basis is used to decide if one string is less than another?

9. Assuming the following declaration:

```
VAR
     X:PACKED ARRAY[1..10] OF CHAR;
```

determine which of the following are valid? If invalid, explain.

(a) READ(X);

(b) WRITE(X);

(c)
```
FOR I:= 1 TO 5 DO
    BEGIN
        READ(X[i]);
        WRITE(X[i]);
    END;
```

(d) `X:= 'John';`

10. Is the following valid? If not, explain.

```
VAR
    X:PACKED ARRAY[2..10] OF CHAR;
.
.
WRITE(X);
```

⇒ **You may now proceed to Pascal laboratory Activity 31.**

〉 5.6 Multi-dimensional ARRAYs

Recall that the element TYPE of an ARRAY can be any TYPE except a FILE TYPE. In particular, the element TYPE may be another ARRAY. This gives rise to multi-dimensional ARRAYs. For example,

```
TYPE
    matrix = ARRAY[1..5] OF ARRAY[1..3] OF REAL;
    cube   = ARRAY[1..3] OF ARRAY[1..3] OF ARRAY[1..3] OF REAL;
VAR
   table  : matrix;
   object: cube;
```

If an index is used to specify a multi-dimensional ARRAY variable, for example table[4], then the resulting variable is another ARRAY which can again be indexed; for example, table[4][2].

Similarly, three indices may be used to specify the real elements of the three-dimensional ARRAY object, for instance object[i][j][k].

An equivalent form for the above TYPE declarations is

```
TYPE
    matrix = ARRAY[1..5,1..3] OF REAL;
    cube   = ARRAY[1..3,1..3,1..3] OF REAL;
```

Also, the elements of a multi-dimensional ARRAY can be indexed in two equivalent ways: table[4][2] is equivalent to table[4,2] and, similarly, object[i][j][k] can be written equivalently as object[i,j,k].

Example 5C: Pascal's triangle. In Pascal's triangle, as displayed below, each number, except 1, is the sum of the two numbers in the previous row, one being directly above and one to the left. Our problem is to write a program to generate the first *n* rows.

```
1
1    1
1    2    1
1    3    3    1
1    4    6    4    1
1    5   10   10    5    1
1    6   15   20   15    6    1
1    7   21   35   35   21    7    1
1    8   28   56   70   56   28    8    1
1    9   36   84  126  126   84   36    9    1
1   10   45  120  210  252  210  120   45   10    1
```

In the program **PascalsTriangle** below, a two-dimensional **ARRAY** is used to generate the values in the triangle. The **ARRAY** elements corresponding to the diagonal and the left-hand column are set to 1. The rest of the values for each element are calculated by adding the values of the appropriate elements in the row above. Only half of the **ARRAY** is utilised and therefore storage is not used very efficiently. The problem can be done using one-dimensional **ARRAY**s but the algorithm requires more work.

```
PROGRAM PascalsTriangle(INPUT,OUTPUT);
CONST
    n = 10;
VAR
  triangle    : ARRAY [1..n,1..n] OF INTEGER;
  row,column: 1..n;

BEGIN
    FOR row := 1 TO n DO triangle [row,row] := 1; { fill the diagonal }
    FOR row :=2 TO n DO triangle [row,1] := 1;    { fill the first column }
    FOR row := 3 TO n DO
        FOR column := 2 TO n - 1 DO
            triangle [row,column] :=
                triangle [row - 1,column] +      { the only directly above }
                triangle [row - 1,column - 1];   { the one to the left }

    FOR row := 1 TO n DO
        BEGIN
            FOR column := 1 TO row DO WRITE(triangle [row,column]:5);
            WRITELN;
        END;
END.
```

Example 5D: magic squares. Magic squares have fascinated humans from very early times, being particularly popular in India and China. A magic square of order n is a two-dimensional array of n^2 integers which has the property that the sum of the numbers in each row, column or the diagonals add up to the same value. For instance, the array below is a magic square of order 3:

```
4 9 2
3 5 7
8 1 6
```

A method which will generate a magic square of odd order n with elements in the range $1 \ldots n^2$ can be visualised as follows.

Initially, the magic square will comprise an empty two-dimensional array. Start by writing a 1 in the middle of the bottom row. Imagine that the magic square to be constructed is surrounded with identical copies of itself as in a tiling and that every time a number is entered, it also appears in all the corresponding positions in every tile. Now repeat the following process until all the positions have been filled:

> Travel diagonally down and to the right to an adjacent empty cell and write the next integer. If the cell already has an entry, then move one row up instead, keeping in the same column. If you enter a cell of a neighbouring tile outside the magic square, then jump to the corresponding cell position inside the square.

The rule becomes clearer if we look at a bigger magic square, e.g. the 11×11 one below. As soon as we start, we go out into a neighbouring tile and then we jump to enter 2. The numbers 3,4,5,6 are written diagonally and then we jump again to write 7. When we reach 11 the next position is occupied so we jump one row up to write 12, and so on.

```
 56  69  82  95 108 121   2  15  28  41  54
 55  57  70  83  96 109 111   3  16  29  42
 43  45  58  71  84  97 110 112   4  17  30
 31  44  46  59  72  85  98 100 113   5  18
 19  32  34  47  60  73  86  99 101 114   6
  7  20  33  35  48  61  74  87  89 102 115
 16   8  21  23  36  49  62  75  88  90 103
104 117   9  22  24  37  50  63  76  78  91
 92 105 118  10  12  25  38  51  64  77  79
 80  93 106 119  11  13  26  39  52  65  67
 68  81  94 107 120   1  14  27  40  53  66
```

To write a computer program all we need is to work out how to travel diagonally in a two-dimensional array and how to make the jumps to the appropriate positions. This is not very difficult and you are invited to work out the solution and then study the program **magicSquares** which follows. This program is included on the disk under the name MAGICSQ.PAS.

```
PROGRAM magicSquares(INPUT,OUTPUT);
CONST
      n=11;
Type
     dimensions=1..n;
     range      =0..121; {n*n}
VAR
    square                 : ARRAY[dimension,dimension] OF range;
    currRowPos,currColPos: dimension;
    nextRowPos,nextColPos: 1..12; { n+1 }
    number                 : range;
BEGIN
      FOR currRowPos:= 1 TO n DO
          FOR currColPos:= 1 TO n DO
              square[currRowPos,currColPos]:= 0; {square is empty}
      currRowPos:= n;
      currColPos:= 1+(n DIV 2);       {start in the middle of the bottom row}

      FOR number:= 1 TO n*n-1 DO
          BEGIN
                square[currRowPos,currColPos]:= number;
                nextRowPos:= currRowPos+1;
                nextColPos:= currColPos+1;

                {search for a vacant position}
                IF nextRowPos=n+1 THEN nextRowPos:= 1;
                IF nextColPos=n+1 THEN nextColPos:= 1;
                IF square[nextRowPos,nextColPos] <> 0 THEN {cell occupied}
                  BEGIN
                         nextRowPos:= currRowPos-1;
                         nextColPos:= currColPos;
                  END;
                  currRowPos:= nextRowPos;
                  currColPos:= nextColPos;
          END;
      square[currRowPos,currColPos]:= n*n;

      WRITELN('A MAGIC SQUARE OF ORDER ',n,':');
      FOR currRowPos:= 1 TO n DO
          BEGIN
                FOR currColPos:= 1 TO n DO
                     WRITE(square[currRowPos,currColPos]:4);
                WRITELN;
          END;
END.
```

Example 5E: finding routes between cities. Matrices are two-dimensional **ARRAY**s; in what follows we will assume that you have met matrices in a mathematics course and are familiar with matrix multiplication.

Matrices frequently offer a useful way for representing information. For example, consider n cities $1, 2, \ldots, n$ and their connections by various roads and air routes. The air connections can be stored as an n by n matrix **Air**, in which **Air**$[i, j] = 1$ if there is a direct route from city i to city j and **Air**$[i, j] = 0$ if there is none. For example, for the following connections diagram, the matrices **Air** and **Road** are

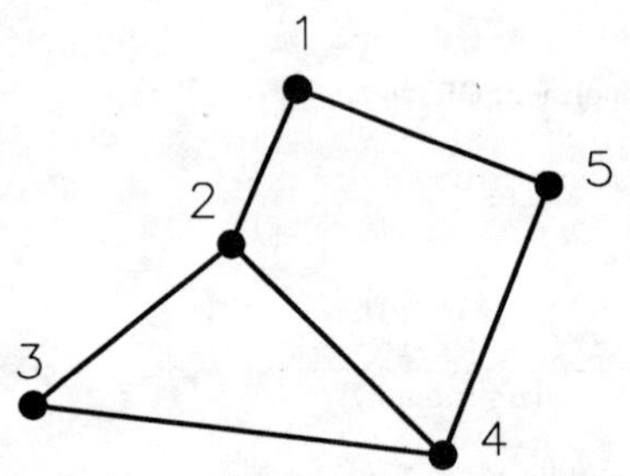

AIR ROUTES

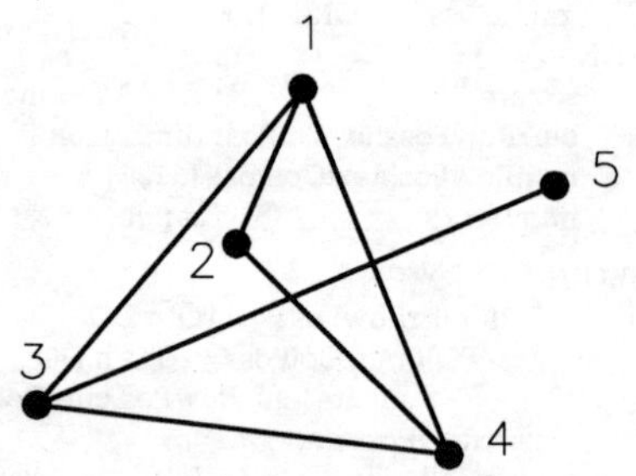

ROAD ROUTES

$$\text{Air} = \begin{matrix} 0 & 1 & 0 & 0 & 1 \\ 1 & 0 & 1 & 1 & 0 \\ 0 & 1 & 0 & 1 & 0 \\ 0 & 1 & 1 & 0 & 1 \\ 1 & 0 & 0 & 1 & 0 \end{matrix} \qquad \text{Road} = \begin{matrix} 0 & 1 & 1 & 1 & 0 \\ 1 & 0 & 0 & 1 & 0 \\ 1 & 0 & 0 & 0 & 1 \\ 1 & 1 & 0 & 0 & 1 \\ 0 & 0 & 1 & 1 & 0 \end{matrix}$$

From these two we can compute the matrix **Path** = **Air** * **Road**, in which the value of **Path**$[i,j]$ gives the number of different ways of going from city i to city j going first by air to some connecting city and then going by road.

Program **Paths** below calculates the matrix **Path** when supplied with the matrices **Air** and **Road**. It comprises three procedures. **PROCEDURE readMatrix** reads the matrices **Air** and **Road**. **PROCEDURE multiply** does matrix multiplication to compute the matrix **Path** and **PROCEDURE writeMatrix** writes it out. In the reading of data we take advantage of the fact that the diagonal terms in our matrices are zero and that they are symmetric, i.e. **Air**$[i,j]$ = **Air**$[j,i]$, etc. Only the values that occur above the main diagonal in each row are supplied so that for the above matrices the input data take the form

```
1 0 0 1 1 1 0 1 0 1
1 1 1 0 0 1 0 0 1 1
```

For this input, the matrix **Path** is computed as

```
1 0 1 2 0
2 2 1 1 2
2 1 0 1 1
2 0 1 2 1
1 2 1 1 1
```

This tells us, for example, that there are two ways to go from city 2 to city 5. From the connecting diagram we can see that we can go first by air to either city 3 or city 4 and then by road to city 5.

```
PROGRAM Paths(INPUT,OUTPUT);
{Intended to demonstrate matrix input, output and manipulation}
CONST
        numCities = 5;
TYPE
      Matrix = ARRAY [1..numCities,1..numCities] OF 0..MAXINT;
VAR
    Air,Road,Path: Matrix;

PROCEDURE readMatrix(VAR C: Matrix);
{Reads the upper-triangular elements of matrix C and assigns the rest}
VAR
    city1,city2: 1..numCities;
BEGIN
       FOR city1 := 1 TO numCities - 1 DO
            FOR city2 := city1 + 1 TO numCities DO READ(C [city1,city2]);
       FOR city1 := 1 TO numCities DO C [city1,city1] := 0;
       FOR city1 := 2 TO numCities DO
            FOR city2 := 1 TO city1 - 1 DO C [city1,city2] := C [city2,city1];
END; {readMatrix}

PROCEDURE multiply( VAR A,B: Matrix; VAR C: Matrix);
VAR
    i,j,k: 1..numCities;
    sum: 0..MAXINT;
BEGIN
       FOR i := 1 TO numCities DO
            FOR j := 1 TO numCities DO
                 BEGIN
                         sum := 0;
                         FOR k := 1 TO numCities DO sum := sum + A [i,k] * B [k,j];
                         C [i,j] := sum;
                 END;
END; {multiply}
```

```
PROCEDURE writeMatrix(VAR A: Matrix);
{Prints matrix A}
VAR
    i,j: 1..numCities;
BEGIN
        FOR i := 1 TO numCities DO
            BEGIN
                FOR j := 1 numCities DO WRITE(A[i,j]:5);
                WRITELN;
            END;
END; {writeMatrix}
BEGIN
        WRITELN; WRITELN('Enter upper triangular elements of matrix Air:');
        readMatrix(Air);
        WRITELN; WRITELN('Enter upper triangular elements of matrix Road:');
        readMatrix(Road);
        multiply(Air,Road,Path);
        WRITELN; WRITELN('Path = ');
        writeMatrix(Path);
END.
```

Example 5F: the lazy traveller problem. Another interesting problem that can be solved using connection matrices of the **TYPE** given in the last example is this: given the information on road connections between n cities, what is the least number of cities that must be visited in order to go from city i to city j $(i \neq j)$? To fix ideas, let us consider the following matrix which describes the road connections between eight cities.

$$\text{Road} = \begin{matrix} 0 & 1 & 0 & 0 & 0 & 1 & 0 & 1 \\ 1 & 0 & 0 & 1 & 0 & 0 & 0 & 0 \\ 0 & 0 & 0 & 0 & 0 & 1 & 0 & 1 \\ 0 & 1 & 0 & 0 & 1 & 0 & 1 & 0 \\ 0 & 0 & 0 & 1 & 0 & 0 & 1 & 0 \\ 1 & 0 & 1 & 0 & 0 & 0 & 0 & 0 \\ 0 & 0 & 0 & 1 & 1 & 0 & 0 & 1 \\ 1 & 0 & 1 & 0 & 0 & 0 & 1 & 0 \end{matrix}$$

For convenience, let us refer to the matrix **Road** as A. The solution to this problem involves computing the powers $A, A^2, A^3, \ldots, A^{n-1}$ and finding the least value of p for which $A^p[i, j] > 0$. If such a p cannot be found, then there is no road connection linking city i and city j.

Note that in solving this problem we do not necessarily have to compute all the powers of A as far as $p = n - 1$. For a particular choice of i, j we stop at the first value of p which produces a non-zero element at the position $[i, j]$. To have the solution for all choices of i, j, we stop the calculation as soon as all the non-diagonal terms become positive. For example, for the above matrix **Road**, all the non-diagonal terms become positive when A is raised to power 4 hence the solution for all choices of i, j becomes available at this stage. This solution is shown below.

$$\text{Least} = \begin{matrix} 0 & 1 & 2 & 2 & 3 & 1 & 2 & 1 \\ 1 & 0 & 3 & 1 & 2 & 2 & 2 & 2 \\ 2 & 3 & 0 & 3 & 3 & 1 & 2 & 1 \\ 2 & 1 & 3 & 0 & 1 & 3 & 1 & 2 \\ 3 & 2 & 3 & 1 & 0 & 4 & 1 & 2 \\ 1 & 2 & 1 & 3 & 4 & 0 & 3 & 2 \\ 2 & 2 & 2 & 1 & 1 & 3 & 0 & 1 \\ 1 & 2 & 1 & 2 & 2 & 2 & 1 & 0 \end{matrix}$$

Matrix Least tells us, for example, that in going from city 6 to city 5, we have to visit at least four other cities.

Below we give a program to solve this problem. It makes use of a **PROCEDURE** to compute the matrix **Least**. Also, a **FUNCTION** is utilised to check if at any stage during the calculation of powers all the non-diagonal elements have become positive. If so, the solution has become available.

```
PROGRAM LazyTraveller(INPUT,OUTPUT);
CONST
        numCities = 8;
TYPE
      Matrix = ARRAY [1..numCities, 1..numCities] OF 0..MAXINT;
VAR
     Road,Least: Matrix;

FUNCTION allPositive(VAR A: Matrix): BOOLEAN;
{Checks to see if all the non-diagonal terms in matrix A have become positive}
LABEL 10;
VAR
      i,j: 1..numCities;
BEGIN
        allPositive := FALSE;
        FOR i := 1 TO numCities DO
             FOR j := 1 TO numCities DO
                   IF (i <> j) AND (A[i,j] <= 0) THEN GOTO 10;
        allPositive := TRUE;
10:
END; {allPositive}
```

```
PROCEDURE computeLeast(VAR A: Matrix; VAR L: Matrix);
{Computes of matrix least}
VAR
   C: Matrix; {Holds the successive powers of A}
   i,j,counter: 1..numCities;
BEGIN
      {Initialise C to the identity matrix:}
      FOR i := 1 TO numCities DO
          FOR j := 1 TO numCities DO C[i,j] := 0;
      FOR i := 1 TO numCities DO C[i,i] := 1;
      {Initialise L to zero matrix}
      FOR i := 1 TO numCities DO
          FOR j := 1 TO numCities DO L[i,j] := 0;

      counter := 1; {counter is the power to which A is raised}
      WHILE (counter < numCities) AND NOT(allPositive(C)) DO
            BEGIN
                  multiply(A,C,C); { As in Example 5E }
                  FOR i := 1 TO numCities DO
                      FOR j := 1 TO numCities DO
                          IF (L[i,j] = 0) AND (i <> j) AND (C[i,j] <> 0)
                          THEN L[i,j] := counter;
                  counter := counter + 1;
            END;
END; {computeLeast}

BEGIN
      readMatrix(Road);       { As in Example 5E }
      writeMatrix(Road);      { As in Example 5E }
      computeLeast(Road,Least);
      writeMatrix(Least);
END.
```

Example 5G: sorting words. As a final example on **ARRAY**s of **ARRAY**s we examine a program that does the following: a sentence of up to 70 characters is read and separated into words. Words are considered to be strings containing letters only and are separated by blanks. The words contained in the sentence are then sorted in alphabetical order and printed.

The algorithm used in the program **WordSort** is as follows:

Read the sentence into an array and pad any remaining spaces with blanks (this is done using **PROCEDURE readLine**).

Validate to check that the sentence contains only letters and blanks (this is done using **FUNCTION**s **valid** and **letter**).

Calculate the left and right positions of each word and copy successive elements into an array of words. Keep a count of the number of words (This is done using **PROCEDURE separateWords**).

Sort the array of words in alphabetical order (this is done using bubble sort in the **PROCEDURE sort**).

Print the sorted array.

```
PROGRAM WordSort(INPUT,OUTPUT);
CONST
        stringSize = 71;
        maxWords = 35;
        blank = ' ';
TYPE
      range      = 1..stringSize;
      wordTotal = 1..maxWords;
      sentence  = PACKED ARRAY[range] OF CHAR;
      Words      = ARRAY[1..maxWords] OF sentence;
VAR
     L     :sentence;
     W    :words;
     ok   :BOOLEAN;
     nW:  wordTotal;

PROCEDURE readLine(VAR Line: sentence);
VAR
     i,j: range;
BEGIN
       i := 1;
       WHILE NOT EOLN DO
             BEGIN
                      READ(Line[i]);
                      i := i + 1;
             END;
       READLN;
       For j := 1 TO stringSize DO Line[j] := blank;
END; {readLine}

FUNCTION letter(c: CHAR): BOOLEAN;
BEGIN
       letter := c IN ['A'..'Z','a'..'z'];
END; {letter}

FUNCTION valid(VAR L: sentence): BOOLEAN;
VAR
    i: range;
```

```
BEGIN
      i := 1;
      WHILE (i < stringSize) AND
            (letter(L[i]) OR (L[i] = blank)) DO i := i + 1;
      valid := letter(L[i]) OR (L[i] = blank);
END; {valid}

PROCEDURE copy(left,right: range; VAR L,s: sentence);
VAR
    i: range;
BEGIN
      FOR i := 1 TO stringSize DO s[i] := ' ';
      FOR i := left TO right DO s[i - left + 1] := L[i];
END; {copy}

PROCEDURE separateWords(VAR L: sentence; VAR W: words; VAR m:
wordTotal);
VAR
    i          : wordTotal;
    left,right,j: range;
BEGIN
      FOR i := 1 TO maxWords DO
            FOR j := 1 TO stringSize DO W[i][j] := ' ';
      left := 1;
      i := 1;
      REPEAT
                right := left;
                WHILE (right < stringSize) AND
                      NOT(L[right] = blank) DO right := right + 1;
                IF L[right] = blank THEN { end of word }
                  BEGIN
                      copy(left,right - 1,L,W[i]);
                      i := i + 1;
                  END;
                left := right;
                WHILE (left < stringSize) AND
                      (L[left] = blank) DO left := left + 1;
      UNTIL left = stringSize;
      m := i - 1;
END; {separateWords}

PROCEDURE sort(VAR W: words; numWords: wordTotal);
Var
    i,j  : wordTotal;
    aux: sentence;
BEGIN
      FOR i := 1 TO numWords - 1 DO
            FOR j := i + 1 TO numWords DO
                  IF W[i] > W[j] THEN
```

```
                BEGIN
                        aux := W [i];
                        W [i] := W [j];
                        W [j] := aux;
                END;
END; {sort}

PROCEDURE writeWords(VAR W: words, numWords: wordTotal);
VAR
    i: wordTotal;
BEGIN
        FOR i := 1 TO numWords DO WRITELN(W [i]);
END; {writeWords}

BEGIN {----- Main -----}
        REPEAT
                WRITELN('Enter line (at most 70 characters long):');
                readLine(L);
                WRITELN('The line you entered is ');
                WRITELN(L);
                ok := valid(L);
                IF ok THEN
                  BEGIN
                        separateWords(L,W,nW);
                        sort(W,nW); { in lexicographic order }
                        WRITELN('The ',nW,' words you entered are: ');
                        writeWords(W,nW);
                  END
                ELSE
                  WRITELN('Invalid data, type again.');
        UNTIL ok;
END.
```

〉5.7 Conformant ARRAY parameters

In writing general applications involving processing of **ARRAY**s in **PROCEDURE**s and **FUNCTION**s one would like to have the facility to pass **ARRAY**s of variable sizes. For example, the same **PROCEDURE** that sorts an **ARRAY** may be supplied with the task of sorting 100 or 1000 elements.

In Pascal, there is an optional feature, not often implemented, which facilitates this to some extent; this goes under the name of **conformant ARRAY parameters**. The idea is to declare **ARRAY** parameters as conformant **ARRAY**s. An example of such a declaration is

```
PROCEDURE P(VAR A: ARRAY [low..high: INTEGER] OF REAL);
```

Here the parameter **A** is a conformant **ARRAY**. An **ARRAY** parameter is said to be conformant if it has the same number of dimensions, the same **TYPE** of indices and components and the same state of packing as that of an **ARRAY** declared in an outer block via a **TYPE** or a **VAR** declaration. For example, **A** is conformant with the **ARRAY**s **X**, **Y** declared as

```
VAR
    X: ARRAY[-10..10] OF REAL;
    Y: ARRAY[1..5] OF REAL;
```

It will be valid to write P(x) and, with this invocation, low will be set to -10 and high to $+10$.

On the other hand, **A** does not conform to any of the **ARRAY**s declared as below:

```
VAR
    X: ARRAY[-10..10] OF INTEGER;     { different element type }
    Y: ARRAY['A'..'E'] OF REAL;       { different index type }
    Z: ARRAY[1..10,1..8] OF REAL;     { different dimensionality }
    W: PACKED ARRAY[1..10] OF REAL; { differs in packing }
```

For one-dimensional **ARRAY**s the general form for a conformant **ARRAY** parameter is

ARRAY [*lowerBoundVariable..upperBoundVariable*: *indexType*] of *elementType*

Note that the **ARRAY** bounds are not constant, they must be identifiers. Their values are worked out at the time the procedure is called and can be used inside the procedure. They cannot be treated as variables and changed inside the procedure.

Conformant **ARRAY** parameters can be multi-dimensional. For example, the following is a two-dimensional conformant **ARRAY** parameter:

```
VAR X: ARRAY[min1..max1: INTEGER; MIN2..MAX2: INTEGER] OF REAL;
```

Notice the semicolon which separates the two indices; this is inconsistent with the normal practice where one would expect to find a comma.

Conformant **ARRAY** parameters are not of great use and do not provide dynamic **ARRAY** bounds. An **ARRAY** which can be passed to such a parameter has to be declared with fixed bounds in its own **TYPE** or **VAR** declaration. We have discussed them purely for the sake of completeness. In practice it is far more convenient to declare oversize **ARRAY**s and then to supply the needed size as parameters; for example, to sort an **ARRAY A** of **TYPE list** we might have a **PROCEDURE** heading:

PROCEDURE Sort(VAR A: list; size: INTEGER);

where **size** would provide the actual number of elements to be sorted in a particular call.

We complete this chapter by giving an example on the use of conformant **ARRAY** parameters. **PROCEDURE readString** below reads a string of any length or any **PACKED ARRAY OF CHAR**.

```
PROCEDURE readString(VAR String: PACKED ARRAY[first..last: INTEGER] OF CHAR);
VAR
   index: INTEGER;
BEGIN
      WRITELN('Enter ',last - first + 1,' characters: ');
      FOR index := first TO last DO READ(String[index]);
END; {readString}
```

Quickies

11. Determine which of the following are valid. If invalid, explain.

(a) VAR Num1,Num2: INTEGER
            X: ARRAY[1..Num1,1..Num2] OF INTEGER;

(b) VAR X: PACKED ARRAY[1..10,1..20] OF REAL;

(c) VAR X,Y: ARRAY[1..10,1..2] OF BOOLEAN;
   .
   .
   IF NOT(X = Y) THEN ..

(d) VAR X: ARRAY[1..10,BOOLEAN] OF INTEGER;

12. Calculate the number of elements in the following **ARRAY**s.

(a) TYPE matrix = ARRAY[1..2,1..5] OF CHAR;

(b) TYPE vector = ARRAY[−5..5] OF INTEGER;

(c) TYPE X = ARRAY[BOOLEAN,'a'..'e'] OF REAL;

⇒ You may now proceed to Pascal laboratory Activities 31–32.

〉 Pascal laboratory

Activity 28. Program TUTOR27 is a copy of program **Computer-Dating** in Example 5A. Study the program and predict what the output will be if the data entered are such that the same item is selected as an interest and a dislike. Verify. Extend the program so that it selects those applicants who do not dislike any in the set [Books, Opera, Drinking]. Also, a list of interests and dislikes should be printed if an applicant is judged as being suitable.

Activity 29. Program TUTOR28 is an incomplete program to do a bubble sort. Complete the program and test it. Modify it so that it sorts characters in descending order.

Activity 30. Program TUTOR29 is an incomplete shell based around the procedure insertSort given in the text. Complete the program and test it. Modify the program so that it will also print the partially sorted list at the intermediate steps. Change the FUNCTION findWhere so that it uses a binary search.

Activity 31. Program TUTOR30 is an incomplete program. It is intended to read a string and to write it out. Run the program. You will find that it will probably print some trailing junk. Extend the program so that the string is padded with blanks to make it of the right length.

Activity 32. Program TUTOR 31 is the same program as the one in Example 5E. Write a general-purpose procedure to supply row by row input to a matrix and incorporate it in the program. Typically, the prompts might be given as

```
ENTER MATRIX Air:
Row 1:
Row 2:
.
.
```

〉 Exercises

1*. Write a program that will, given two positive integers, write out the digits that occur in each of them and also the digits that are common to them. For example, given 45984 and 6259, it should output

```
digits in 45984 are [ 4 5 8 9]
digits in 6259 are [ 2 5 6 9]
digits common to both are [ 5 9]
```

2*. Write a procedure which will reverse the elements in an array, e.g. 72 36 56 −10 should become −10 56 36 72. You are not allowed to declare another array.

3*. Write a program to generate prime numbers from 2 to n using the sieve of Eratosthenes. This method, named after its inventor, the Greek mathematician Eratosthenes, works as follows:

Start by putting all the numbers into the sieve.
Repeat the following step until the sieve is empty.
Remove the smallest remaining number, which will be a prime, and discard all its multiples which will be non-primes.

4*. Write a program, using only one one-dimensional **ARRAY**, to generate the first n lines of the Pascal's triangle as shown in Example 5C.

5. Write a program that reads nine integers and determines if they can form a magic square of order 3.

6. In Pascal's triangle, if instead of adding we subtract and disregard the sign, we get the following pattern, where, to enhance the visual effect, we have replaced the 1s with the character ▮. Describe how the pattern grows. Write a program to generate it.

7. Consider the 'non-equation'

$$123456789 = 100$$

The only way to turn this into an equation by inserting a mixture of 7 plus or minus signs between the digits on the left-hand side is

$$1+2+3-4+5+6+78+9=100$$

Write a program to discover how to do the same task using a mixture of only three plus or minus signs.

8. Complete the following sentence:

In this sentence, the number of occurrences of 0 is ___, of 1 is ___, of 2 is ___, of 3 is ___, of 4 is ___, of 5 is ___, of 6 is ___, of 7 is ___, of 8 is ___ and of 9 is ___.

Each blank is to be filled with a number of one or more digits.

9. Explain the fact that $11^4 = 14641$ in terms of Pascal's triangle.

10. The scalar product of two vectors A and B of size n is defined as

$$A \cdot B = \sum_{i=1}^{n} A[i] * B[i].$$

Using conformant **ARRAY** parameters, write a **FUNCTION** which will calculate the scalar product of two vectors of arbitrary size.

11. Information concerning the road connections between 10 cities is provided as follows: for each pair of cities i, j, an integer d is given such that, if $d = 0$, there is no direct road from city i to city j. If $d \neq 0$, then there is a direct road from city i to city j and its length is d. Write a program that determines for each pair of cities the minimum road distance between any two cities.

Answers to Quickies

1. (a) [], [1], [2], [1,2]
   (b) [], [cat], [dog], [bird], [cat, dog], [cat, bird], [dog, bird], [cat, dog, bird]
   2^n.

2. (a) Invalid. The **SET** constructor symbol [] can only be used in an assignment. **SET** declaration and **SET** assignment must be done separately.
   (b) Valid.
   (c) Invalid, because of the first **TYPE** statement. Grades cannot be defined by listing constants, they must be identifiers.
   (d) Invalid. No structured type constants allowed.
   (e) Invalid. **Staff** is defined as a set of sets. The set elements can only be of ordinal type.
   (f) Invalid. It should be written **NOT (x IN** [0..10]).
   (g) Invalid. Type mismatch.
3. (a) []
   (b) [7..10]
   (c) [1,4..10,20..30]
   (d) TRUE
   (e) FALSE.
4. (a) p IN ['0'..'9']
   (b) s IN [p, q, r]
   (c) [p, q, r] = [s].
5. (a) Invalid. Index should be a subrange.
   (b) Valid.
   (c) Valid.
   (d) Invalid. A **FUNCTION** must produce a single scalar value.
   (e) Invalid. **ARRAY**s must be passed via a **TYPE** declaration.
   (f) Valid!
6. (a) Finds the average of **ExamMark** and **ProjectMark** for each student.
   (b) Finds the position of each letter in the alphabet.
   (c) Finds the sum of all positive elements in the **ARRAY A**.
7. Relational operations and **WRITE** and **WRITELN**.
8. The ordinal value of the first character which is not common to the two of them.
9. (a) Invalid in standard Pascal. A string must be read one element at a time.
   (b) Valid.
   (c) Valid.
   (d) Invalid. Only strings of equal length can be assigned.
10. Invalid. The lower bound of the index must be 1 to make X a string.
11. (a) Invalid. The indices must be constants.
    (b) Valid but not very useful.

(c) Invalid. No relational or Boolean operators for ARRAYs.
(d) Valid.

12. (a) 10
(b) 11
(c) 10.

〉 Chapter 6

〉 Files

In the previous chapters, it was assumed that all input will take place via the keyboard and all output will be directed to the screen. The purpose of this chapter is to show how information may be read from and sent to a storage device such as a disk.

〉 6.1 Files in general

A **file** is a structure comprising a sequence of items which are all of the same type. We can picture a file as in the following diagram:

```
[ITEM1] [ITEM2] [ITEM3] ... [ITEMn] [EOF]
```

in which EOF stands for an End Of File marker. The nature of the marker is implementation dependent and is not specified by Pascal.

A file is a dynamic structure in that its size is not fixed and may grow indefinitely. For this reason, information from a file stored on an external device is transferred in blocks of items into an area known as the **file buffer** in the computer's main memory. The size of the block is not fixed and is dictated by the operating system. As we shall see later, Pascal utilises a file buffer that stores only one item at a time.

There are two types of files: **sequential files** and **random access** (or **direct access**) files. In a sequential file the items can only be accessed in the same sequence in which they are stored. In constrast the values in a random access file can be accessed in any order. Standard Pascal only supports sequential files.

〉 6.2 Files in Pascal

In Pascal all input/output is done using files and in general the names of the files have to be explicitly included in all input and output statements such as **READ**, **WRITE**, **EOLN**, etc. For example, to read an integer i from a file named **myFile**, we have to write

```
READ(myFile,i);
```

and a statement of the form

```
IF NOT EOF(myFile) THEN ..
```

is used to check for the end of **myFile**.

This fact has so far been hidden since we have assumed that all input will come from the predefined file **INPUT** and that all output will be written to the predefined file **OUTPUT**.

If a file name is not included in an input/output statement then Pascal assumes that we are referring to these default files. In the previous chapters the input/output statements could have been written in the form

```
READLN(INPUT,i,j,k);
WRITELN(OUTPUT,i,j,k);
```

but this is optional and hence unnecessary.

Something else we have assumed is that the file **INPUT** is connected to the keyboard and the file **OUTPUT** to the screen. This is the standard situation but is by no means compulsory. The files **INPUT** and **OUTPUT** may be connected to other external devices such a disk or a printer. How this connection is to be made is determined by a particular implementation and you should find out the procedure adopted by your system.

The files **INPUT** and **OUTPUT** are TEXT files. TEXT is a predefined Pascal **TYPE** exactly as INTEGER, REAL, BOOLEAN and CHAR. A TEXT file is one whose components are characters, i.e. they are of type CHAR — ASCII or whatever character set the computer is using. A TEXT file has the further property that it is organised into 'lines'; what this means is that there is a special character, which separates other characters and denotes the end of a line. The BOOLEAN **FUNCTION** **EOLN**, which is only relevant in the context of a TEXT file, is used in detecting this character. We can picture a TEXT file as follows:

CHARACTERS	EOLN	MORE CHARACTERS	EOLN	..	EOF

TEXT files are the ones that are used most frequently since, in practice, they are the only files that are intelligible to the human eye when viewed.

Such files can be created and altered using an editor of the kind that you have already been using in producing Pascal programs.

The fact that we have been able to handle not only the input and output of characters but also of numbers may be puzzling to the thoughtful reader at this stage, since, as we said, the components of a TEXT file are of type CHAR. It is possible not only to read characters but also to read REALs and INTEGERs from TEXT files. Also, not only can we write values of type CHAR but also of type REAL, INTEGER, BOOLEAN and **PACKED ARRAY OF CHAR**. This privilege is only allowed to TEXT files. In all other file TYPEs only one type of item can be written to or read from. The extended facility is available because, for TEXT files, and only for TEXT files, the procedures **READ**, **READLN**, **WRITE** and **WRITELN** do automatic type conversion during input and output. For example, when a number is read, what happens in the first instance is that a string of characters is read and is then converted to the appropriate type REAL or INTEGER. Typically, a simple TEXT file may look something like

3.1415 2	EOLN	EOF

This file may be read one character at a time using the statement **READ(myFile, ch)** where **ch** is of type CHAR but it may also be read using the statement **READ(myFile,x,i)** where **x** is of type REAL and **i** is of type INTEGER. In the latter case, the string of characters 3.1415 is automatically converted to the type REAL and similarly 2 is converted from a character to an INTEGER.

Likewise during output, REALs and INTEGERs are transformed into strings before being written in a TEXT file.

Files which are not character coded are referred to as **binary files**. Binary files are created by computer programs rather than typed directly. Binary files are much faster to read because no conversion is involved but they have the disadvantage that when viewed by the human eye they appear incomprehensible. They are also more compact and do not give rise to inaccuracies which can result from type conversion.

In general, before a file can be used for input or output, there are three preliminary requirements. These are

file nomination,
file declaration,
file opening.

We shall now examine each of these.

File nomination

A file which exists before a program has been executed or a file which is required to exist after the program has ended is called an **external file**. Temporary file which may be needed only during the execution of a program and which reside in the memory of the computer are called **internal files**. Such files are deleted at the end of the execution. Every external file must be nominated in the program heading in exactly the way that we have been doing for the files **INPUT** and **OUTPUT**. For example, suppose that we want to read data from a file called **myData** and send the results to a file called **myResults**, then the nomination would look something like

```
PROGRAM fileUsage(OUTPUT,myResults,myData);
```

The order in which we list the files is immaterial. Even if the file **OUPUT** is not being used to print the results, it should be nominated so that error messages are displayed on the screen.

The names listed in the heading are the logical names to be used in the input and output statements. The actual names understood by the operating system may be different. For example, if such a declaration is made in VAX Pascal then the operating system will assume that the actual names of the files are myResults.DAT and myData.DAT. With many compilers it is not sufficient to nominate files in the program heading. It is also necessary to associate the nominated file names with the actual file names. For example, in TURBO Pascal this is done using the **PROCEDURE ASSIGN** and to associate the logical name **myResults** with the operating system file name FILEX.DAT the **PROCEDURE** is invoked as

```
ASSIGN(myResults,'FILEX.DAT');
```

This association must be established before a file can be opened for reading or writing.

File declaration

Apart from the files **INPUT** and **OUTPUT**, all files to be used by a program must be declared in the declaration section.

A file type variable is created in the same way as variables of other types, i.e. via a **TYPE** and/or a **VAR** declaration.

The **TYPE** definition has the form:

```
TYPE
        Identifier = FILE OF BaseType;
```

where *BaseType* is the type of the individual components of the file structure. *BaseType* can be any type other than a file itself. Here are some examples:

```
TYPE
   Cars = ( Ford, Mercedes, Jaguar, Renault);
   CarFile = FILE OF Cars;
   Name = PACKED ARRAY[1..10] OF CHAR;
VAR
   CarFileA, CarFileB : CarFile;
   NumFile            : FILE OF INTEGER;
   Pattern            : FILE OF CHAR;
   Data1,Data2        : TEXT;
   Names              : FILE OF Name;
```

Note that **TEXT** is not the same as a **FILE OF CHAR**. As was explained earlier, TEXT files have the further property that they are organised into lines using an end-of-line marker. For this reason, the function **EOLN** is only meaningful in the context of TEXT files.

File opening

Apart from the files **INPUT** and **OUTPUT**, all files must be opened before they can be read or written to. A file is opened for reading using the **RESET** statement which has the form

RESET(*FileName*);

Similarly, a file is opended for writing using the **REWRITE** statement:

REWRITE(*FileName*);

Several files may be opened simultaneously for reading and writing. A file cannot be read and written to at the same time although a file may be opened for writing using **REWRITE** and subsequently read from using a **RESET**. It is illegal to try to open a file which is already open and for this reason it would be a fault to do a **RESET** or a **REWRITE** on the files **INPUT** and **OUTPUT**. These files are opened automatically by the system.

Here is a little example program to illustrate file usage. It reads a set of integers from the file **Numbers** and prints the odd ones into the file **OddNumbers**. The input is supplied as one integer per line.

```
Program FileDemo(OUTPUT,Numbers,OddNumbers);
VAR
   i : INTEGER;
   Numbers, OddNumbers : TEXT;
BEGIN
      RESET(Numbers);
      REWRITE(OddNumbers);
      WHILE NOT EOF(Numbers) DO
         BEGIN
            READLN(Numbers,i);
            IF ODD(i) THEN WRITELN(OddNumbers,i);
         END;
END.
```

As far as TEXT files are concerned the input/output statements now covered are sufficient for their handling. However, to be able to handle files in general, it is sometimes necessary to have to make use of the file buffer and the low level **PROCEDURE**s **GET** and **PUT**. These will now be explained.

File window and file buffer

Since the size of a file is indefinite, the method of access to elements of a file differs from that of an **ARRAY** in which all the elements are available simultaneously. Pascal allows only one item of a file to be accessible at any one time when a file is in use although in the case of TEXT files the single item can be a whole string of characters denoting a number. Conceptually, each access to a file is done by positioning a **window** over an item and storing the value of the item in a **file buffer** as shown below:

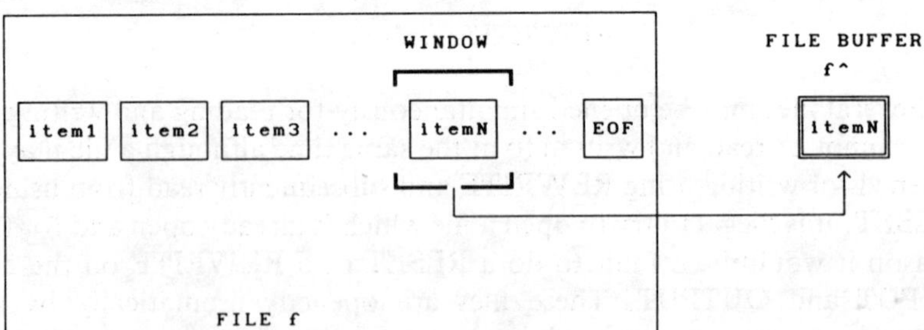

To refer to the current item, the file variable name is followed by the character ^, so, for example, the buffer variable for the file f is denoted

IMPORTANT NOTICE—this information supercedes that given on the back cover of this book

This book contains an MS-DOS format disc for use with IBM PCs and compatible machines, bound into the inside back cover. It is not necessary to order any additional software to use with the text, and no other versions of the software are now available.

Discounts are available for bulk purchases of the book, and site licences are available for multiple or institutional use of the software. Packs consist of two text/software packages and authorised licence form.

Further information and additional copies of this text/software package can be ordered from:

Customer Services Department
IOP Publishing Ltd
Techno House
Redcliffe Way
Bristol
BS1 6NX
United Kingdom

IMPORTANT NOTICE—this information supersedes that given on the back cover of this book.

This book contains an MS-DOS format disc for use with IBM PCs and compatible machines, bound into the inside back cover. It is not necessary to order any additional software to use with the text, and no other versions of the software are now available.

Discounts are available for bulk purchases of this book, and site licences are available for multiple or institutional use of the software. Packs consisting of two texts/software packages and additional [illegible].

Further information and additional copies of this text/software package can be obtained from:

Customer Services Department
IOP Publishing Ltd
Techno House
Redcliffe Way
Bristol
BS1 6NX
United Kingdom

Software Order Form

Pascal: An Interactive Text

Software forms an essential part of this Computer Illustrated Text. It is integrated with 50 activities in the text and is designed to save time in keying programs to allow more time to be given to hands-on experience of working in Pascal.

Software is available for MS-DOS machines on 51/4 disc at £32.50 (inc VAT) per disc. Site licenses are available for multiple use of software at £150.00 (inc VAT). Packs include master disc for copying, back-up disc and two books.

To receive your software complete this form and return with your remittance to: Adam Hilger, IOP Publishing Ltd, Techno House, Redcliffe Way, Bristol BS1 6NX, England Telephone: 0272 297481 Telex: 449149 INST P G

Telephone orders are accepted from customers paying by credit card

Please send me software for *Pascal: An Interactive Text* by S J Abas and J R Mondragon on

☐ MS-DOS disc ☐ Site license MS-DOS

I enclose my cheque for £________ payable to IOP Publishing Ltd

Please charge to my Access/Visa/AmEx/Diners Club card number

☐☐☐☐☐☐☐☐☐☐☐☐☐☐☐☐ Expiry date ________

Name______________________**Signature** ______________________

Address ____

____**Date** ______________

by f^. The file window and the file buffer are used to link the storage device and the main memory of the computer. They are used in two different ways depending on whether we are reading or writing.

GET *statement*

In reading a file, the predefined procedure **GET** is used to advance the window and place the next element in the buffer variable. The **EOF** function is used to detect the end of file. This will be explained with reference to the diagram below and a file named **f**.

Initially, the file buffer and the function **EOF** are undefined. The reading process is initiated by the statement **RESET(f)**. This assigns the value of the first item to the buffer variable f^ and the function **EOF(f)** takes the value FALSE (unless the file is empty). The statement **GET(f)** is used to advance the file window to the next component and correspondingly f^ takes its value. This process is continued until the last item has been read. When **GET(f)** is executed with the file window placed on the

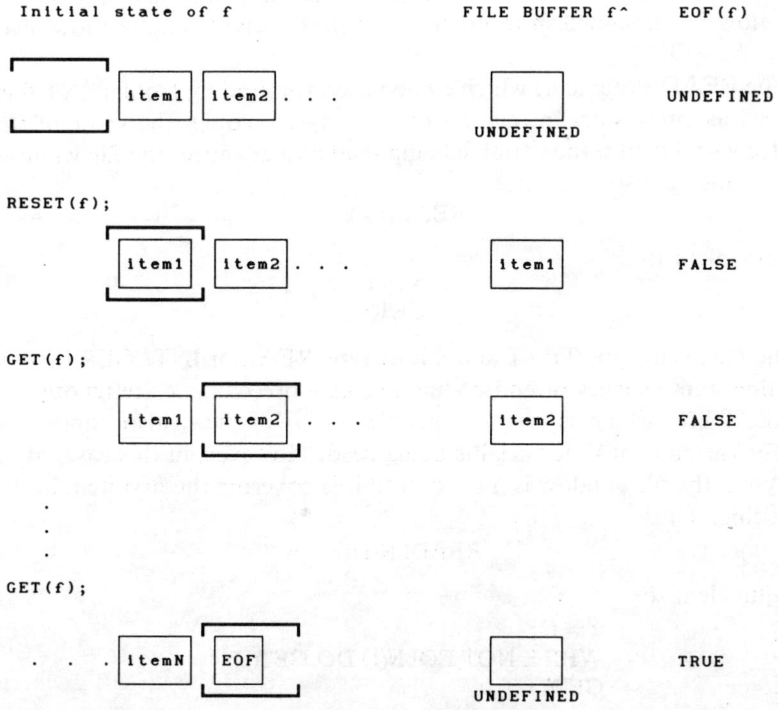

last item, the window moves to the end-of-file marker. At this stage the file buffer becomes undefined and the function **EOF(f)** becomes **TRUE**.

If the file **f** happens to be a TEXT file then there is an extra point to consider. Such a file also contains the end-of-line markers. In this case, if the file window is positioned on an end-of-line marker then the **FUNCTION EOLN(f)** becomes TRUE and the buffer variable is assigned the character value blank, i.e. f^ = ' '.

The statements below, which could be used to sum a set of numbers contained in a file, are intended to illustrate the use of the file buffer and the **GET** statement.

```
RESET(f);
sum := 0;
WHILE NOT EOF(f) DO
    BEGIN
        sum := sum + f^;
        GET(f);
    END;
```

The **READ** and **READLN** statements that have been used previously can now be explained in terms of the buffer variable and the low level procedure **GET**.

The **READ** statement, which can be used for reading from TEXT files as well as binary files in fact does two things: it copies the value of the buffer variable into the variable being read and advances the file window one frame. Thus

```
READ(f,X);
```

is equivalent to

```
x := f^;
GET(f);
```

If the file **f** is of type TEXT and **x** is of type REAL or INTEGER then in reading **x** any spaces or end-of-line markers preceding **x** are ignored.

READLN, which is only applicable to TEXT files, also copies the buffer variable into the variable being read. However, in this case, after copying, the file window is moved until it is covering the first item in the next line. Thus

```
READLN(f,x);
```

is equivalent to

```
x := f^;
WHILE NOT EOLN(f) DO GET(f);
GET(f);
```

To illustrate what has just been said, consider the TEXT file shown in the diagram

and suppose **x** is of type **CHAR**. A **READ(f,x)** will make **x** = **a** and will place the file window on **b**:

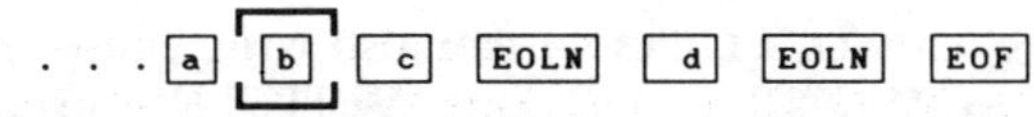

If we follow this with a **READLN(f,x)**, it will make **x** = **b** and will place the file window on **d**, which is the first element of the next line. The character **c** will be ignored:

Suppose we follow this with a **READ(f,x)**. This will make **x** = **d** and will place the file window on **EOLN**:

At this stage, the function **EOLN(f)** will become TRUE and f^ = ' '. A **READ** or a **READLN** from this position will result in error since we will be trying to read the end-of-file marker.

PUT *statement*

The **PUT** statement is used in writing to a file. Initially, a file is opened for writing using a **REWRITE**. A **REWRITE** produces an empty file containing just the end-of-file marker. At this stage the file buffer is undefined. If **REWRITE** is done on a file f which already exists then any information contained in f is erased.

After the file has been opened, information is placed into it in two steps. First, the buffer variable is assigned a value:

```
f^ := item;
```

Then the value of the file buffer is placed in the file using **PUT**:

```
PUT(f);
```

After a **PUT** the value of the file buffer again becomes undefined. The two statements together are equivalent to **WRITE(f,item)**. The process of writing to a file is illustrated below.

```
REWRITE(f);                 [EOF]
f^ := item;    PUT(f);
     or                     [item] [EOF]
WRITE(f,item);
```

When dealing with TEXT files we can also write end-of-line markers. This is done using **WRITELN**. An empty **WRITELN(f)** produces just the end-of-line marker. It is illegal to attempt to produce the end-of-line marker by copying; it can only be produced using a **WRITELN**. The statement **WRITELN(f,item)** will write the item and then write the end-of-line.

In the above diagram, if we were to follow with the statement **WRITE(f,item)** the resulting picture will be:

```
[item] [EOLN] [item] [EOF]
```

Here is a program to illustrate the use of **PUT** and **GET**. The program below reads a **FILE OF REAL** and produces a file in which the numbers have been scaled by a factor.

```
PROGRAM Scale(INPUT,OUTPUT,InFile,OutFile);
VAR
    InFile,OutFile  :  FILE OF REAL;
    factor          :  REAL;
BEGIN
        RESET(InFile);
        REWRITE(Outfile);
        WRITE('Give the scale factor: ');
        READLN(factor);
        WHILE NOT EOF(InFile) DO
            BEGIN
                    OutFile^: = factor*InFile^;
                    PUT(OutFile);
                    GET(InFile);
            END;
END.
```

Procedure **PAGE**

Pascal provides the predefined procedure **PAGE** to send output to a new page during printing. The procedure is only usable with TEXT files and has the form

PAGE(*FileName*);

As usual, if *FileName* is omitted then the file **OUTPUT** is implied.

As to whether it can be utilised depends on the equipment in use. Also, some dialects of Pascal, e.g. TURBO Pascal, do not implement it.

Passing files as parameters to **PROCEDURE***s and* **FUNCTION***s*

A file type can only be passed as a **VAR** parameter to a **PROCEDURE** or a **FUNCTION**.

Here is a program to copy a TEXT file. It uses a **PROCEDURE** which copies only one line.

```
PROGRAM FileCopy(OUTPUT,original,copy)
VAR
    original,copy    :  TEXT;

        PROCEDURE copyOneLine(VAR f1,f2: TEXT);
        VAR
            ch:  CHAR;
        BEGIN
                WHILE NOT EOLN(f1) DO
                    BEGIN
                            READ(f1,ch);
                            WRITE(f2,ch);
                    END;
                READLN(f1);
                WRITELN(f2);
        END;  {copyOneLine}

BEGIN
        RESET(original);
        REWRITE(copy);
        WHILE NOT EOF(original) DO
                copyOneLine(original,copy);
END.
```

Quickies

1. Mark each of the following as true or false.
   (a) TEXT files must be nominated in the program heading if they are external files.
   (b) Files **INPUT** and **OUTPUT** refer to a keyboard and a screen.
   (c) A TEXT file is the same as a **FILE OF CHAR**.

(d) It is illegal to attempt a **RESET** on the file **INPUT** or a **REWRITE** on the file **OUTPUT**.
(e) A file component can be another file.
(f) The **EOF** function becomes TRUE when the last item of a file is in the file window.
(g) A file that is open can be read from or written to at the same time.
(h) We can open as many files as we like simultaneously.

2. Assume that we are reading from a file **f1** and writing into a file **f2**. The two files, their windows and their file buffers appear as follows.

```
f1        17 19 [7] 5  13        [7]

f2        11 7  [ ]              [5]
```

Draw diagrams to illustrate the effect of the following operations.

(a) GET(f1); GET(f1);
(b) PUT(f2);
(c) RESET(f1);
(d) f2^ := 3*f1^; PUT(f2);

3. Assuming that **f** and **fCopy** are TEXT files, is this code correct for copying **f** into **fCopy**? If not, explain why.

```
RESET(f);
REWRITE(fCopy);
WHILE NOT EOF(f) DO
    BEGIN
        READ(f,ch);
        WRITE(fCopy,ch);
    END;
```

⇒ **You may now proceed to Pascal laboratory Activities 33–35.**

Example 6A: Big Letters. Program **BigLetters**, which is the subject of this example, reads a 12-character message from the keyboard and writes out the message in big characters. For example, the output below was produced in response to the message **FILE OF CHAR**.

```
FFFFFFFFFFFFFF      IIIIIIII         LLLLLLLL          EEEEEEEEEEEEEE
  FFFF      FF        IIII             LLLL              EEEE      EE
  FFFF  FF            IIII             LLLL              EEEE  EE
  FFFFFFFF            IIII             LLLL              EEEEEEEE
  FFFF  FF            IIII             LLLL     LL       EEEE  EE
  FFFF                IIII             LLLL    LLLL      EEEE      EE
FFFFFFFF            IIIIIIII         LLLLLLLLLLLLL     EEEEEEEEEEEEEE

                      OOOOOO         FFFFFFFFFFFFFF
                    OOOO  OOOO         FFFF      FF
                  OOOO      OOOO       FFFF  FF
                  OOOO      OOOO       FFFFFFFF
                  OOOO      OOOO       FFFF  FF
                    OOOO  OOOO         FFFF
                      OOOOOO         FFFFFFFF

    CCCCCCCC      HHHH    HHHH          AAAA           RRRRRRRRRRRR
  CCCC    CCCC    HHHH    HHHH        AAAAAAAA           RRRR    RRRR
CCCC              HHHH    HHHH      AAAA    AAAA         RRRR    RRRR
CCCC              HHHHHHHHHHHH      AAAA    AAAA         RRRRRRRRRR
CCCC              HHHH    HHHH      AAAAAAAAAAAA         RRRR  RRRR
  CCCC    CCCC    HHHH    HHHH      AAAA    AAAA         RRRR    RRRR
    CCCCCCCC      HHHH    HHHH      AAAA    AAAA       RRRRRR    RRRR
```

The big letters are stored in the file **CharData** which is included under the name LETTERS.DAT on your disk. Each of the big letters is an 8 by 18 array of CHAR. There is a blank line separating the data for each of the letters in the file.

To output the message, the screen is thought of as a 24 by 72 array containing 12 subarrays of 8 rows and 18 columns as shown.

1	2	3	4
5	6	7	8
9	10	11	12

PROCEDURE ReadLetterData opens the file **CharData** and stores the data in the 3D array **Letters**. **Letters** is a 1D array whose elements are themselves 2D arrays.

PROCEDURE readMessage is straightforward. It simply reads the 12-character message into the array message.

PROCEDURE writeMessage does two things. It fills the 2D array **Screen** and writes it out. The filling is done using the **PROCEDURE WriteToScreen** which maps the *i*th character in the message into the *i*th cell shown in the above diagram. **WriteToScreen** in turn makes use of the **PROCEDURE** map to work out the rows and columns of the array **Screen** in which to copy the big character.

```
PROGRAM BigLetters(INPUT,OUTPUT,CharData);
TYPE
    range    = 32..126;
    BigChar = ARRAY[1..8,1..18] OF CHAR;
VAR
   Letters     :  ARRAY[range] OF BigChar; { This is a 3D ARRAY }
   message     :  ARRAY[1..12] OF CHAR;
   CharData    :  TEXT;
PROCEDURE readLetterData;
VAR
   ASCII     :  range
   row       :  1..8;
   column    :  1..18;
BEGIN
     RESET(CharData);
     FOR ASCII := 32 TO 126 DO { Printable ASCII characters }
          BEGIN
                 READLN(CharData);
                 FOR row := 1 TO 8 DO
                      BEGIN
                           FOR column := 1 TO 18 DO
                                  READ(CharData,Letters[ASCII][row,column]);
                           READLN(CharData);
                      END;
          END;
END; {readLetterData}
PROCEDURE readMessage;
VAR
   i:  1..12;
BEGIN
     FOR i := 1 TO 11 DO READ(message[i]);
     READLN(message[12]);
END; {readMessage}
PROCEDURE writeMessage;
VAR
   panel  :  ARRAY[1..24,1..72] OF CHAR;
   row    :  1..24;
   column:  1..72;

          PROCEDURE map(c: CHAR; position: INTEGER);
          VAR
                row          :  1..8;
                column       :  1..18;
                firstColumn,firstRow:  INTEGER;
```

```
        BEGIN
            firstRow := 8*((position - 1) DIV 4);
            firstColumn := 18*((position - 1) MOD 4);
            FOR row := 1 to 8 DO
                FOR column := 1 TO 18 DO
                    panel [row + firstRow,column + firstColumn] :=
                        Letters [ORD(c)] [row,column];
        END;  {map}

        PROCEDURE writeToScreen;
        VAR
            c          :  CHAR;
            i          :  1..12;
        BEGIN
            FOR i := 1 TO 12 DO
                BEGIN
                    c := message [i];
                    map(c,i);
                END;
        END;  {writeToScreen}

BEGIN
    writeToScreen;
    FOR row := 1 TO 24 DO
        BEGIN
            FOR column := 1 TO 72 DO WRITE(panel [row,column]);
            WRITELN;
        END;
END;  {writeMessage}

BEGIN
    readLetterData;
    WRITE('Type 12 characters: ');
    readMessage;
    writeMessage;
END.
```

Example 6B: File merge. The following algorithm may be used to merge two sorted files to produce a third ordered file. For example, if File1 and File2 contain the integers:

$$-10\ 4\ 23\ 117$$
$$-20\ -5\ \ 3$$

then File3 will contain:

$$-20\ -10\ -5\ 3\ 4\ 23\ 117$$

Open File1 and File2 for reading.
Open File3 for writing.
While File1 and File2 are both non-empty do the following:

if File1^ ≤ File2^ then write File1^ to File3 and move the next item from File1 into the File1 buffer. Otherwise, write File2^ to File3 and move the next item from File2 into the File2 buffer.

If File1 is not empty then write out the rest of the items into File3.
If File2 is not empty then write out the rest of the items into File3.

```
PROGRAM Merge(File1,File2,File3);
VAR
   File1,File2,File3: FILE OF INTEGER;
BEGIN
      RESET(File1);
      RESET(File2);
      REWRITE(FILE3);
      WHILE (NOT EOF(File1)) AND (NOT EOF(File2)) DO
         IF File1^ < = File2^ THEN
           BEGIN
                 WRITE(File3,File1^);
                 GET(File1);
           END
         ELSE
           BEGIN
                 WRITE(File3,File2^);
                 GET(File2);
           END;
      WHILE NOT EOF(File1) DO
         BEGIN
                 WRITE(File3,File1^);
                 GET(File1);
         END;
      WHILE NOT EOF(File2) DO
         BEGIN
                 WRITE(File3,File2^);
                 GET(File2);
         END;
END.
```

〉 Pascal laboratory

Activity 33. TUTOR32 produces a shell for writing Pascal programs. It writes the program heading and places the words **CONST**, **TYPE** and **VAR**. **FUNCTION** names and also the words **BEGIN** and **END** are suitably placed. Run the program and study its code. Modify the program so that it also writes out the shell for **PROCEDURE**s as done for **FUNCTION**s. You may like to speed up your programming by utilising an initial shell of this kind.

Activity 34. TUTOR33 is intended to read a set of integers from the keyboard and write them out into a TEXT file named **MyFile**. The program is incomplete. Introduce the necessary statements to make it perform. Use the program to create a file containing some positive and negative integers. Modify the program so that it reads **MyFile** and writes all the negative integers to another TEXT file called **Negatives**. Type out the file **Negatives** to verify.

Activity 35. Repeat activity 34 but this time declare **MyFile** to be a **FILE OF INTEGER**. Try typing it out!

〉 Exercises

1. As done in the text for the case of reading from a file using **GET**, draw a diagram for writing to a file using **PUT**.

2*. Write a program to copy, character by character, a TEXT file **f** into another TEXT file **fCopy**.

3. Write a program that reads a file of REALs and creates a new file that contains only the positive REALs.

4. Replace **READ** and **WRITE** by **GET** and **PUT** in the following:

```
WHILE NOT EOF(f) DO
  BEGIN
      READ(f,x);
      Sum := Sum + x;
  END;
```

```
FOR i := 1 TO 100 DO
  BEGIN
      x := i*i;
      WRITE(f,x);
  END;
```

5. Write a program that will read a **FILE OF INTEGER** and separate the contents into two files: one containing the odd integers and the other the even ones.

6. Let the TEXT file f contain the text of a Pascal program. Write a program that will copy f into **fShort** in which all blank lines and any trailing blanks at the end of lines have been removed. Hint: read each line from f into an **ARRAY**. Keeping count of the index, scan the **ARRAY** from right to left until the first non-blank character is met. Write out the remainder.

Answers to quickies

1. (a) T, (b) F, (c) F, (d) T, (e) F, (f) F, (g) F, (h) T.

2.

(a)	f1	17 19 7 5 [13]	[13]
(b)	f2	11 7 [5]	[?]
(c)	f1	[17] 19 7 5 13	[17]
(d)	f2	11 7 [21]	[?]

3. No. The **EOLN** character cannot be copied. It must be produced using **WRITELN**.

〉 Chapter 7

〉 RECORDs and Variants

ARRAYs and **SET**s, which we met earlier, comprise collections of data items which are all of the same type. By contrast, a **RECORD** structure groups several different types of data items into a single structure. The purpose of this chapter is to teach you about **RECORD**s.

〉 7.1 RECORDs

The **RECORD** type in Pascal is used to group together logically related data items of different type under a single identifier. This has the great advantage that data with components of different types can be manipulated as a single entity. Suppose, for example, that we are involved in a computation with persons characterised by their name, sex and age. A suitable **RECORD** type to handle the situation may be defined as

```
TYPE
    Person = RECORD
                 name: PACKED ARRAY[1..20] OF CHAR
                 sex  : (male, female);
                 age  : 18..65
             END;
```

Each variable of **TYPE person** will now have three components: **name** **sex** and **age**. The components of a **RECORD** are called its **fields**. Here, **name**, **sex** and **age** are the fields of **Person**.

In general the **TYPE** declaration for a **RECORD** has the form

```
TYPE
    Identifier = RECORD
                     field,field,..field: type;
                     . . . .
                     field,field,..field: type;
                 END;
```

The **TYPE** of a field can be anything. In particular, it can be another **RECORD**. In any single **RECORD** every field identifier is required to be unique. The same identifier, however, may be used for some other purpose outside the **RECORD** including the specification of a field name in a different record. For example, it is valid in the same **TYPE** definition to write

```
RecordA = RECORD                    RecordB = RECORD
              x,y: REAL;                          x,z: INTEGER;
              p: (This, That);                    p,q: 1..10;
          END;                                END;
```

The fact that the same identifiers **x** and **p** are used as field names in different **RECORD**s is legal but such usage must be avoided as it may lead to error and confusion. On the other hand, it would be illegal to try to define another **RECORD** as

```
RecordC = RECORD
              x,z: CHAR;
              z  : REAL;
          END;
```

since there are now two fields denoted with the same identifier **z**.

The work **PACKED** may be optionally added before the word **RECORD** and implies the same as it does when used with **ARRAY**s. A **PACKED RECORD** may occupy less space in memory, but a price has to be paid in retrieval time during execution.

Components of **RECORD**s are accessed through field names preceded by a dot which is referred to as the **field selection operator**. Field names play an analogous role to the one played by indices in accessing components of **ARRAY**s, except that unlike indices, field names cannot be calculated. They are fixed identifiers. To demonstrate the method let us declare a variable p1 of **TYPE** Person:

```
TYPE
      Person = RECORD
                     name: PACKED ARRAY[1..10] OF CHAR;
                     sex  : (male, female);
                     age  : 18..65;
                 END;
VAR
    p1: Person;
```

The assignment statements below illustrate how the three components of p1 are referenced:

```
p1.name := 'John Jones';
p1.sex := male;
p1.age := 25;
```

If **RECORD**s are nested then several dots are used in an analogous way to access the inner field. For example, with the following declarations:

```
TYPE
      string  = PACKED ARRAY[1..10] OF CHAR;
      Names = RECORD
                     first,last: string;
                  END;
      Person = RECORD
                     name: Names;
                     sex   : (male, female);
                     age   : 18..65;
                  END;
VAR
      p1,p2: Person;
```

the assignments of values to name will take the form

```
p1.name.first := 'John      ';
p1.name.last := 'Jones     ';
```

It is valid to assign a whole **RECORD** to another of the same **TYPE**. However, exactly as discussed in the case of **ARRAY**s, 'same **TYPE**' means that the declaration must be via the same **TYPE** statement or must occur in the same list in a **VAR** declaration. For example, with the above declaration it would be legal to write

```
p2 := p1;
```

WITH *statement*

Having to refer to components of **RECORD**s via long chains such as **p1.names.first...**, is clearly very tedious. The **WITH** statement factorises out the common part in statements involving such chains and provides a more compact and readable method of reference. It has the form

WITH *RecordName* DO *Statement*;

where *Statement* will usually be a compound statement. For example,

```
WITH p1.name DO
   BEGIN
         first:= 'John          ';
         last:= 'Jones         ';
   END;
```

The scope of the **WITH** statement extends between **BEGIN** and **END**. Within this scope, references to the fields of the **RECORD p1.name** can be made without the prefix **p1.name**.

A **WITH** statement is also allowed to factor out more than one record name. For example, with two records it has the form

WITH *RecordName1*, *RecordName2* DO *Statement*;

where *RecordName2* may be a component of *RecordName1*. This form is equivalent to the nested form

WITH *RecordName1* DO
  WITH *RecordName2* DO *Statement*;

For example, with our definitions above we can write

```
WITH p1,Name DO
   BEGIN
         first:= 'John          ';
         last := 'Jones         ';
         sex := male;
         age := 25;
   END;
```

or alternatively in nested form as

```
WITH p1 DO
   WITH Name DO
      BEGIN
               first := 'John        ';
               last  := 'Jones       ';
               sex   := male;
               age   := 25;
      END;
```

Care must be taken, however, in using a **WITH** statement with multiple **RECORD**s to ensure that no ambiguity arises due to clashes in field names. For example, if we have defined

```
VAR
   R1 = RECORD
            x: REAL;
            y: BOOLEAN;
        END;

   R2 = RECORD
            x: INTEGER;
            z: CHAR;
        END;
```

and we try to write

```
WITH R1,R2 DO
   BEGIN
        x := 2;
        y := TRUE;
        x := -10;
        z := 'c';
   END;
```

then it is not clear which **x** is intended. In such cases the compiler will add the name of the last record listed in the **WITH** statement so that in this case all the references to **x** will be taken to mean **R2.x,** which may not be what we had intended. For the purposes of defining the scope rules, field names in a nested **WITH** statement are treated in the same way as local and global identifiers in nested blocks.

Input/output of RECORD*s*

As with **ARRAY**s, a complete **RECORD** cannot be read or written using **READ**, **WRITE** and standard **INPUT** and **OUTPUT**. When using TEXT files we must resort to handling individual components. However, whole **RECORDS**s may be read or written from binary files using **READ**, **WRITE** or **PUT** and **GET**.

The example below shows how a **RECORD** of type person defined above can be read and written using standard **INPUT** and **OUTPUT**.

```
PROGRAM RecordIO(INPUT,OUTPUT);
TYPE
      str     = PACKED ARRAY [1..10] OF CHAR;
      Names = RECORD
                  first,last:str;
               END;
      Person = RECORD
                  name: Names;
                  sex  : (male, female);
                  age  : 18..65;
               END;
VAR
    p1: Person;

PROCEDURE readPerson(VAR aPerson: Person);
VAR
     i: 1..10;
     s: CHAR;
BEGIN
       WITH aPerson,name DO
          BEGIN
                 WRITE('Enter first name (10 characters)   ');
                 FOR i := 1 TO 10 DO READ(first [i]);
                 READLN;
                 WRITE('Enter last name (10 characters)   ');
                 FOR i := 1 TO 10 DO READ(Last [i]);
                 READLN;
                 REPEAT
                        WRITE('Give sex. Male(M) or Female(F) ');
                        READLN(s);
                 UNTIL s in ['M','m','F','f'];
                 CASE s OF
                        'M','m': sex := male;
                        'F','f':   sex := female;
                 END;
                 WRITE('Enter age: ');
                 READLN(age);
          END;
END; {readPerson}
```

```
PROCEDURE writePerson(VAR aPerson: Person);
BEGIN
      WITH aPerson,name DO
         BEGIN
               WRITELN('first name: ',first);
               WRITELN('last name: ',last);
               WRITE('sex        : ');
               CASE sex OF
                    male   : WRITELN('male');
                    female: WRITELN('female');
               END;
               WRITELN('age        : ',age);
         END;
END; {writePerson}

BEGIN
      readPerson(p1);
      writePerson(p1);
END.
```

Quickies

1. Write **TYPE** definitions using **RECORD**s for the following data;

   (a) Point with fields x, y, z all real.
   (b) Date with fields day, month and year.
   (c) Person with fields name and dateOfBirth which is of type Date in (b).

2. Which of the following are valid? If invalid, explain.

   (a)
```
TYPE
      Point: RECORD
                  x,y: INTEGER;
              END;
```

   (b)
```
Type
      Point = RECORD
                  x,y: REAL;
               END;
      Line  = RECORD
                  First: Point;
                  x,y: REAL;
               END;
```

(c)
```
TYPE
     Book = RECORD
              ISBN: INTEGER;
              Author = RECORD
                          Name: PACKED ARRAY [1..20] OF CHAR
                          Telephone: INTEGER;
            END;
```

3. Use a **WITH** statement to assign a value to a variable of **TYPE Person** as defined in your answer to question 1(c) above.

4. Given the following definitions:

```
TYPE
     R1 = RECORD
            x: INTEGER;
            y: REAL;
          END;

     R2 = RECORD
            p: INTEGER;
            q: BOOLEAN;
          END;

VAR
   A: R1;
   B: R2;
```

write **WITH** statements in two equivalent forms to make **A.x = B.p**, **A.y = 1.5** with **B.q = FALSE**.

⇒ **You may now proceed to Pascal laboratory Activities 36–37.**

〉7.2 ARRAYs of RECORDs

A very important structure that is frequently of interest is an **ARRAY OF RECORD**s. For example, given the declarations

```
TYPE
     str    = PACKED ARRAY [1..10] OF CHAR;
     Names = RECORD
                first,last: str;
             END;
```

```
Person = RECORD
           name: Names;
           sex  : (male, female);
           age  : 18..65;
         END;
```

we can declare the variable **Client** as

```
VAR
    Client: ARRAY [1..size] OF Person;
```

Client is an **ARRAY** whose elements are **RECORD**s of type **Person**. To access a value stored in an element we have to specify the index of the component along with the field. For example,

```
x := Client [5].age;
WRITELN(x);
```

will pick out the age in the fifth component of the **ARRAY**.

Example 7A: sorting **ARRAY***s of* **RECORD***s.* One frequent activity in connection with **ARRAY**s of **RECORD**s is that of sorting. We have already met some sorting algorithms in our discussions of **ARRAY**s. In sorting **RECORD**s only a portion of information is utilised in producing the ordered list; for example, if we are sorting **RECORD**s which involve names and addresses, we may sort alphabetically using names or we may sort according to the postal code in the address. The relevant piece of information on which comparisons are made is called the **key**, so that if we were sorting by names then names would constitute the key.

In sorting **RECORD**s, the most efficient thing to do is to set up an **ARRAY** of pointers to the **RECORD**s and to interchange these pointers rather than the **RECORD**s themselves. Since swapping **RECORD**s involves the swapping of more than one item, this is faster. The method is explained in the diagram that follows on p176.

Program **Clients** given on p176, also included on the disk under the name CLIENTS.PAS, implements the above method. It reads an **ARRAY OF RECORD**s from a file and initialises pointers to them. The pointers are then sorted on the key **Names.last** using the bubble sort method which was discussed in Chapter 5. The format of the input file is shown and the output produced is shown after the listing of the program.

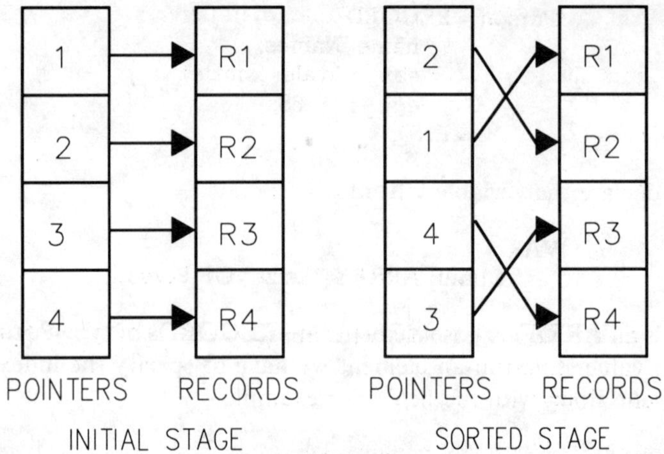

INPUT FILE:

John
Jones
m
25
Winston
Zeedmore
m
38
Griselda
Campbell
f
28
Egon
Spengler
m
35
Ray
Stanz
m
32
Peter
Venkman
m
27
Janine
Alcock
f
45

```
PROGRAM Clients(INPUT,OUTPUT,nameFile);
CONST
        numClients = 7;
TYPE

      str      = PACKED ARRAY [1..10] OF CHAR;
      Names = RECORD
                  first,last: str;
               END;
      Person = RECORD
                  name: Names;
                  sex   : (male, female);
                  age   : 18..65;
               END;
VAR
     Client      : ARRAY [1..numClients] OF Person;
     NameFile: TEXT;
     pointers  : ARRAY [1..numClients] OF 1..numClients;


PROCEDURE readClients;
VAR
     i : 1..numClients;
     s: CHAR;
     j : 1..10;
BEGIN
       RESET(NameFile);
       FOR i := 1 TO numClients DO
            WITH Client [i], name DO
               BEGIN
                      FOR j := 1 TO 10 DO READ(NameFile,first [j]);
                      READLN(NameFile);
                      FOR j := 1 TO 10 DO READ(NameFile,last [j]);
                      READLN(NameFile);
                      READLN(NameFile,s);
                      CASE s OF
                           'M','m': sex := male;
                           'F','f'  : sex := female;
                      END;
                      READLN(NameFile,age);
               END;
END; {readClients}
PROCEDURE sortClients;
VAR
     i,j,k: 1..numClients;
```

```
BEGIN
      FOR i := 1 TO numClients DO pointers[i] := i;
      FOR i := 1 TO numClients - 1 DO
          FOR j := i + 1 TO numClients DO
              IF Client[pointers[i]].name.last >
                 Client[pointers[j]].name.last THEN
                   BEGIN
                         k := pointers[i];
                         pointers[i] := pointers[j];
                         pointers[j] := k;
                   END;
END; {sortClients}

PROCEDURE writeClients;
VAR
    i: 1..numClients;
BEGIN
      FOR i := 1 TO numClients DO
          WITH Client[pointers[i]], name DO
              BEGIN
                   WRITE(last,first);
                   CASE sex OF
                        male   : WRITE('male':10)
                        female: WRITE('female':10);
                   END;
                   WRITELN(age:5);
              END;
END; {writeClients}

BEGIN { ---- main ---- }
      readClients;
      sortClients;
      writeClients;
END.
```

Output from the program:

```
Alcock     Janine       female  45
Campbell   Griselda     female  28
Jones      John           male  25
Spengler   Egon           male  35
Stanz      Ray            male  32
Venkman    Peter          male  27
Zeedmore   Winston        male  38
```

〉7.3 Variants

It is often logically desirable to regard two **RECORD** variables as being of the same **TYPE**, even though they may show some variation in the number and type of their fields. For example, suppose that a **RECORD** variable is related to details of persons. Depending on whether or not they were employed, we may wish to have an extra field to record their occupation. In Pascal a **RECORD** that allows for this kind of variation is known as a **variant**. Consider, for example the following definitions:

```
TYPE
      String  =PACKED ARRAY[1..10] OF CHAR;
      Status  –(Unemployed, Employed);
      Person =RECORD
                   Name             : String;
                   Age              : 16..65;
                   CASE JobStatus : Status OF
                      Unemployed : ( );
                      Employed       (Occupation : String);
                END;
```

We can examine the definition of **Person** to illustrate the key features of a variant **RECORD**. The structure of such a **RECORD** in general has two parts: a fixed part and a variant part. The fixed part, if there is one, must precede the invariant part. Only one variant part is allowed in a list of fields following the fixed part although variants may be nested. In this example the fixed part consists of the two fields **Name** and **Age**.

The variant part starts with the keyword **CASE** which is followed by the special field known as the **tag field**. Here, **JobStatus** is the tag field and is of the enumerated type **Status**. In general, a tag field can be any ordinal type. It is the value of the tag field which decides which fields in the variant part are valid. Here if the value of the tag field is **Unemployed** then no other fields are available, which is specified by the empty brackets. If the tag field has value **Unemployed** then the extra field **Occupation** of **TYPE String** is available.

Note that there is only one **END** that completes the definition of such a **RECORD**. Because the variant part has to be last, the same **END** serves to close the words **CASE** and **RECORD**.

We now illustrate how the tag field is used in accessing the variant fields. Suppose with the above **TYPE** definition we make the following declaration:

```
VAR
    p: Person;
```

and then make the assignment

p.JobStatus := Employed;

Then, and only then, we are entitled to access the variant field **Occupation**. For example, we can now write

p.Occupation := 'Student   ';

Had we assigned

p.JobStatus := UnEmployed;

it would be invalid to try to access the field **Occupation**.

Example 7B: **FILE**s *of variants.* Program **CreateShapeData** in this example is intended to show the input and output of variant **RECORD**s. The variant **TYPE shapeInfo** is defined to handle three different types of shapes, namely triangles, rectangles and circles. For each case appropriate fields are introduced. **PROCEDURE getData** obtains the data interactively and stores them into the **ARRAY Shapes**. **PROCEDURE saveData** saves the data into the binary file **ShapeFile**. **PROCEDURE readData** reads the data and puts them back into the **ARRAY Shapes**. **PROCEDURE showData** prints the components of the **ARRAY Shapes** on the screen.

```
PROGRAM CreateShapeData(INPUT,OUTPUT,shapeFile);
CONST
        numShapes = 10;
TYPE
      shape = (triangle,rectangle,circle);
      point  = RECORD
                  x,y: REAL;
               END;
      shapeInfo = RECORD
                     CASE s: shape OF
                        triangle   : (side1,side2,angle: REAL);
                        rectangle : (width,height: REAL);
                        circle      : (centre: point;
                                           radius: REAL);
                  END;
VAR
     Shapes   : ARRAY[1..numShapes] OF shapeInfo;
     shapeFile: FILE OF shapeInfo;

PROCEDURE getData;
VAR
     i : 1..numShapes;
     c: CHAR;
```

```
BEGIN
	WRITELN('Enter T for triangle, R for rectangle and C for circle');
	WRITELN;
	FOR i:= 1 TO numShapes DO
		WITH Shapes[i] DO
			BEGIN
				REPEAT
					WRITE('Shape ',i,': '); readln(c);
				UNTIL c in ['t','T','r','R','c','C'];
				CASE c OF
					'T','t' : BEGIN
							s:= triangle;
							WRITE('Enter side1,side2 and angle: ');
							READLN(side1,side2,angle);
						END;
					'R','r' : BEGIN
							s:= rectangle;
							WRITE('Enter width and height: ');
							READLN(width,height);
						END;
					'C','c': BEGIN
							s:= circle;
							WRITE('Enter xC,yC and radius: ');
							READLN(centre.x,centre.y,radius);
						END;
				END;
			END;
END; {getData}

PROCEDURE saveData;
VAR
	i: 1..numShapes;
BEGIN
	REWRITE(shapeFile);
	For I:=  TO numShapes DO WRITE(shapeFile,shapes[i]);
END; {saveData}

PROCEDURE readData;
VAR
	i: 1..numShapes;
BEGIN
	RESET(shapeFile);
	FOR I:= 1 TO numShapes DO READ(shapeFile,shapes[i]);
END; {readData}

PROCEDURE showData;
VAR
	i: 1..numShapes;
BEGIN
	FOR i:= 1 TO numShapes DO
		WITH Shapes[i] DO
			CASE s OF
				triangle  : WRITELN('shape ', i ,' triangle,     side1 = ',side1:4:1,
							'  side2 = ',side2:4:1,'    angle = ',angle:4:1);
```

```
            rectangle: WRITELN('shape ', i ,' rectangle,  width = ',width,
                                    '  height = ',height);
            circle    : WRITELN('shape ', i ,' circle, centre = (',centre.x:4:1,
                                    ',',centre.y:4:1,')  radius = ',radius:4:1);
        END;
END; {showData}

BEGIN    { ---- Main ---- }
    getData;
    saveData;
    readData;
    showData;
END.
```

Comments. Although it was said that the variant fields in a **RECORD** depend on the value of the tag field in fact the tag field is optional. For example, we can write

```
VAR
    rec: RECORD
            CASE BOOLEAN OF
                FALSE: (ch: CHAR);
                TRUE : (int: INTEGER);
         END;
```

Such a **RECORD** with no explicit tag field is called a **free union**. It is usually used by experienced programmers to do naughty things such as convert a value of one **TYPE** to a value of another **TYPE**. Free unions are error-prone in use and for this reason we will not discuss them any further.

Quickies

5. Assuming the following:

```
TYPE
    str    = PACKED ARRAY[1..10] OF CHAR;
    Names = RECORD
                first,last: str;
            END;
    Person = RECORD
                name: Names;
                sex  : (male,female);
                age  : 18..65;
            END;
VAR
    p,q: Person;
    List: ARRAY[1..50] OF Person;
```

state which of the following are valid. If invalid, explain.

(a)
```
WITH p, name DO
    WRITELN(first,last);
```

(b)
```
WITH List[i] DO
    WRITELN(p.name.first);
```

(c)
```
WITH List[i] DO
    WRITELN(sex);
```

(d)
```
WITH p,q DO
    WRITELN(name.first, age);
```

6. Define a variant **RECORD** to cater for the following.

   (1) The fixed part has one field of TYPE REAL.
   (2) The tag field is of TYPE 1..2. If the tag field has value 1 then no extra field is defined. If the tag field has value 2 then an extra field of TYPE BOOLEAN is available.

⇒ **You may now proceed to Pascal laboratory Activities 38–40.**

〉 Pascal laboratory

Activity 36. TUTOR34 is an incomplete program. Complete the program by writing **PROCEDURE readPart** which will read a variable of type part from the keyboard and a **PROCEDURE writePart** which will print the variable on the screen.

Activity 37. TUTOR35 is a program that sets out to add two vectors. Study the program and decide what the correct output should be for the two vectors given. Run the program. Why does it not produce the right result? Correct and verify.

Activity 38. Run TUTOR 36 which is the same as the program in Example 7B. Extend the program to handle an extra shape **ellipse** defined by a centre and major and minor axes.

Activity 39. In TUTOR36 introduce an extra field **Area** as follows:

```
shapeInfo = RECORD
              Area: REAL;
              CASE s: shape OF
                triangle  : (side1,side2,angle: REAL);
                rectangle: (width,height: REAL);
                circle    : (centre: point;
                             radius: REAL);
          END;
```

Modify the program so that, in reading data, after the shape has been specified, the appropriate area is calculated and assigned to the field **Area**. Modify the **PROCEDURE**s **saveData**, **readData** and **showData** appropriately.

Activity 40. Insert a **PROCEDURE sortData** in the version produced in Activity 39 to sort the data using **Area** as the key. Modify **showData** so that it prints the sorted data.

〉 Exercises

1. Write suitable **RECORD** declarations for

   (a) **Employee** to contain **name**, **IDNumber** and **salary**.
   (b) **Person** to contain name, **sex**, **age** and **marital status**.

2*. Write a variant **RECORD** that could be used to store information about a person on name, sex and whether single, married, widowed or divorced. If the person is married, it should also record the name of the spouse. In the case of a divorced person, the date of the divorce should be recorded and, in the case of a widowed person, the date on which the spouse died should be recorded.

3. Suppose that, in an input file, data on a person appear as follows. The name appears in the first 20 columns followed by a letter m or f to indicate male or female followed by an integer which gives the age followed by another letter which indicates whether the person is single, married, divorced or widowed. For example:

```
Steve Jones         m25s
Mary Smith          f82w
```

Write a **PROCEDURE readPerson(VAR p: person)** to read a **RECORD** of **TYPE person.**

4. Unlike FORTRAN, Pascal does not possess the **TYPE Complex.** The **RECORD** structure

```
TYPE
      Complex = RECORD
                      realPart,imaginaryPart: REAL;
                  END;
```

can be used to provide for complex arithmetic. Write procedures to implement addition, subtraction and multiplication of complex numbers.

5*. The following data structure is used by an estate agent to record the name of the manager and the number of properties in various locations.

```
CONST
      nLocations = 5;
TYPE
    str = PACKED ARRAY [1..20] OF CHAR;
    branch = RECORD
                 brName,manager: str;
                 houses,bungalows,cottages: INTEGER;
             END;
business = ARRAY [1..nLocations] OF branch;
```

Write two **PROCEDURE**s as follows:

(1) **PROCEDURE readBusiness(VAR b: business)** to read all the data for the business **b**. In the **INPUT** file assign **brName** and **manager** in 20 columns each, followed by three integers to give numbers of houses, bungalows and cottages.

(2) **PROCEDURE totals(VAR b: business)** to print the manager's name and the total number of properties of each type in each branch and also the grand total of all the properties in the business.

6. A computer dating service uses the following structure to record its

clients:

```
TYPE
        pursuits = (Eating,Drinking,Dancing,Travel,TV,
                    Fashion,Books,Opera,Religion,Jogging);
        client = RECORD
                    name: PACKED ARRAY[1..20] OF CHAR;
                    sex  : (male,female);
                    age  : 17..70;
                    interests: SET OF pursuits;
                 END;
```

Suppose that data for each client are input in the following form:

name	in columns 1 to 20
sex	in column 22, m = male, f = female
age	in columns 24 to 25
interests	indicated by characters X in columns 27 to 36.

For example, an **X** in column 29 will indicate that the person indulges in dancing.

Write a program to store information about clients. Given information about a particular client, the program should also print out a list of all compatible clients where compatibility is defined as follows.

Is of opposite sex.
The age difference is not greater than five years.
Has at least three interests in common.
If the client for whom compatibles are being sought is interested in religion then a compatible client must also be interested in it.

Answers to Quickies

1. (a)

```
Type
      Point = RECORD
                 x,y,z: REAL;
              END;
```

(b)

```
TYPE
      Months = (Jan,Feb,Mar,Apr,May,Jun,Jul,Aug,Sep,Oct,Nov,Dec);
      Date   = RECORD
                  day   : 1..31;
                  month: Months;
                  year  : 1900..2000;
               END;
```

(c)
```
TYPE
      Person = RECORD
                 name: PACKED ARRAY [1..10] OF CHAR;
                 dateOfBirth: Date;
               END;
```

2. (a) Invalid. Equals sign after **RECORD** instead of a colon.
   (b) Valid.
   (c) Invalid. Colon after **Author**; also, another **END** needed.

3.
```
WITH p, dateOfBirth DO
    BEGIN
        Name := 'Jack Bird ';
        day := 8;
        month := Jun;
        year := 1960;
    END;
```

4.
```
WITH A,B DO                 WITH A DO
   BEGIN                       WITH B DO
     x := p;                      BEGIN
     y := 1.5;                       x := p;
     q := FALSE                      y := 1.5;
   END;                              q := FALSE;
                                  END;
```

5. (a) Valid.
   (b) Invalid. List [i] is not connected with p.
   (c) Invalid. **Sex** is an enumerated type and is not a valid parameter to **WRITELN**.
   (d) Valid but not recommended as it is ambiguous. The field **name.first** and **age** are common to **p** and **q**. The compiler will assume that **q.name.first** and **q.age** is intended and **p** will be redundant.

6.
```
TYPE
    range = 1..2;
    r = RECORD
           f1: REAL;
           CASE f2: range OF
              1: ( );
              2: (f3: BOOLEAN);
      END;
```

Chapter 8

A Second Look at FUNCTIONs and PROCEDUREs

The purpose of this chapter is to introduce you to more advanced uses of FUNCTIONs and PROCEDUREs than has been covered so far. In particular, we will examine the important concept of recursion, which some would argue is even more fundamental than repetition.

8.1 Subprograms as parameters

Thus far, we have only seen two types of parameters: value parameters which essentially supply constants to subprograms and VAR parameters which supply variables. Pascal, in fact, allows two additional types of parameters: **FUNCTION parameters** and **PROCEDURE parameters**. These provide for the passing of subprograms as parameters. How this is done will now be explained.

Consider the following problem. We want to write a Boolean function which will be TRUE if some arbitrary function $f(x)$ lies in the range -1 to $+1$ for all integer values of x in the range 0 to 10. FUNCTION inRange given below does the job.

```
FUNCTION inRange( FUNCTION f(x:INTEGER):REAL ):BOOLEAN;
VAR
   i:  INTEGER;
BEGIN
        i := 0;
        WHILE (i <=  10) AND (f(i) >= -1) AND (f(i) <= 1) DO
        i := i + 1;
        inRange := 1 > 10;
END;{inRange}
```

Here we are passing the **FUNCTION** f as a parameter to the function **inRange**. Note that the **FUNCTION** parameter has exactly the same form as a **FUNCTION** heading. Any number and type of **FUNCTION** parameters may be passed and there is no restriction on the number and type of parameters contained in each of them. The names of arguments used in **FUNCTION** parameters are not significant. Their only purpose is to list the number and type of parameters involved. Thus, in our example if we replace **f(x:INTEGER)** with **f(y:INTEGER)** then this will not alter the performance of **inRange** in any way. One restriction on a **FUNCTION** parameter is that it cannot be a predefined function of Pascal. For example, f could not be the functions **SIN** or **COS** in a call to **inRange**.

A typical call to the **FUNCTION inRange** would be

IF inRange(*SomeFunction*) THEN . .

where *SomeFunction* would have been declared to correspond in its parameters and TYPE with f, i.e. it must have only one value parameter of TYPE INTEGER and be itself of TYPE REAL. The program below gives examples of actual function parameters that would be suitable. The version of **inRange** in the program has been slightly generalised in that it checks to see if **f(x)** lies between − 1 and + 1 for all integer values of **x** in the range lower...upper, rather than in the range 0...10 which we took above.

```
PROGRAM DemoParameters(OUTPUT);

FUNCTION sineX(x:INTEGER):REAL;
BEGIN
      sineX := sin(x);
END; {sineX}

FUNCTION xSineX(x:INTEGER):REAL;
BEGIN
      xSineX := x*sin(x);
END; {xSineX}

FUNCTION inRange(lower, higher : INTEGER;
                        FUNCTION f(x:INTEGER):REAL):BOOLEAN;
VAR
   i: INTEGER;
```

```
BEGIN
      i := lower;
      WHILE (i <= higher) and (f(i) >= -1) AND (f(i) <= 1) DO
      i := i + 1;
      inRANGE := i > higher;
END; {inRange}

BEGIN {---- Main ---- }
      IF inRange(0,10,sineX) THEN WRITELN ('sineX is in range')
                              ELSE WRITELN ('sineX is not in range');
      IF inRange(0,10,xSineX) THEN WRITELN ('xSineX is in range')
                               ELSE WRITELN ('xSineX is not in range');
END.
```

Comments. It is frequently the case that the facility to pass subprograms as parameters is not available in a compiler. Also, the syntax for subprogram parameters has been modified from the original ISO standard. The old method did not require a listing of the parameters of the subprogram which is being passed as a parameter. Thus in our example, had we been using the old method, **FUNCTION inRange** would have been declared as

```
FUNCTION inRange(FUNCTION f:REAL);
```

Another restriction in the old method was that the parameters of the subprogram to be passed had to be value parameters. **VAR** parameters were not allowed. In our example f would only be allowed to have value parameters.

Although the passing of subprograms as parameters is a very important concept and is of great value in a number of advanced topics which are outside the scope of this book, it is difficult to find realistic examples of applications at this level without going into specialist areas. This is particularly true when it comes to the passing of **PROCEDURE**s as parameters. The examples given in textbooks can usually be done in a less cumbersome way using constructions such as the **CASE** statement.

〉8.2 Recursion

Consider the following definition to produce a sequence of integers $s(n)$:

$$s(0) = 0$$
$$s(n) = s(n-1) + 2 \qquad n = 1, 2, 3, 4, \ldots$$

Starting with $n = 0$, the above definition will generate the sequence of even numbers

$$0, 2, 4, 6, 8, \ldots.$$

Supposing now that, instead of starting with $n = 0$ we try to calculate $s(4)$ by working backwards and making substitutions to obtain $s(n-1)$ from $s(n)$ in the right-hand side:

$$\begin{aligned} s(4) &= s(3) + 2 \\ &= s(2) + 2 + 2 \\ &= s(1) + 2 + 2 + 2 \\ &= s(0) + 2 + 2 + 2 + 2 \\ &= 0 + 2 + 2 + 2 + 2 \\ &= 8. \end{aligned}$$

The definition of $s(n)$ given above is an example of a **recursive definition**. It has two essential features: a **base clause**, $s(0) = 0$, which specifies explicitly how the initial term of the sequence is to be calculated and a **recursion clause**, $s(n) = s(n-1) + 2$, which gives a general term in terms of its predecessor.

The method of solving a problem recursively is typified by the method used just now to calculate $s(4)$. To find $s(4)$ we tried to solve the simpler problem of finding $s(3)$, to find $s(3)$ we tried to solve again the simpler problem of finding $s(2)$, and so on until the problem was reduced to finding $s(0)$. We succeeded at this stage since $s(0)$ was given explicitly by the base clause $s(0) = 0$.

It is easy to see that in this manner of working a base clause is essential because it provides the terminating condition; without a base clause, the definition would be **circular** rather than recursive and the process of reduction would never end.

By generalising the notions we have just discussed, we can define what is meant by a **recursive algorithm**. An algorithm is recursive if it is *expressed in terms of the same algorithm* applied to some simplified version of the data (recursion clause) and *contains an explicit statement* about the simplest version of the data(base clause). For example, here is a non-numerical recursive algorithm to print a word W in reverse order:

TO PRINT A WORD W IN REVERSE ORDER DO THE FOLLOWING:

If W has only one letter then print W. Otherwise

print the word obtained by removing the first letter of W in reverse order and then print the first letter of W.

In computer programming, the term **recursion** is used when a subprogram calls itself, either directly in its body or indirectly when a subprogram **X** calls another subprogram **Y** which in turn calls **X**. Not all programming languages allow for recursion but in Pascal the scope of a **FUNCTION** or a **PROCEDURE** extends from its heading to the end of the block in which it is defined. A Pascal subprogram is therefore allowed to do recursion by invoking itself. This makes it possible for recursive algorithms to be transcribed very directly into Pascal code. For example, the algorithm

$$s(0) = 0$$
$$s(n) = s(n-1) + 2 \quad n = 1,2,\ldots$$

which we met earlier, can immediately be coded as

```
FUNCTION s(n: INTEGER): INTEGER;
BEGIN
        IF n = 0 THEN s := 0
        ELSE s := s(n - 1) + 2;
END; {s}
```

Without some further explanation, it is not immediately obvious as to how a recursive subprogram actually works. The secret of success lies in the fact that every time a subprogram calls itself, a new set of formal parameters and local variables (if any) are created in an area of the computer's memory known as the **stack**. At the completion of the call, the program returns to where it was called from and the previous values of formal parameters and local variables are remembered. The unfinished business is then completed with the old values of these parameters and variables. We will explain this process of stacking and unstacking of parameters and local variables with reference to the function s above. Refer to the diagram below when reading what follows.

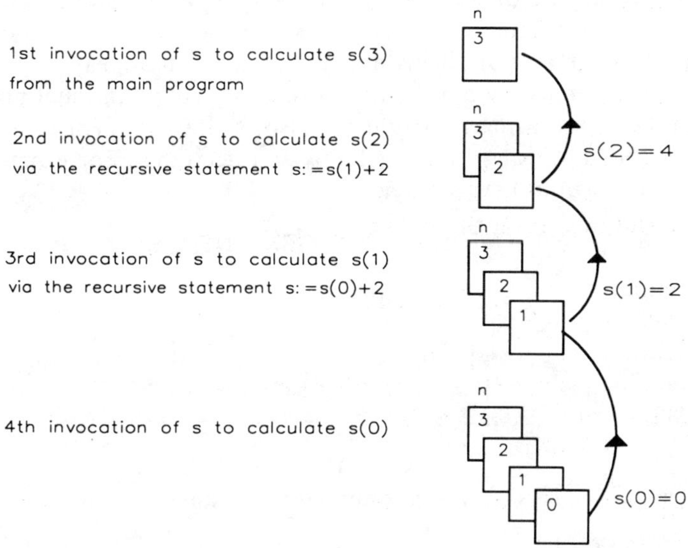

Suppose that in the main program a call is made to calculate **s(3)**. In the first instance the formal parameter n takes the value 3. When the **FUNCTION** is executed then, since **n** is not equal to 0, a recursive call is made to calculate **s(2)**. This postpones the complete execution of the **FUNCTION** for the stage when **n** = 3.

In response to this recursive call, new storage is allocated on the stack to create a fresh **n** and the value of the current parameter **n** is set to 2. The old value **n** = 3 is kept in the previously allocated memory and remembered. Again, the **FUNCTION** is executed but, since the new **n** is still not equal to 0, another call is made to calculate **s(1)** and, again, fresh storage is allocated to create a new **n**. This time the new **n** takes the value 1 and the previous value **n** = 2 is remembered. The next time, a recursive call is made to calculate **s(0)**. Since **s(0)** can be calculated explicitly at this stage the job is successfully completed.

Execution now returns to complete the previous stage in which **n** had the value 1. This time **s** can be calculated because **s(0)** is known and the execution of this stage is now completed with **s** = 2. The execution then returns to the next unfinished stage when **n** was equal to 2 and **s** is calculated as 4. Finally, all the steps in the computation are completed with the completion of the initial stage where n is taken as 3. At last s returns with the value 6.

Once this method of stacking and unstacking of parameters and local variables for each unfinished stage of a subprogram is understood, the mystery of a subprogram being able to call itself disappears.

A point that must be appreciated is that any computational problem that can be solved using recursion can also, at least in theory, be solved without recursion using loops or loops and decisions. For example, to compute s we could have written

```
FUNCTION s(n: INTEGER): INTEGER;
VAR
    s1,i: INTEGER;
BEGIN
        s1 := 0;
        FOR i := 1 TO n DO s1 := s1 + 2;
        s := s1;
END; {s}
```

An even shorter version would only have one statement in the body:

```
s := 2*n;
```

The question arises as to which is preferable, a recursive solution to a problem or a non-recursive one? Since for each recursive invocation of a subprogram, space has to be allocated on the stack, it should be clear that a recursive subprogram will use more space than a non-recursive one. In fact, recursive subprograms generally use more space and more execution time, the latter through overheads incurred in PROCEDUREs or FUNCTIONs being called repeatedly. For this reason, recursion is to be avoided whenever possible, although it has to be said that the penalty to be paid in doing recursion can sometimes depend substantially on the compiler being used. Some compilers are designed to handle recursion far more efficiently than others.

Having warned against recursion, there remains the fact that there are many algorithms which are naturally recursive and can only be coded in a comprehensible manner in this way. Many problems which would be extremely difficult to solve without recursion can be solved almost trivially when recursion is employed. We shall meet several such problems in the next chapter. The rest of this chapter will be devoted to highlighting the elegance of recursion through a range of examples. The greatest virtue of recursion is that it makes things look so easy, hiding all the the messy work that the computer has to do behind the scenes.

Example 8A: Euclid's algorithm. Perhaps the oldest recursive algorithm is Euclid's algorithm to find the highest common factor (HCF) of two positive integers. Let us illustrate the algorithm with an example. Suppose we want to find the HCF of the integers 30 and 154. To proceed, find the remainder when 154 is divided by 30:

$$154 \text{ MOD } 30 = 4.$$

As long as the remainder is not zero, repeat the process by substituting the first number by the divisor and the divisor by the remainder; in this case, substitute 30 for 154 for 4 for 30:

$$30 \text{ MOD } 4 = 2.$$

Repeating this again by substituting 40 for 30 and 2 for 4 we get

$$4 \text{ MOD } 2 = 0.$$

When the remainder is 0, the HCF is given by the divisor, i.e. 2.

The algorithm is readily coded as

```
FUNCTION hcf(n,m: INTEGER): INTEGER;
VAR
    nModm: INTEGER;
BEGIN
        nModm := n MOD m;
        IF nModm = 0 THEN hcf := m
        ELSE hcf := hcf(m,nModm);
END; {hcf}
```

An alternative version is

```
FUNCTION hcf2(n,m:INTEGER):INTEGER;
BEGIN
        IF m = 0 THEN hcf2 := n
        ELSE hcf2 := hcf2(m,n MOD m);
END; {hcf2}
```

in which the base clause to stop the execution is set one step deeper. **FUNCTION hcf2** will make one extra recursive call compared to **FUNCTION hcf** to do the same task. The example is intended to make the point that the base clause should be chosen carefully to avoid unnecessary computation.

Example 8B: recursive pictures. In recent years, recursion has found all sorts of new applications in computer graphics. In particular, in fractal geometry, which was invented by the French mathematician Benoit Mandelbrot during the 1970s, and which has been used to model many natural forms such as rocks, clouds and trees. These are difficult to model using the traditional Euclidean geometry. Most of the algorithms used in producing fractal pictures are naturally recursive.

Unfortunately, standard Pascal does not contain any predefined procedures to support the drawing of pictures. For this reason, in any discussion of graphics it is necessary to assume that we have available some basic procedures for graphical output. For the discussion in this section we shall assume the existence of the following:

```
PROCEDURE initialise; { To initialise the graphics device }

PROCEDURE show(xMin,xMax,yMin,yMax: REAL);
{ This maps the screen into a rectangle whose bottom left hand corner is
the point (xMin,yMin) and the top right hand corner is the point
(xMax,yMax) }

PROCEDURE move(x,y: REAL); { To move the 'pen' to the point (x,y) }

PROCEDURE draw(x,y: REAL);
{ To draw a line from the current position of the pen to the point (x,y) }
```

For the users of TURBO Pascal, we have made these procedures available in the unit **MINIGRAF** on the disk.

Our problem is to draw the picture shown opposite:

Here is the algorithm:

> Draw a frame consisting of n small squares to fit on each of the sides of a given square. This will produce an empty square region in the middle of the original square. If $n = 1$ then stop, otherwise
>
> Draw a frame consisting of $n - 1$ small squares to fit on each of the sides of the empty square produced in the previous step.

In the program that follows, this algorithm is implemented in the **PROCEDURE nest. PROCEDURE drawFrame**, as the name implies, is used to actually draw the frame consisting of n small squares on each of the sides of the square whose lower corner is the point A, B.

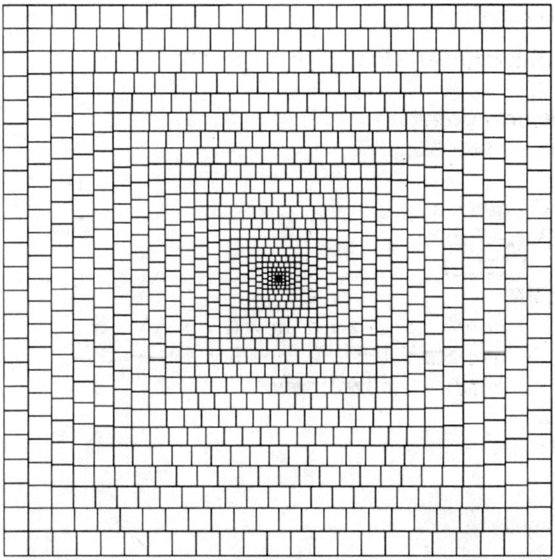

```
PROGRAM recursiveSquares(INPUT,OUTPUT);
USES MINIGRAF;          { provided for the users of Turbo Pascal }
TYPE
      point = RECORD
                 x,y; REAL;
              END;
VAR
    n   : INTEGER;
    A,B: point;

PROCEDURE drawFrame(n: INTEGER; A,B: point);
VAR
    i,j: INTEGER;
    d : REAL;
BEGIN
      d := (B.x - A.x)/n;
      FOR i := 0 TO n - 1 DO
          FOR j := 0 TO n - 1 DO
              IF (i = 0) OR (j = 0) OR (i = n - 1) OR (j = n - 1) THEN
                BEGIN
                      move(A.x + d*i,A.y + d*j);
                      draw(A.x + d*(i + 1),A.y + d*j);
                      draw(A.x + d*(i + 1),A.y + d*(j + 1));
                      draw(A.x + d*i,A.y + d*(j + 1));
                      draw(A.x + d*i,A.y + d*j);
                END;
```

```
END; {drawFrame}

PROCEDURE nest(n: INTEGER; A,B: point);
VAR
    newA,newB: point;
    d         : REAL;
BEGIN
      drawFrame(n,a,b);
      d := (B.x - A.x)/n;
      IF n > 1 THEN
        BEGIN
              newA.x := A.x + d; newA.y := A.y + d;
              newB.x := B.x - d;  newB.y := B.y + d;
              nest(n - 1,newA,newB);
        END;
END;  {nest}

BEGIN
      initialise;
      n := 23;
      show(0,n,0,n);
      A.x := 0;          A.y := 0;
      B.x := n - 1;      B.y := 0;
      nest(n,A,B);
      READLN;
END.
```

Example 8C: A chess challenge. A problem which has occupied many chess enthusiasts involves the placing of eight queens on a chessboard such that no queen is under attack from any of the others. A solution to the problem is shown below

<table>
<tr><td></td><td></td><td></td><td>Q</td><td></td><td></td><td></td><td></td></tr>
<tr><td></td><td></td><td></td><td></td><td></td><td>Q</td><td></td><td></td></tr>
<tr><td>Q</td><td></td><td></td><td></td><td></td><td></td><td></td><td></td></tr>
<tr><td></td><td></td><td></td><td></td><td>Q</td><td></td><td></td><td></td></tr>
<tr><td></td><td>Q</td><td></td><td></td><td></td><td></td><td></td><td></td></tr>
<tr><td></td><td></td><td></td><td></td><td></td><td></td><td></td><td>Q</td></tr>
<tr><td></td><td></td><td>Q</td><td></td><td></td><td></td><td></td><td></td></tr>
<tr><td></td><td></td><td></td><td></td><td></td><td></td><td>Q</td><td></td></tr>
</table>

Our problem is to find all the solutions. A recursive algorithm to solve the problem can be constructed as follows. Suppose we search for a solution by first placing a queen in column 1, then placing a queen in a safe position in column 2 and so on. Having found a solution as far as column $n-1$, the following algorithm will find *all* the solutions which exist in the region spanned by columns n to 8.

TO SOLVE THE PROBLEM FOR THE REGION SPANNED BY COLUMNS N TO 8 DO:

For each safe position in column n;
place a queen in position
if $n < 8$ then solve the problem for the region spanned by columns $n + 1$ to 8. Otherwise, print the board.

To find all the solutions we choose $n = 1$ in the above algorithm.

Program **Queens**, given below and also provided on the disk, implements this algorithm. The two-dimensional BOOLEAN **ARRAY** board is used to model the chessboard. A TRUE value indicates the presence of a queen. **PROCEDURE printBoard** is used for printing a solution. **FUNCTION safe** checks to see if a position in a given row and column is safe for placing a queen. This is done by establishing, if, in any of the previous columns, a queen exists which occupies the same row as the given row or occupies a cell which lies along one of the two diagonals emanating from the given position.

PROCEDURE putQueen implements the above algorithm recursively. The variable counter is used to keep a count of the number of solutions found so far. There are in fact 92 solutions. A small sample of the output is shown at the end of the program.

The fact that we have chosen an 8×8 board is not a restriction on the program. It will work for any $n \times n$ square. Also, the algorithm itself does not say anything about a square board or what is meant by a safe position; by redefining the meaning of 'safe' the program may be converted to solve many other kinds of interesting problems.

```
PROGRAM Queens(INPUT,OUTPUT);
CONST
        boardSize = 8;
TYPE
      position = 0..9;              { 0..boardSize + 1 }
```

```
VAR
   board       : ARRAY[1..boardSize,1..boardSize] OF BOOLEAN;
   row,column : position;
   success     : BOOLEAN;
   counter     : INTEGER;
PROCEDURE printBoard;
VAR
   r,c: position;
BEGIN
      WRITELN('SOLUTION ',counter);
      FOR r := 1 TO boardSize DO
         BEGIN
               FOR c := 1 TO boardSize DO
                  IF board[r,c] THEN WRITE('Q ') ELSE WRITE('. ');
               WRITELN;
         END;
END; {printBoard}

FUNCTION safe(row,column: position): BOOLEAN:
VAR
   r,c: position;
BEGIN
      safe := TRUE;
      FOR c := 1 TO column - 1 DO
         FOR r := 1 TO boardSize DO
            IF board[r,c] THEN
               IF (r = row) OR (ABS(r - row) = column - c) THEN safe := FALSE;
END; {safe}

PROCEDURE putQueen(column: position; VAR successful: BOOLEAN);
VAR
   row: position;
   s   : BOOLEAN;
BEGIN
      successful := TRUE;
      IF column < = boardSize THEN
         BEGIN
               succesful := FALSE;
               FOR row := 1 TO boardSize DO
                  IF safe(row,column) THEN
                     BEGIN
                           board[row,column] := TRUE;
                           putQueen(column + 1,s);
                           IF s THEN
                              BEGIN
                                    successful := TRUE;
                                    IF column = boardSize THEN
```

```
                                    BEGIN
                                          printBoard;
                                          counter := counter + 1;
                                    END;
                             END;
                           board [row,column] := FALSE;
                    END;
        END;
END; {putQueen}

BEGIN       { ---- Main ---- }
      FOR row := 1 to boardSize do
          FOR column := 1 TO boardSize DO
               board [row,column] := false;      { board empty }
      counter := 1;
      putQueen(1,success);
END.
```

```
SOLUTION 1

Q . . . . . . .
. . . . . . Q .
. . . . Q . . .
. . . . . . . Q
. Q . . . . . .
. . . Q . . . .
. . . . . Q . .
. . Q . . . . .
         ⋮
SOLUTION 92

. . Q . . . . .
. . . . . Q . .
. . . Q . . . .
. Q . . . . . .
. . . . . . . Q
. . . . Q . . .
. . . . . . Q .
Q . . . . . . .
```

Example 8D: Quicksort. The bubble sort and the insertion sort algorithms that we met earlier in Chapter 5 are not very efficient for sorting a large amount of data. The quicksort algorithm, which will now be described in its simplest form, is the most heavily used sorting algorithm. The reason for its popularity is that it requires very little extra memory apart from the memory required for data and its average performance is superior to other methods. The algorithm is inherently recursive. It succeeds by employing a divide and conquer strategy to reduce the problem of sorting a large list into the problem of sorting a series of lists that get smaller and more orderly at each stage. The algorithm is not very quick if the list is not too disordered to begin with. For this reason the data to be sorted are often randomly permuted at the start!

For the case when data are to be sorted in ascending order, the quicksort algorithm can be stated as follows:

TO SORT A LIST OF ITEMS IN ASCENDING ORDER DO THE FOLLOWING:

If the list to be sorted has only one item then the task is complete, otherwise

take the first element of the list as the TEST element and, rearranging the list if necessary, place the TEST element in its correct position so that every item to the left of the TEST element is less than or equal to the TEST element and every item to the right is greater than or equal to it.

Now sort the two sublists produced in the last step; the one to the left of the TEST element and the one to the right.

To illustrate, we will first take a list that requires no rearranging to place the TEST element in the correct position. Suppose we want to sort the array of integers

13 9 5 56 34 27

The correct position for the TEST element is the third position and by placing it there we obtain the new list:

9 5 13 56 34 27

Next we apply the same process to the two sublists 9 5 and 56 34 27. It is easy to see that in two more steps the whole list will be sorted. Of course, we have not said anything yet about how the TEST element is to be placed in the correct position in general, but let us postpone that and for the time being assume that we have available a **PROCEDURE** of the form

```
PROCEDURE placeTest(VAR correctPosition:INTEGER; VAR A:List;
                                        leftIndex, rightIndex:INTEGER);
```

which will, given an array **A** with its index spanning the range **leftIndex..rightIndex**, place the TEST element in the correct position, rearranging the elements of **A** if necessary. Given such a **PROCEDURE**, we can easily turn the above algorithm into a **PROCEDURE** to do quicksort:

```
PROCEDURE QuickSort(VAR A:List; leftIndex, rightIndex:INTEGER);
VAR
   position:INTEGER;
BEGIN
       IF leftIndex <> rightIndex THEN
       BEGIN
       placeTest(position,a,leftIndex,rightIndex);
       QuickSort(A,leftIndex,position - 1);
       QuickSort(A,position + 1,rightIndex);
       END;
END; {QuickSort}
```

Any method of finding the correct position for the TEST element will work with this **PROCEDURE**, but let us now explain the method used in quicksort.

Consider now the modified list of integers shown below.

13 9 5 56 3 27

It is not possible now to place 13 in the correct position without rearranging the list. We proceed as follows.

Set two index pointers L and R (for left and right). L will always point to a position which is either to the left of the correct position of the TEST element, or is the correct position. Similarly, R will point to a position on the right of or at the correct position.

We start by setting the TEST element equal to the first element 13 and placing L and R at the two extreme ends of the list as shown:

```
L          R
↓          ↓
13 9 5 56 3 27
```

Now move R to the left until an element is found whose value is less than or equal to the value of the test element 13. This will happen when R points at 3. Swap the elements pointed at by L and R, which is this case results in the interchange of 3 and 13. The picture now looks like this:

```
L           R
↓           ↓
3 9 5 56 13 27
```

Now move L to the right until an element is found whose value is greater than or equal to the TEST element. This will occur when L reaches 56. Again swap the elements pointed at by L and R to interchange 56 and 13. This results in the picture

```
      L  R
      ↓  ↓
3 9 5 13 56 27
```

The next time R is moved to the left it coincides with L. We stop when L and R are pointing at the same element

```
              LR
              ↓↓
3    9    5    13    56    27
```

We see that, at this stage, every element to the left of the TEST element has a value less than 13 and every element to the right has a value which is greater.

The method used to place the TEST element in the correct position can be stated algorithmically as follows.

TO PLACE THE TEST ELEMENT IN THE CORRECT POSITION DO THE FOLLOWING

Initialise index pointers L and R to the two ends of the array to be sorted.

REPEAT
  Move R to the left until an element is pointed at whose value is less than or equal to TEST. Swap this element, with TEST.
  Move L to right until an element is pointed at whose value is greater than or equal to TEST. Swap this element, with TEST.
UNTIL L = R

This part of the Quicksort algorithm is iterative rather than recursive although one can turn it into a recursive version if desired. A non-recursive **PROCEDURE** for finding the correct position of the TEST element is given below.

```
PROCEDURE placeTest(VAR correctPosition:INTEGER; VAR a:list;
                                        leftIndex,rightIndex:INTEGER);
VAR
   test,L,R:INTEGER;
PROCEDURE swap; {interchanges a[L] and a [R]}
VAR
   temp:INTEGER
BEGIN
      temp := a[L];
      a[L] := a[R];
      a[R] := temp;
END; {swap}
BEGIN
      {set test to the first element and initialise L and R}
      test := a[leftIndex}; L := leftIndex; R := rightIndex;
      {now move R and L and swap}
      WHILE R <> L DO
            BEGIN
                  WHILE (R > L) AND (a[R] > = test) DO R := R - 1;
                  IF R <> L THEN swap;
                  WHILE (L < R) AND (a[L] <= test) DO
                  L := L + 1;
                  IF L < > R THEN swap;
            END;
      correctPosition := L;
END; {placeTest}
```

〉 8.3 Mutual recursion and the directive FORWARD

If a subprogram *x* calls a subprogram *y* and *y* calls *x* then this is known as **mutal recursion**. How are we to cater for this chicken/egg predicament if we stick to the rule that a subprogram must be declared before it can be referenced?

The escape clause that is available to bail us out is the **FORWARD declaration**. This declaration is done as follows.

Only the heading of the subprogram is declared in the first instance followed by the word **FORWARD**.

When the actual code for the subprogram is written then the parameter list is omitted.

For example,

```
PROCEDURE chicken(feathers;INTEGER); FORWARD;     {FORWARD declaration of
                                                    chicken}
PROCEDURE egg(hatchtime:REAL);
VAR
  f:INTEGER;
BEGIN
     .
     .
     chicken(f);
     .
END;{egg}
PROCEDURE chicken; {code for chicken. Note no parameter list}
VAR
  h:REAL;
BEGIN
     .
     egg(h);
     .
END;{chicken}
```

Quickies

1. List the four types of parameter allowed in Pascal.
2. Write recursive **FUNCTION**s for the following where n and r are integers and a is real.
   (a) Factorial(0) = 1
   Factorial(n) = $n \times$ Factorial($n-1$), $n = 1, 2, \ldots$.
   (b) Power(a, 0) = 1
   Power(a, n) = 1/Power($a, -n$), $n < 0$
   Power(a, n) = $a \times$ Power($a, n-1$), $n > 0$.
   (c) Binomial(n, 0) = 1
   Binomial(n, n) = 1
   Binomial(n, r) = Binomial($n-1, r$) + Binomial($n-1, r-1$) for $0 < r < n$.

3. Explain what the following **PROCEDURE** will do if called as UpToP('f')

```
PROCEDURE UpToP(x: CHAR);
BEGIN
        IF x < = 'p' THEN
          BEGIN
                WRITE(x);
                UpToP(SUCC(x));
          END;
END; {UpToP}
```

4. Write a recursive algorithm to calculate the sum $1 + 2 + \cdots + n$.

⇒ **You may now proceed to Pascal laboratory Activities 41–45.**

〉 Pascal laboratory

Activity 41. Examine and run TUTOR37. Alter **PROCEDURE tabulate** so that it takes two **FUNCTION**s $f(x)$ and $g(x)$ as parameters and tabulates the two sets of values $f(g(x))$ and $g(f(x))$. (You will not be able to carry out this activity if your compiler does not allow subprograms as parameters, in which case treat this as an exercise on paper.)

Activity 42. TUTOR38 is meant to show the stacking and unstacking process involved in recursion and described in the text. Run the program and observe.

Activity 43. The medieval number theorist and algebraist Leonardo Fibonacci (1170–1250) who introduced arabic numerals in Europe studied the following infinite sequence:

$$0, 1, 1, 2, 3, 5, 8, 13, 21, 34, 55, \ldots.$$

These numbers, known as Fibonacci numbers, turn up in many natural objects such as spirals in pine cones and also in classical art and architecture. Each number in the sequence starting from 0 and 1 is the sum of the two previous numbers in the sequence.

TUTOR39 is a recursive program to generate the sequence. Study the program and run it. Modify the program so that it prints instead a list of the ratios of the nth element divided by the $(n - 1)$th element. What do you observe? If you are producing the right answer, this sequence should be approaching a number known as the **golden ratio**. Write a non-recursive **PROCEDURE Fibo2** to produce Fibonacci numbers.

Activity 44. TUTOR40 is an incomplete program to sort integers using Quicksort. Write a **PROCEDURE** to read data from the keyboard into an **ARRAY** and another to print an **ARRAY**. Read ten integers and print the unsorted and sorted data. Modify the program so that it sorts strings and test it by sorting ten names.

Activity 45. (This activity is for TURBO Pascal users.) TUTOR41 is a recursive program to produce a diagrammatic representation of Pascal's triangle as shown below. Study the program and write in algorithmic form the method used in there. Run the program for various values of *n*. Modify the program so that instead of drawing a triangle at any of the recursive stages, it draws three lines joining the centre of the triangle to the three vertices.

〉 Exercises

1*. Write a **FUNCTION SumF** which will calculate the sum of the values of an arbitrary function $f(i)$ for $i = 1$ to n, i.e.

$$\sum_{i=1}^{n} f(i).$$

Test **SumF** with $f = i$ and $f = \mathbf{SQRT}(i)$.

2. The trapezoidal rule for calculating the integral I of a function $f(x)$ between the limits a and b is

$$I = h(f(a)/2 + f(a+h) + f(a+2h) + \cdots + f(a+(n-1)h) + f(b)/2)$$

where the interval $[a, b]$ is divided into n equal intervals of width $h = (b-a)/n$.

Write a function that will use the trapezoidal rule to calculate the integral of an arbitrary function in a given interval.

3. Illustrate, for each recursive stage, the values allocated on the stack to the parameters **n** and **m** and the variable **nModm** when the **FUNCTION hcf** given in the text is called with **n** = 7 and **m** = 5.

4*. Denoting the nth Fibonacci number as $F(n)$, $n = 1, 2, \ldots$, work out how many times $F(1)$, $F(2)$, $F(3)$ and $F(4)$ have to be calculated in the recursive **PROCEDURE Fibo**, given in TUTOR39, to calculate $F(5)$.

5*. A partition of a given positive integer n consists of a sequence of positive integers which add up to n. The sequence is written in a sorted decreasing fashion. For example, the partitions of 5 are

$$\begin{array}{l} 4+1 \\ 3+2 \\ 3+1+1 \\ 2+2+1 \\ 2+1+1+1 \\ 1+1+1+1+1 \end{array}$$

Write a program to generate the partitions of n. Hint: the first number x in any partition takes values from $n-1$ to 1 and appears with all the partitions of $n-x$.

6*. A Diophantine equation (named after the mathematician Diophantus of Alexandria, 250 AD) is an equation in one or more variables with integer coefficients. Furthermore, its solutions are sought consisting only of integers. For example, the Diophantine equation

$$2x_1 + 3x_2 = 11$$

has a solution $x_1 = 1$, $x_2 = 3$. It has infinitely many others, e.g. $x_1 = -2$, $x_2 = 5$.

Given a Diophantine equation, can we tell if it can be solved? This problem was raised by a very distinguished German mathematician, David Hilbert, in 1900. It occupied the labours of many mathematicians and it was not until 1970 that a Russian mathematician, named Yuri Matyasevich, proved it could not be done. You are invited to follow in this great tradition by attempting to solve the following problem: Given the Diophantine equation

$$a_1x_1 + a_2x_2 + \cdots + a_mx_m = b$$

in which all the *a*s and the *b* are positive integers, write a program to find all the positive integer solutions. Hint: x_m can take a value in the range $0, \ldots, b/a_m$. Then the probem reduces to solving the Diophantine equation:

$$a_1x_1 + a_2x_2 + \cdots + a_{m-1}x_{m-1} = b - a_mx_m.$$

7*. (This exercise is for TURBO Pascal users.)
(a) Use recursion to subdivide a square into $2^n \times 2^n$ squares. The case $n = 4$ is shown in the diagram. Hint: write a **PROCEDURE nest(n: INTEGER; A,B,C,D: point)** which, if $\mathbf{n} = 1$, will call a **PROCEDURE drawFrame(A,B,C,D)** to draw a square with vertices at the points A, B, C and D. If $\mathbf{n} > 1$ then the **PRO-**

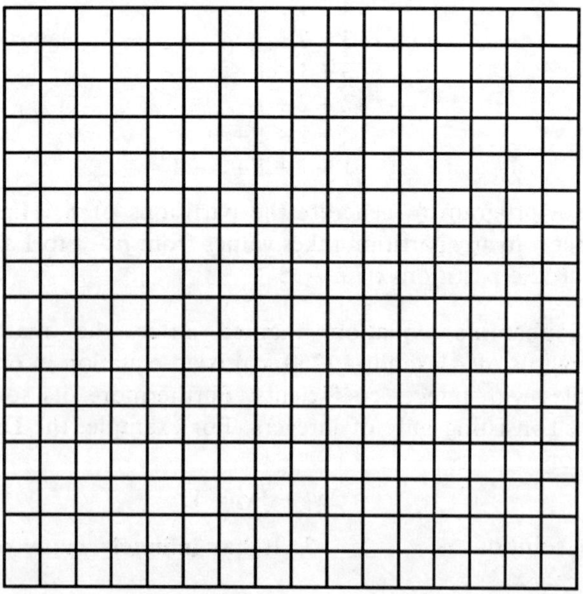

CEDURE nest will make four recursive calls to itself with suitable choices of A B, C and D.

(b) By modifying your **PROCEDURE drawFrame** (a), produce the two pictures shown below.

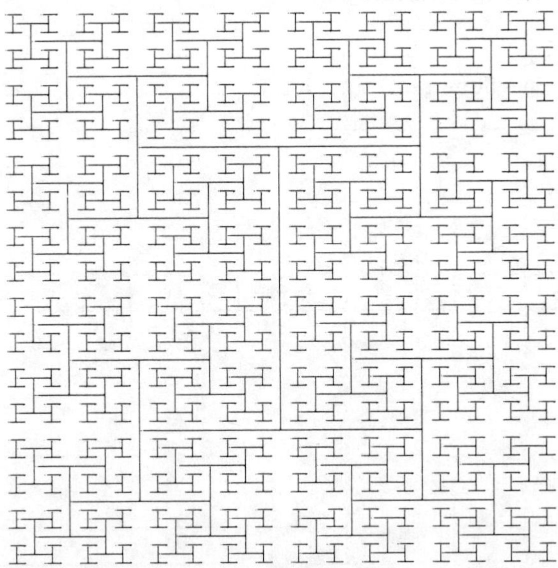

Answers to quickies

1. Value, **VAR**, **FUNCTION** and **PROCEDURE**.
2. (a)

```
FUNCTION Factorial(n: INTEGER): INTEGER;
BEGIN
        IF n = 0 THEN Factorial := 1
        ELSE Factorial := n*Factorial(n - 1);
END; {Factorial}
```

(b)

```
FUNCTION Power(a: REAL; n: INTEGER): REAL;
BEGIN
        IF n = 0 THEN Power := 1
        ELSE IF n < 0 THEN Power := 1/Power(a, - n)
        ELSE Power := a*Power(n - 1);
END; {Power}
```

(c)

```
FUNCTION Binomial(n,r: INTEGER): INTEGER;
BEGIN
        IF (r = 0) OR (r = n) THEN Binomial := 1
        ELSE Binomial := Binomial(n - 1,r) + Binomial(n - 1,r - 1);
END; {Binomial}
```

3. It will write **fghijklmnop**

4. Sum(1) = 1
   Sum(n) = n + Sum(n − 1)   n = 2,3 . .

〉 Chapter 9

〉 Manipulating Dynamic Data

The two structures **FILE**s and **ARRAY**s, which are suitable for storing large amounts of data have their limitations. Neither of them allow for efficient run-time management of memory requirements nor do they allow for insertion and deletion of individual data items without the whole structure having to be shifted. The purpose of this chapter is to introduce you to dynamic data structures which can grow and contract in size during program execution and in which individual items can be easily manipulated.

〉 9.1 Pointers

Apart from the data type FILE, all other data types we have met so far are **static**. Their sizes remain fixed during program execution. For example, an **ARRAY** with ten components remains an **ARRAY** with ten components. This is unsatisfactory in situations where the memory requirements are not known in advance.

The size of a FILE does of course vary but, because files reside on external mediums, operations on data held on files consume more execution time than on data held in the internal memory of a computer.

By contrast, dynamic variables, which we shall now discuss, are created and removed dynamically, i.e. during the execution of a program. Creation and manipulation of dynamic variables is done using **pointers**. Unlike a static variable, a pointer does not store data but instead stores an address where the data is to be found in memory.

A pointer is declared by prefixing the type of value to be pointed at with the symbol ^ (in books this is often denoted by the up arrow symbol

↑). For example,

```
VAR
    p: ^INTEGER; { pronounced pointer to INTEGER }
```

This declares **p** as a pointer to point at a memory location which will store an INTEGER. What we have done here is to declare a **dynamic** INTEGER variable. The variable cannot be referred to directly but only indirectly via the pointer variable as will shortly be explained.

A dynamic variable can be of any TYPE. The **TYPE** definition has the general form

ProgramIdentifier = ^ *TypeIdentifier*;

where a special feature of this declaration is that *TypeIdentifier* may refer to an identifier that is defined later in the same block. This violates the normal requirement in Pascal that an identifier must be declared before it can be referenced. For example, in the following declaration **aPointer** is defined to point to the **RECORD TYPE Node**, which is defined afterwards.

```
TYPE
    aPointer = ^Node;
    Node = RECORD
               item: INTEGER;
               next: aPointer;
           END;
```

Note that here the definition of **Node** also contains a reference to **aPointer**, so that **aPointer** is defined in terms of **Node** and **Node** is defined in terms of **aPointer**. Without this facility to refer forwards such a declaration would not be possible. This is not a perverse example but, as we shall see in the next section, represents the most useful case in which pointers are used to link a whole chain of **RECORD**s. In all such cases the pointer type has to be defined prior to the **RECORD** type to which it points.

As mentioned earlier, unlike static variables, dynamic variables are not referenced directly using identifiers; they can only be referred to indirectly using pointers. The contents of the memory to which a pointer p points are referenced by placing ^ as a suffix to the name of the pointer. In the diagram below the pointer **p** is pointing at the dynamic INTEGER variable **p^** whose current value is −26. Thus **p^** is the symbol that has to be used to refer to the value pointed at by the pointer **p**.

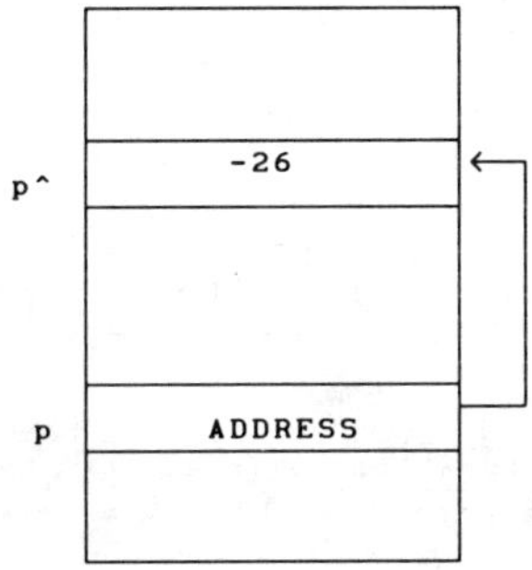

The address associated with a pointer p is allocated by the system and held in internal format. For this reason values of pointer variables are anonymous and cannot be examined or printed.

The declaration of a pointer p serves only to reserve storage for p. The value of p at this stage remains undefined, i.e. p as yet does not refer to any memory location. The storage is allocated dynamically during program execution (dynamic variables are stored in an area of computer's memory known as the **heap**). This is done via a call to the standard procedure NEW. The statement NEW(p) assigns a value to p and simultaneously allocates storage for the variable pointed at by p, i.e. the storage for p^.

The storage allocated to a dynamic variable may be deallocated, for possible reuse by the system. This is achieved via a call to the standard procedure DISPOSE. The statement DISPOSE(p) causes the pointer p to become undefined. Thus DISPOSE is the inverse of NEW.

The various processes we have just described are illustrated diagrammatically below

The declaration of a pointer p reserves storage for p. At this stage p is undefined

```
VAR
  p: ^INTEGER;
```

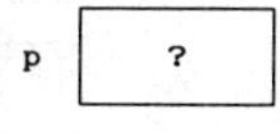

The execution of the statement NEW(p), causes an address in memory to be assigned to p. The pointer p now points to a specific memory location. However, the memory location pointed at has no value associated with it at this stage.

```
NEW(p)
```

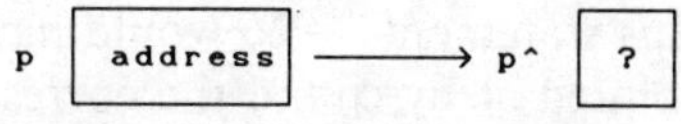

p^ can be treated exactly like any other INTEGER variable and, if, for example, we make the assignment p^:=-26 then the memory location pointed at by p will now have the value -26 written into it.

p^:=-26

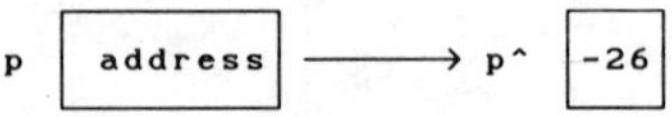

To free the memory location pointed at by p, the statement DISPOSE(p) is used. This removes the link between the pointer and the location pointed at. Once more p becomes undefined.

DISPOSE(p)

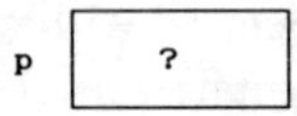

A pointer variable can be assigned to another pointer variable of the same TYPE. For example, the declaration

```
VAR
    p,q: ^INTEGER;
```

makes possible the assignment q := p. This has the effect of making q and p both point at the same address. For example, if p and q are pointing in the manner shown

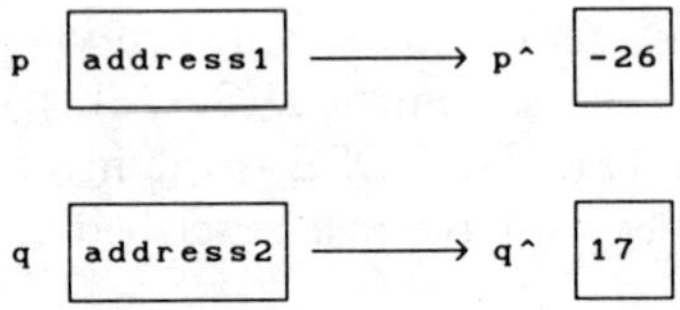

then the assignment q := p will change this picture into

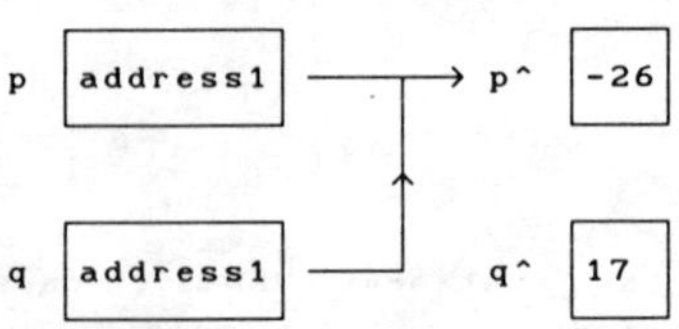

making q point at the same memory location as p. Remember that the assignment q^ := p^ means something quite different. Had we instead executed this statement, −26 would have been written into the memory location pointed at by q and the corresponding picture would be

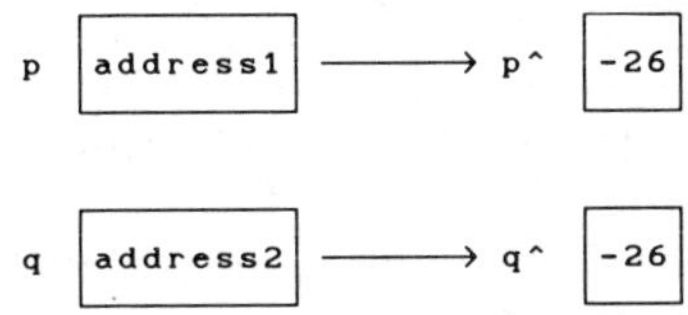

There is one special predefined pointer in Pascal denoted by the identifier **NIL**. It is used to point at nothing. It has no TYPE associated with it and any pointer variable can be assigned to it. It must be understood, however, that an undefined pointer is not the same as one whose value is NIL. It is an error to try to use a pointer which is undefined, hence an assignment of the form p:= NIL is used for initialisation to change the status of p if it is undefined. The other important use of NIL is for indicating the end of linked data structures, as we shall see in the next section.

Apart from the operation of assignment, pointer values can be compared using the two comparison operators = and <>. Two pointer values are equal if they are both NIL or if they both point at the same memory location. For example, the following statement checks to see if the pointers p and q are equal:

```
IF p = q THEN
        IF p <> NIL THEN
              WRITE('p and q point to the same memory location')
        ELSE
              WRITE(' p and q are both NIL ')
ELSE
      WRITE(' p and q are unequal ');
```

Pointers may be passed as parameters to subprograms. Also, a FUNCTION may return a pointer result. Examples of these will be given later.

〉9.2 Linked linear structures

Having covered the basics of pointers we are now ready to study linked data structures. In these structures pointers are utilised to link many RECORDSs together. The linking is achieved by declaring RECORDs in which at least one of the fields is itself a pointer.

Linked data structures offer the following advantages:

They can expand and contract during program execution as the need arises.
New elements can easily be inserted and deleted.
The structures reside in the internal memory of the computer and can be accessed quickly.

The simplest of these structures is the stack, which we shall look at now.

Stacks
A stack is a data structure which is frequently utilised in systems software, e.g. compilers. It comprises a list of a variable number of items and is characterised by the requirement that items are added to and removed from only at one end of the list (the top). This implies that the last item to be added is the first one that is removed (last-in first-out or LIFO). For historical reasons the actions of adding and deleting items are referred to as **Push** and **Pop**, respectively.

We will now construct a stack and, to keep things simple, we will take the items in the stack to be integers. The question may be raised as to why we do not use an ARRAY. The answer is that a stack can grow and shrink but with an ARRAY we would be occupying all the storage needed to accommodate the largest size stack. By creating a dynamic stack we use only as much memory as needed and release the space as soon as an item has been removed.

We start by introducing the following declarations:

```
TYPE
      stackPtr = ^node;
      node = RECORD
                   item: INTEGER;
                   next: stackPtr;
             END;
VAR
      TopPtr,newPtr: stackPtr;
```

These definitions will be utilised to construct the stack shown below. Note how the pointer NIL marks the end of the stack.

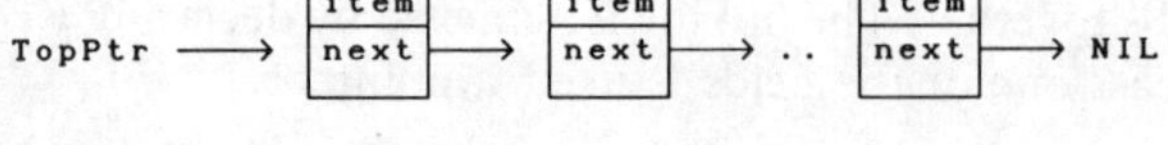

To illustrate how to create a node and link it into the stack (push) we shall go through the steps involved in the initial creation of two nodes. The general method to be used should then become clear.

Initially, when the stack is empty, the first node is created using the following statements:

```
NEW(TopPtr);
TopPtr^.item := item1;
TopPtr^.next := NIL;
```

which results in the picture

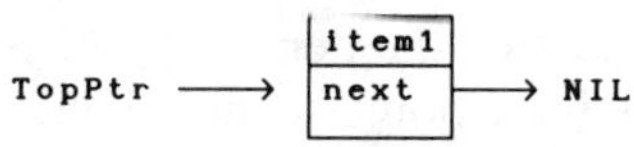

Here, the first statement creates the pointer **TopPtr**, i.e. allocates storage for **TopPtr^** and makes **TopPtr** point to it. This pointer will always be set to point to the top node in the stack and will be our one 'named handle' on this dynamic structure which will otherwise remain concealed and nameless. The next two statements assign values to the two fields of this first node. Item1 will be some INTEGER value. The field next is assigned the value **NIL** since at this stage there is nothing else to point to.

To add the second node we use the following statements:

```
NEW(newPtr);
newPtr^.item := item2;
newPtr^.item := TopPtr;
TopPtr := newPtr;
```

The explanation is as follows. The first statement creates a new pointer **newPtr** to point to a fresh node. The second statement assigns a value to the field item of this node. The third statement makes the field next to this node point at the previously added node (which was being pointed at by **TopPtr**). This achieves the linking of the newly created node into the structure and placing it at the top. Finally, the last statement updates the pointer **TopPtr** by making it point at the fresh node. Our picture now looks like this

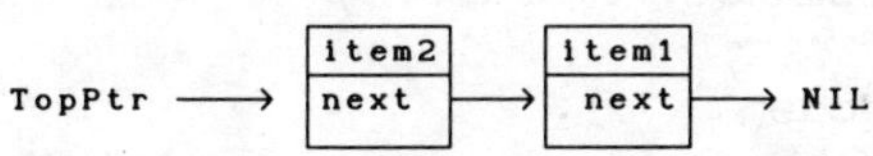

The program **demoStack** demonstrates the process of adding items to the stack, deleting items from the stack and printing the stack.

PROCEDURE push is used to place an item on the top and, after the discussion above, its functioning should be quite clear.

FUNCTION pop is used to dispose an item from the top. A **FUNCTION** rather than a **PROCEDURE** is used so as to obtain the value of the field *item* in the node being disposed. The use of a **FUNCTION** is made possible only because in this simple example the stack items are INTEGERs.

The algorithm employed in **FUNCTION pop** goes as follows.

IF THE STACK IS NOT EMPTY THEN

Assign to **pop** the value of the item being disposed.
Make a temporary pointer point at the second node.
Dispose the pointer which was pointing at the old top.
Make the new top pointer the same as the temporary pointer.

IF THE STACK IS EMPTY THEN

Print an error message and assign the value zero to **pop**.

PROCEDURE writeStack writes out all the items currently in the stack. It employs an auxiliary pointer which is made to point in sequence at consecutive nodes starting from the top. The method of moving from node to node using a running pointer is central to any algorithm employed for scanning a linked structure and is referred to as **traversal**. Note how we had no choice but to start the traversal at the top. The meaning of the remark made earlier, that **TopPtr** is our only 'handle' on this dynamic structure should now be clear.

Note that in the main program **TopPtr** is first initialised to **NIL**. This is necessary, otherwise it will be undefined when **PROCEDURE push** is called and an error message will result.

To demonstrate the functioning of the program, the integers −26, 75 and 58 are pushed onto the stack; the last two are then popped and each time the stack is displayed. The output for this sequence of actions is shown after the listing.

```
PROGRAM demoStack(INPUT,OUTPUT);
Type
    stackPtr = ^node;
    node = RECORD
                item: INTEGER;
                next: stackPtr;
            END;
```

```
VAR
    TopPtr: stackPtr;

PROCEDURE push(VAR Top: stackPtr; n: INTEGER);
VAR
    newPtr: stackPtr;
BEGIN
      new(newPtr);
      newPtr^.item := n;
      newPtr^.next := Top;
      Top := newPtr;
END; {push}

FUNCTION pop(VAR Top: stackPtr): INTEGER;
VAR
    tempPtr: stackPtr;
BEGIN
      IF TOP <> NIL THEN
        BEGIN
              pop := Top^.item;
              tempPtr := Top^.next;{pointer to second item}
              DISPOSE(Top); {delete the top node}
              Top := tempPtr; {update the top pointer}
        END
      ELSE
        BEGIN
              WRITELN('Error-tried to pop an empty stack');
              pop := 0;
        END;
END; {pop}

PROCEDURE writeStack(Top: stackPtr);
VAR
    auxPtr: stackPtr;
BEGIN
      auxPtr := Top;
      WHILE auxPtr <> NIL DO
         BEGIN
               WRITE(auxPtr^.item,' ');
               auxPtr := auxPtr^.next;
         END;
      WRITELN;
END; {writeStack}
```

```
BEGIN
        NEW(TopPtr);
        TopPtr := NIL;
        push(TopPtr, -26);
        WRITELN('OPERATION      STACK');
        WRITE('push -26       '); writeStack(TopPtr);
        push(TopPtr,75);
        WRITE('push 75        '); writeStack(TopPtr);
        push(TopPtr,58);
        WRITE('push 58        '); writeStack(TopPtr);
        WRITE('pop ',pop(TopPtr),'         '); writeStack(TopPtr);
        WRITE('pop ',pop(TopPtr),'         '); writeStack(TopPtr);
END.
```

```
OPERATION      STACK

push -26       -26
push 75        75  -26
push 58        58  75  -26
pop 58         75  -26
pop 75         -26
```

Example 9A: huge integers. The largest known prime number at the time of writing of this book requires 6505 digits to write it out. This number is

$$2^{216091} - 1$$

How do you handle such a number on a computer? Even large computers offer you something like 13 digits to hold an integer.

As an application of the stack we will now develop a method for storing and printing positive integers of arbitrary length. The program hugeIntegers listed after the discussion (and also given on the disk) will use the method to calculate powers of a digit. For example, the output from the program for 5 raised to the power 100 is shown below.

```
1577721810442023610823457130565572459346412870218046009540557861328125
```

The items in our stack will be the digits 0, ..., 9. To make things clear, let us assume that we are calculating powers of 5 and that we have calculated $5^2 = 25$. Our stack will look like this:

stack1 ⟶ [5] ⟶ [2] ⟶ NIL

Note that the number 25 is written in reverse order. This is in keeping with the behaviour of a stack in which the first item gets pushed below the second one and so on. To go from here to calculate 5^3, let us consider first what happens when we multiply 25 by 5:

$$\begin{array}{r} 25 \\ \underline{5} \\ 125 \end{array}$$

5 is multiplied by 5 to get 25, we write 5 and carry 2. Next, 5 is multiplied by 2 to get 10 to which we add the number carried, i.e. 2, and we get 12. We write 2 and 1 is carried. Since there is nothing else left to multiply, we simply put down the number carried, i.e. 1 which gives us the final answer. Note that the functions **DIV** and **MOD** can be used to calculate the digit that is written and the carry. For example, when we multiply 5 times 5 to get 25, then **25 MOD 10** gives the digit 5 and **25 DIV 10** gives the carry 2.

The same process is applied in the creation of a new stack. We take out the top digit 5, multiply by 5 to get 25 and, instead of writing 5, we push 5 onto a new stack. 2 is carried as previously. We then take out the number 2, multiply it by 5 to get 10, add 2 to it to get 12. We push 2 onto the stack and carry 1. The stack is now empty so we push the number we carried, i.e. 1, onto the new stack. The new stack has the following appearance:

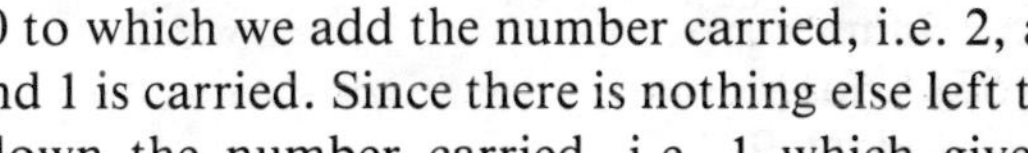

Note that in the new stack the answer is written in the correct order.

To proceed to calculate 5^4, we create a new stack in which the digits are written in reverse order, i.e.

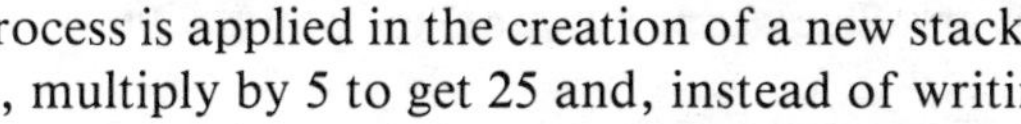

In the program **hugeIntegers**, the **FUNCTION multiply** does exactly what has been described above. It receives the pointer to the top of the current stack (stack1) and calculates the new stack (stack3) in the correct order which will be needed for the next multiplication.

FUNCTION multiply is called from **PROCEDURE upToPower** repeatedly to calculate all the powers of the base from 0 to 100.

PROCEDURE upToPower also calls **PROCEDURE printNum** to print out the digits making up the current stack.

FUNCTION multiply and **PROCEDURE printNum** both call **FUNCTION reverseStack**. In this, we simply traverse the input stack and write out the items consecutively into a new stack which, of course, reverses all the digits.

```
PROGRAM hugeIntegers(INPUT,OUTPUT);
TYPE
    numberPtr = ^number;
    number = RECORD
                digit: 0..9              ;
                next: numberPtr
             END;
VAR
   base: 0..9
FUNCTION reverseStack(top: numberPtr): numberPtr;
VAR
   newPtr,auxPtr: numberPtr;
BEGIN
    auxPtr := nil;
    WHILE top < > nil DO
       BEGIN
          NEW(newPtr);
          newPtr^.digit := top^.digit;
          newPtr^.next := auxPtr;
          auxPtr := newPtr;
          top := top^.next;
       END;
    reverseStack := auxPtr;
END; {reverseStack}

PROCEDURE printNum(top: numberPtr);
VAR
   auxPtr: numberPtr;
BEGIN
    auxPtr := reverseStack(top);
    WHILE auxPtr < > nil DO
       BEGIN
          write(auxPtr^.digit);
          auxPtr := auxPtr^.next;
       END;
    WRITELN;
END; {printNum}
```

```
FUNCTION multiply(top: numberPtr): numberPtr;
VAR
    stack2,newPtr        :numberPtr;
    carry,product,dig    :INTEGER;
BEGIN
      stack2 := nil;
      carry := 0;
      WHILE top <> nil DO
          BEGIN
                product := top^.digit * base + carry;
                dig := product MOD 10;
                carry := product DIV 10;
                new(newPtr);
                newPtr^.digit := dig;
                newPtr^.next := stack2;
                stack2 := newPtr;
                top := top^.next;
          END;
      IF carry > 0 THEN
          BEGIN
                new(newPtr);
                newPtr^.digit := carry;
                newPtr^.next := stack2;
                stack2 := newPtr;
          END;
      multiply := reverseStack(stack2); { multiply is now stack3 }
END; {multiply}
PROCEDURE upToPower(n: INTEGER);
VAR
    i       : INTEGER;
    topPtr: numberPtr;
BEGIN
      new(topPtr); topPtr^.digit := 1; topPtr^.next := nil;
      FOR i := 0 TO n - 1 DO
          BEGIN
                WRITE(base,'^',i,' = '); printNum(topPtr);
                topPtr := multiply(topPtr);
          END;
END; {upToPower}
BEGIN
      WRITE('Enter base (a digit): ');
      READLN(base);
      upToPower(100);
END.
```

Queues

Queues of people are very familiar in everyday life. People join the back of a queue and leave from the front. The data structure queue behaves similarly. In it, elements are inserted at one end (back) and removed from the other (front). This is called first-in first-out, or FIFO for short. We can picture a queue as shown below:

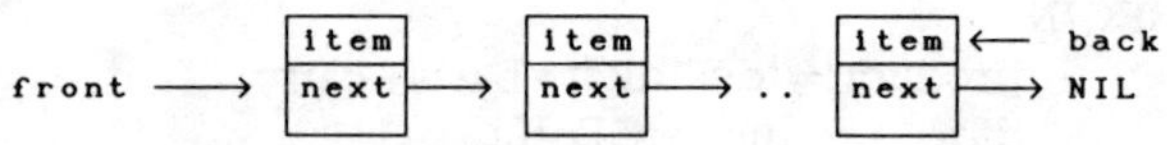

To simulate a queue of persons characterised by their names, we make the following declarations:

```
TYPE
    name  = PACKED ARRAY[1..15] OF CHAR;
    qPtr  = ^node;
    node  = RECORD
              item:name;
              next:qPtr;
            END;
    queue = RECORD
              front,back:qPtr;
            END;
```

Note that this time we are using two pointers to keep a handle on the structure. The two primary operations on a queue involve adding an item to the back of the queue and removing an item from the front.

PROCEDURE joinQ given below adds items to the back of the queue and **PROCEDURE leaveQ** removes an item from the front. The algorithms used are quite straightforward and are explained with comments in the code.

```
PROCEDURE joinQ(thisName:name; VAR q:queue);
VAR
   newPtr:qPtr;
BEGIN
      WITH q DO
         IF back = NIL THEN                {If q is empty then we do the following}
           BEGIN
              NEW(back);                   {create a new node}
              front := back;               {make the front pointer point to it}
              back^.item := thisName;      {write the name of the newcomer}
              back^.next := NIL;           {set marker for the end of queue}
           END
         ELSE
```

```
        BEGIN                       {If q is not empty we do the following}
            New(newPtr);            {create a new node}
            back^.next := newPtr;   {link it to the back}
            back := newPtr;         {make the new node the new back}
            back^.item := thisName; {write the name of the newcomer}
            back^.next := NIL;      {set marker for the end of queue}
        END;
END; {joinQ}

PROCEDURE leaveQ(VAR q:queue);
VAR
    tempPtr: qPtr;
BEGIN
    WITH q DO
      IF front = NIL THEN
        WRITELN('this queue is empty')
      ELSE
        BEGIN
          temPtr := front;                        {save the front pointer}
          front := front^.next;                   {point front at the second person}
          IF front = NIL THEN back := NIL;        {If the queue has become empty,
                                                   then set the pointer back to NIL}
          DISPOSE(tempPtr);                       {release storage}
        END;
END; {leaveQ}
```

Quickies

1. Suppose that pointers p and q are pointers to characters as shown:

Draw diagrams to illustrate the difference between q := p and q^ := p^.

2. State the two actions which occur when the statement new(p) is executed.

3. Which of the following are valid? If invalid, explain.

(a)
```
Type
    road = RECORD
             length: REAL;
             junctions: ^road;
           END;
```

(b)
```
VAR
      x: INTEGER;
      y: ^INTEGER;
  .
  .
x := ^y;
```
(c) (assuming x, y are both pointers)
```
IF x < y THEN ..
```
(d)
```
TYPE
      x: ^INTEGER;
      y: ^x;
VAR
      a: x; b: y;
  .
  .
a := b^;
```
4. Write a recursive **PROCEDURE printQueue(q: queue)** to print a queue backwards.

⇒ **You may now proceed to Pascal laboratory Activities 46–47.**

Linked lists

Stacks and queues require that data be added and removed in a special way. There is no fundamental reason why a linked structure should have data inserted in and removed from any particular position. Also, there is no reason as to why the process of retrieval from a node should necessarily destroy the node.

Linked lists are similar to stacks and queues in that they comprise chains of **RECORD**s linked together by pointers but, unlike stacks and queues, the nodes may be accessed in a random order. For example, whereas in a stack we always add items at the top, in a linked list of names we may add a name in alphabetical order. Also, in a linked list, the operation of retrieval does not destroy the node. We can search for a name to see if it is there without removing it. A node may only be destroyed by a specific disposal operation.

There are two types of linked lists, singly linked lists and doubly linked lists. The diagrammatical representation of a singly linked list, shown below, does not look any different from a stack. The difference lies in the operations that we perform on it rather than the structure.

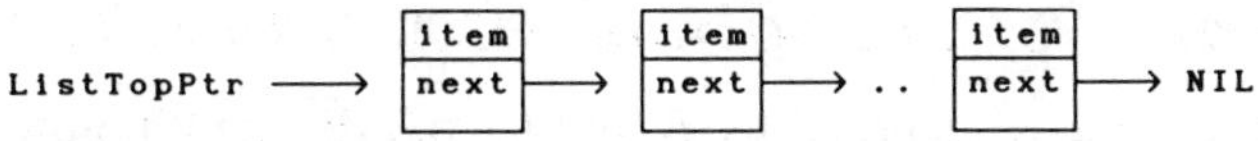

A major drawback of singly linked lists is that they cannot be traversed in reverse order. This makes the operations of insertion and deletion inefficient. For this reason, singly linked lists are not used very extensively. A more widely used linked list structure is the doubly linked list shown below. It consists of nodes that are linked to both the next node and the previous one.

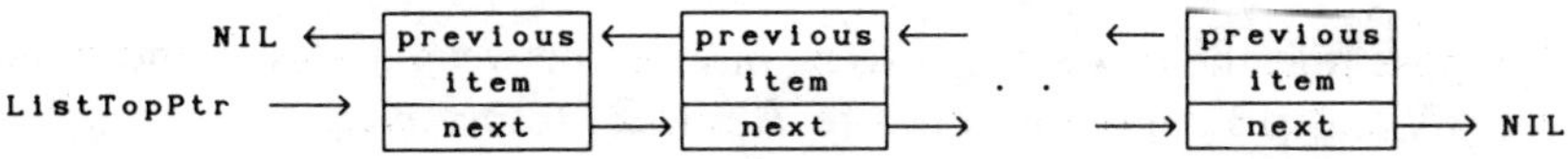

As an example, a double linked list of names can be built up using the following declarations:

```
TYPE
     name = PACKED ARRAY[1..15] OF CHAR;
     listPtr = ^node;
     node = RECORD
               previous: listPtr;
               item    : name;
               next    : listPtr;
            END;
```

The basic operations on a linked list are those involving insertion, deletion, searching, sorting and printing. We will now demonstrate the process of insertion in a doubly linked list. In the **PROCEDURE** to be developed, we will supply a pointer to a node and a new node will be inserted after it. In the algorithm that follows we will assume that p is a pointer of type **listPtr**. There are three cases to consider.

ALGORITHM TO INSERT A NODE IN A DOUBLY LINKED LIST

CASE 1: LIST IS EMPTY

```
NEW(p);
p^.previous := NIL;
p^.item := item;
p^.next := NIL;
ListTopPtr := p;
```

CASE 2: THE NODE BEING ADDED IS AFTER THE LAST NODE

Let the last node be denoted by A and let pA denote a pointer to A.

```
NEW(p);
pA^.next:= p;
p^.previous:= pA;
p^.item:= item;
p^.next:= NIL;
```

CASE 3: THE NODE BEING ADDED IS IN THE MIDDLE OF TWO NODES

Suppose that the new node is to be inserted between nodes A and B and let pA and pB denote pointers to A and B, respectively,

```
NEW(p);
p^.next:= pB;
p^.item:= item;
p^.previous:= pA;
pA^.next:= p;
pB^.previous:= p;
```

```
PROCEDURE insertAfterNode(thisName: name; VAR pA: listPtr);
VAR
    p,pB: listPtr;
BEGIN
      IF pA = NIL THEN { CASE 1 }
        BEGIN
              NEW(p);
              p^.previous:= NIL;
              p^.item:= item;
              p^.next:= NIL;
              pA:= p;
        END
      ELSE
        IF pA^.next = NIL THEN { CASE 2 }
          BEGIN
                NEW(p);
                pA^.next:= p;
                p^.previous:= pA;
                p^.item:= item;
                p^.next:= NIL;
          END
        ELSE
```

```
        BEGIN    { CASE 3 }
                pB := pA^.next;
                NEW(p);
                p^.next := pB;
                p^.item := item;
                p^.previous := pA;
                pA^.next := p;
                pB^.previous := p;
        END;
END; {insertAfterNode}
```

〉9.3 Binary trees

Apart from the linearly linked structures of the kind in which each node points to a single node there are many other useful structures in which a node can point to several nodes. The most important of these is the **binary tree** which we shall first describe in general terms.

A typical binary tree is shown in the diagram below:

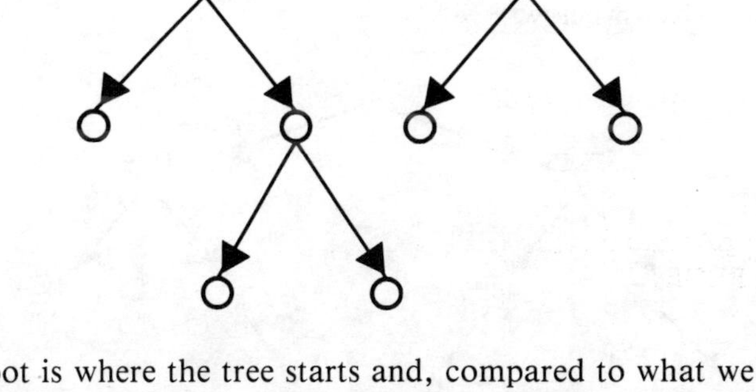

The root is where the tree starts and, compared to what we normally think of as a tree, the binary tree is drawn upside down. Note that a tree is a recursive structure: each node can be thought of as the root of a subtree. The importance of the binary tree arises from the fact that it allows for very rapid access to data.

The data in the nodes of a binary tree are inserted in some systematic way to produce a sorted tree. There are several ways of doing this but the procedure which is most commonly used involves constructing the structure so that the subtree on the left contains nodes that are less than or equal to the root while those on the right are greater than the root. We shall first study an example of the generation of such a tree.

Consider the set of numbers

57 104 33 97 45 81 76 108 22 26 12 56 48

To construct a sorted binary tree to hold these numbers we proceed as follows.

Bring the first number 57 and place it at the root node.
Bring the second number 104 to the root node. Since 104 > 57 go right at the root node and make a new node there to hold it.
Bring the third number 33 to the root node. Since 33 < 57 go left and make a new node to hold it.
Bring the fourth number 97 to the root node. Since 97 > 57 go right to the next node. Since 97 < 104 go left to this node and make a new node to hold it.

.

.

The process should now be clear. Every time we wish to insert a new node we compare the item with the existing nodes starting at the root. If the item is less than the item at an existing node we go left, otherwise we go right. The resulting tree arising from the input of the above integers in that order is shown below.

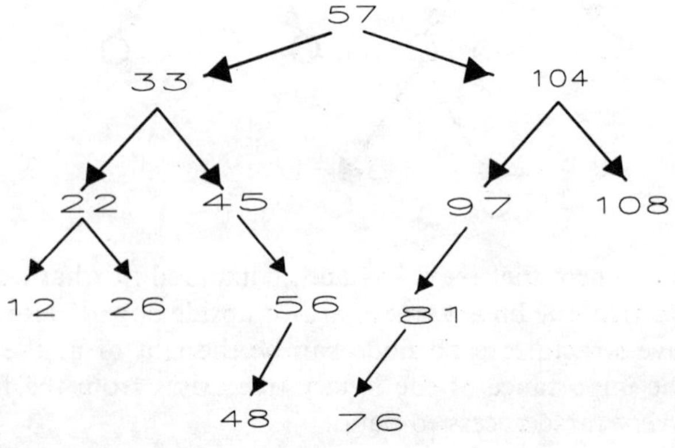

Sorted data can be extracted from the above tree by the following process:

We start at the root and keep going left to find the leftmost node, which is 12. Write out 12.
Visit the root of 12, which is 22. Write out 22.
Visit the right subtree of this root, which is 26. Write out 26.
We have now completely visited the subtree with nodes 12, 22 and 26.
Now visit the root of the completed subtree which is 33. Write out 33.
Now visit the right subtree of 33, whose root is 45. This subtree has no element to its left, so we write out 45.
Visit the right subtree of 45, the leftmost element of which is 48. Write out 48.
Visit the root 56. Write out 56.
Etc.

The algorithm for traversing the sorted tree just described is called **in-order traversal** and can be written more concisely as:

Traverse the left subtree.
Process the root.
Traverse the right subtree.

Here, the process involves doing whatever is required for the data being held in a node. In our example, we were printing out what was in a node. We could, for example, have subtracted 5 or whatever.

It should be obvious that the shape of the tree depends on the order of input. For example, if the input is completely in order then we obtain a linearly linked list.

A special case of a binary tree is that of a **perfectly balanced binary tree**. Such a tree, constructed from the input of data

Green Baker Abdul Buckingham Taylor Wong Smith

is shown in the diagram below.

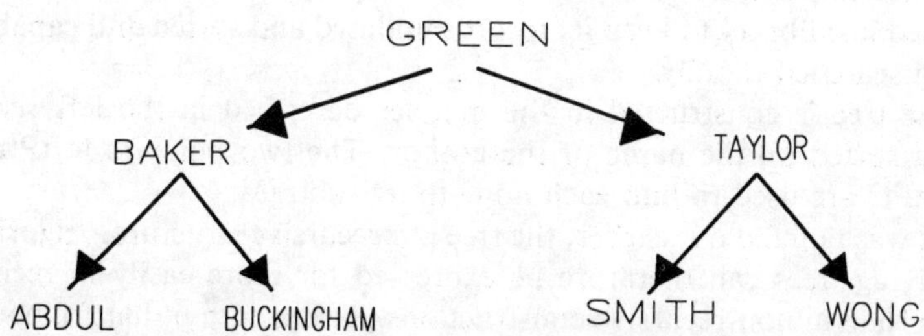

Note that in such a tree there are 2^{n-1} nodes at level n. For example, at the first level, since $2^0 = 1$, we have just the one node which is the root. At the second level, $2^1 = 2$ and we have two nodes and so on. A node is said to be a **leaf node** if it is not pointing at any other existing node. For example, in the above diagram, Abdul is a leaf node. We can now say more precisely what a perfectly balanced tree is. A binary tree is perfectly balanced if each node points to exactly two nodes or is a leaf node and every leaf node is at the same level.

The importance of perfectly balanced trees arises from the fact that, if there are in total $2^m - 1$ items held in such a tree, then any item can be found by making at most $m - 1$ moves. For example, $m = 20$ makes $2^m - 1 = 1048\,575$ so that any item in a balanced tree holding more than 1 million data items can be located in just 19 moves.

Example 9B: a library index. Having described in general terms what binary trees are, let us now consider an application. We introduce the following declarations:

```
TYPE
        str30 = PACKED ARRAY [1..30] OF CHAR;
        book = RECORD
                    title,author: str30;
                    numCopies: INTEGER;
               END;
        treePtr = ^num;
        node = RECORD
                    bookInfo: book;
                    leftPtr, rightPtr: treePtr;
               END;
```

These declarations will be utilised in the program bookTree that follows. The program constructs a binary tree to store information about books. Each node in the tree holds the title and the author of the book and also the number of copies in stock. A program of this type could be utilised in a library to keep its records updated and sorted and capable of being searched rapidly.

The tree is constructed in the manner described in the left section, being sorted on the name of the author. The two pointers leftPtr and rightPtr are used to link each node to its subtrees.

As was pointed out earlier, the tree is a recursive structure. Algorithms involving trees can therefore be expressed far more easily in recursive form than in non-recursive constructions. The program that follows will demonstrate the use of recursion in the construction and printing of a tree structure.

Program **bookTree** contains three **PROCEDURE**s and one **FUNCTION**. The **FUNCTION** is merely used to compare if the fields **author** and **title** in two **RECORD**s involving book information are identical. The **PROCEDURE**s serve the following purposes.

PROCEDURE makeTree reads book information from the TEXT file **bookFile**. The format of the data in the file is shown below. The first 30 columns contain the title, the next 30 the name of the author; this is followed by an integer which corresponds to the number of copies. In the construction of the tree, if the same book is entered again, then this does not lead to the creation of a new node. Only the number of copies is suitably updated. For example, for the data below, the book *The Double Helix* will be held in the tree with the number of copies being recorded as 3.

```
The Double Helix            Watson J.D.         2
I Bought a Mountain         Firbank T.          1
The Double Helix            Watson J.D.         1
The Coming of the Chip      Hyman A.            1
Draw!                       Hanks/Belliston     2
```

The algorithm used in **PROCEDURE makeTree** is as follows.

Open **bookFile** for reading.
Initialise **rootPtr** to NIL.
Repeat until end of **bookFile**:
  Read title, author and number of copies.
  Call **PROCEDURE addNode** to add this information to the tree.

PROCEDURE addNode adds a node to the tree in the manner that was described in the example in the last section. It receives two input parameters: **rootPtr** which points to a node and the **RECORD thisBook** which contains information about the book to be added. It employs the following algorithm.

If **rootPtr** is NIL then do the following:
  Construct a new node.
  Add information about this book to the new node.
  Set **leftPtr** and **rightPtr** to NIL.
If **RootPtr** is pointing to a node which contains the same book as **thisBook** then update the number of copies.

If **rootPtr** is pointing to a node which contains a different book then, if the name of the author of **thisBook** is alphabetically less than the name of the author of the book being pointed at then add **thisBook** to the left subtree. Otherwise add it to the right subtree.

PROCEDURE printTree prints the book information contained in the tree in alphabetical order based on the name of the author. It uses the traversal algorithm which was described in the last section. The output for the data shown above is given at the end of the listing.

```
Program bookTree(INPUT,OUTPUT,bookFile);
TREE
    str30 = PACKED ARRAY[1..30] OF CHAR;
    book = RECORD
            title,author: str30;
            numCopies: INTEGER;
          END;
    treePtr = ^node;
    node = RECORD
            bookInfo: book;
            leftPtr, rightPtr: treePtr;
          END;
VAR
   bookFile: TEXT;
   rootPtr  : treePtr;

FUNCTION equal(book1,book2: book): BOOLEAN;
BEGIN
     equal := (book1.title = book2.title) AND (book1.author = book2.author);
END; {equal}

PROCEDURE addNode(VAR rootPtr: treePtr: thisBook: book);
VAR
   newPtr: treePtr;
BEGIN
     IF rootPtr = NIL THEN
       BEGIN
            new(newPtr);
            WITH newPtr^.bookinfo DO
              BEGIN
                    title := thisBook.title;
                    author := thisBook.author;
                    numCopies := thisBook.numCopies;
              END;
            WITH newPtr^ DO
              BEGIN
                    leftPtr := NIL;
                    rightPtr := NIL;
              END;
            rootPtr := newPtr;
       END
```

```
        ELSE
          WITH rootPtr^ DO
            IF equal(bookInfo,thisBook) THEN
              bookInfo.numCopies := bookInfo.numCopies + thisBook.numCopies
            ELSE
              IF thisBook.author < bookInfo.author THEN
                addNode(leftPtr,thisBook)
              ELSE addNode(rightPtr,thisBook);
END; {addNode}

PROCEDURE printTree(rootPtr: treePtr);
BEGIN
        IF rootPtr < > NIL THEN
          WITH rootPtr^ DO
            BEGIN
                printTree(leftPtr);
                WITH bookInfo DO WRITELN(title,author,numCopies);
                printTree(rightPtr);
            END;
END; {printTree}

PROCEDURE makeTree(VAR rootPtr: treePtr);
VAR
      thisBook: book;
      i       : 1..30;
BEGIN
        RESET(bookFile);
        rootPtr := NIL;
        WHILE NOT EOF(bookFile) DO
            WITH thisBook DO
              BEGIN
                  FOR i := 1 TO 30 DO READ(bookFile,title [i]);
                  FOR i := 1 TO 30 DO READ(bookFile,author [i]);
                  READLN(bookFile,numCopies);
                  addNode(rootPtr,thisBook);
              END;
END; {makeTree}

BEGIN
        makeTree(rootPtr);
        printTree(rootPtr);
END.
```

```
I Bought a Mountain        Firbank T.        1
Draw!                      Hanks/Belliston   2
The Coming of the Chip     Hyman A.          1
The Double Helix           Watson J.D.       3
```

⇒ You may now proceed to Pascal laboratory Activities 48–50.

〉 Pascal laboratory

Activity 46. TUTOR 42 is the same as the program demoStack given in the text. Use this program to do the following:

(1) push 3, −42 and 17
(2) pop
(3) push 99
(4) pop pop

Modify the program so that the stack comprises an item of TYPE plate defined by

plate = (white,black,invisible);

(invisible has been included to cope with FUNCTION pop in the case when the stack is empty.) Verify your program by doing the following operations:

(1) push white, black and white
(2) pop pop
(3) push black
(4) pop pop pop

Activity 47. TUTOR43 is an incomplete program containing PROCEDUREs to add items to a queue, delete items from a queue and to print a queue. Complete the program and use it to do the following:

(1) Add the following persons to the queue in that order:

Jill Smith
Philip Thompson
Judy Hartman

(2) Print the queue.
(3) Take two persons away from the front.
(4) Print the queue.

Activity 48. TUTOR44 is the same as the program bookTree given in the text. Create your own data file to run the program.

Activity 49. Modify TUTOR 44 to construct a tree holding information about airline passengers who are characterised by a name and a seat number.

Activity 50. A **leaf node** in a tree is a node which is not pointing to any other node. Write a **PROCEDURE** to print the leaf nodes in a binary tree and test it in TUTOR44.

〉 Exercises

1. Write a **FUNCTION countStack** to count the number of items in a stack.

2*. Write a **FUNCTION** of the form

```
FUNCTION searchQ(q: queue; thisName: name; VAR place: INTEGER):
                                    BOOLEAN;
```

where the TYPEs being used are the same as those introduced in the section on queues in the text. The **FUNCTION** will search the queue from the front to find if a person having **thisName** as name is in the queue. If the person is found, then the **FUNCTION** will take the value TRUE and place will take the value of the position occupied by the person. If the person is not found, then **searchQ** will take the value FALSE and place will take the value zero.

3. Assume that a book is a **RECORD** containing the two fields title and author which are both **PACKED ARRAY**s **OF CHAR**. Write a **PROCEDURE** to insert a book alphabetically according to the surname of the author in a singly linked list. Write another procedure to search and report if a book exists and another one to search and delete a book. Finally, write a **PROCEDURE** to print the whole list. Test your **PROCEDURE**s in a main program.

4. Write a **PROCEDURE deleteAfterNode(VAR pA: listPtr);** to delete a node pointed at by the pointer **pA** in a doubly linked list. After deletion, **pA** should be set to point at the node before the one deleted. If there is no such node then **pA** should be set to point at the one after. If the list has become empty, then **pA** should be set to NIL.

5*. Assuming the declarations used in the program **bookTree**, write a recursive **PROCEDURE** to search for a book stored in the tree.

6. The **level** of the root of a binary tree is given the value 1. The level of the nodes pointed at by the root is 2 and, in general, the level of any node is one more than the level of the node pointing at it. The **height** of a tree is the maximum level in it. Write a recursive FUNCTION to find the height of a binary tree. Hint: height (treePtr) = max(height(treePtr^.left),height(treePtr^.right)).

Answers to quickies

1.

```
q:=p;

q^:=p^;
```

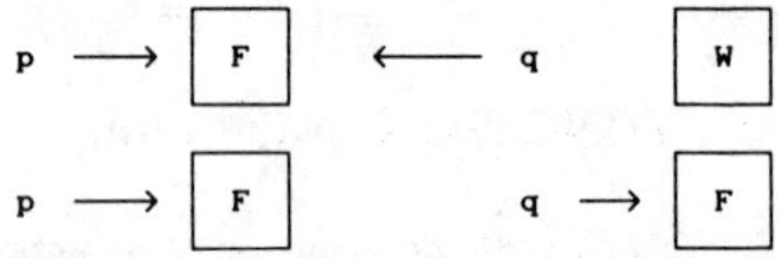

2. Storage is allocated for p^ and p is made to point at it.
3. (a) Invalid. A pointer must be declared before the RECORD to which it points.
   (b) Invalid. The symbol ^ never comes first in an identifier in an assignment, it only comes first in a declaration.
   (c) Invalid. Pointers may only be compared using = and <>.
   (d) Valid.
4.

```
PROCEDURE printQueue(q: queue);
BEGIN
      WITH q DO
         IF front <> NIL THEN
            BEGIN
                    printQueue(front^.next);
                    WRITELN(front^.item);
            END;
END; {printQueue}
```

› Appendix 1

› Reserved Symbols and Words

Reserved symbols

The table below lists those symbols and combination of symbols which have predefined meanings in Pascal. Note that, where two symbols occur together, they must be written without a gap. It would be an error, for example, to write < = when <= is intended.

+	:=	:	<>	(	(*
–	.	=	<=	)	*)
*	;	<	>=	[	{
/	,	>	(	]	}

Reserved words

The table below lists the reserved words of ISO Pascal. These are also called **keywords** or **delimiters**. Like the reserved symbols, the reserved words have fixed meanings. The programmer is not allowed to use them in any other way except as defined by Pascal.

AND	ARRAY	BEGIN	CASE	CONST
DIV	DO	DOWNTO	ELSE	END
FILE	FOR	FUNCTION	GOTO	IF
IN	LABEL	MOD	NIL	NOT
OF	OR	PACKED	PROCEDURE	PROGRAM
RECORD	REPEAT	SET	THEN	TO
TYPE	UNTIL	VAR	WHILE	WITH

〉 Appendix 2

〉 Predefined Identifiers

Predefined or **standard** identifiers are the names of a set of frequently used data types, FUNCTIONs and PROCEDUREs which are provided in Pascal. Unlike the reserved symbols and words, the programmer may choose to use the name of a predefined identifier for his own purposes by declaring it suitably. This, however, must be avoided. It is in bad style to use predefined identifiers for other than standard purposes and it can lead to confusion. The table below lists the predefined identifiers provided by ISO Pascal. Various dialects of Pascal provide many others apart from these.

CONSTANTS:	FALSE	TRUE	MAXINT
TYPES:	ARRAY	BOOLEAN	CHAR
	INTEGER	REAL	TEXT
FUNCTIONS:	ABS	ARCTAN	CHR
	COS	EOF	EOLN
	EXP	LN	ODD
	ORD	PRED	ROUND
	SIN	SQR	SQRT
	SUCC	TRUNC	
PROCEDURES:	GET	PAGE	READLN
	NEW	PACK	PUT
	READ	READLN	RESET
	REWRITE	UNPACK	WRITE
	WRITELN		
FILES:	INPUT	OUTPUT	

Functions

The table below gives the meaning of each of the predefined **FUNCTION**s available in ISO Pascal and lists the TYPEs of parameters that can be supplied and the TYPEs of the results produced. The word ORDINAL refers to any scalar type other than **REAL**.

FUNCTION	Parameter	Result	Description
ABS(x)	INTEGER, REAL	Same as x	Absolute value of x
ARCTAN(x)	INTEGER, REAL	REAL	Arctangent of x
CHR(i)	INTEGER	CHAR	Character with ordinal value i
COS(x)	INTEGER, REAL	REAL	Cosine of x
EOF(f)	FILE	BOOLEAN	TRUE if end of file f
EOLN(f)	TEXT FILE	BOOLEAN	TRUE if end of line f
EXP(x)	INTEGER, REAL	REAL	e raised to power x
LN(x)	INTEGER, REAL	REAL	Log of x to base e
ODD(i)	INTEGER	BOOLEAN	TRUE if i is odd
ORD(j)	ORDINAL	INTEGER	Ordinal value of j
PRED(j)	ORDINAL	Same as j	Predecessor of j
ROUND(x)	REAL	INTEGER	Rounded value of x
SIN(x)	INTEGER, REAL	REAL	Sine of x
SQR(x)	INTEGER, REAL	Same as x	Square of x
SQRT(x)	INTEGER, REAL	REAL	Square root of x
SUCC(j)	ORDINAL	Same as j	Successor of j
TRUNC(x)	REAL	INTEGER	Truncated value of x

〉 Appendix 3

〉 ASCII Table

The table below gives the American Standard Code for Information Interchange (ASCII) for the first 128 characters. The character set designated by ASCII is now supported by the majority of computer systems. For any given code c, **CHR**(c) gives the character associated with the numerical value c and for any given character ch, **ORD**(ch) gives the ASCII code of that character.

Apart from printing characters, the ASCII code is also used in transmitting data between computers and devices such as terminals and printers. This is done using the first 32 characters (ASCII codes 0–31). On some computers these characters are not printable but on IBM compatibles they can (apart from the NUL character) be printed as IBM graphics characters. The characters with ASCII codes 32–125 are printable on all machines which support ASCII. In the United Kingdom the hash character # is often replaced by the pound currency symbol £.

The characters with ASCII codes 128–255 (not listed in the table) are known as the **extended ASCII** character set and are also frequently available.

Code	Char	Code	Char	Code	Char	Code	Char
0	NUL	32		64	@	96	'
1	SOH	33	!	65	A	97	a
2	STX	34	"	66	B	98	b
3	ETX	35	#	67	C	99	c
4	EOT	36	$	68	D	100	d
5	ENQ	37	%	69	E	101	e
6	ACK	38	&	70	F	102	f
7	BEL	39	'	71	G	103	g
8	BS	40	(	72	H	104	h
9	HT	41	)	73	I	105	i
10	LF	42	*	74	J	106	j
11	VT	43	+	75	K	107	k
12	FF	44	,	76	L	108	l
13	CR	45	–	77	M	109	m
14	SO	46	.	78	N	110	n
15	SI	47	/	79	O	111	o
16	DLE	48	0	80	P	112	p
17	DC1	49	1	81	Q	113	q
18	DC2	50	2	82	R	114	r
19	DC3	51	3	83	S	115	s
20	DC4	52	4	84	T	116	t
21	NAK	53	5	85	U	117	u
22	SYN	54	6	86	V	118	v
23	ETB	55	7	87	W	119	w
24	CAN	56	8	88	X	120	x
25	EM	57	9	89	Y	121	y
26	SUB	58	:	90	Z	122	z
27	ESC	59	;	91	[	123	{
28	FS	60	<	92	\	124	|
29	GS	61	=	93	]	125	}
30	RS	62	>	94	^	126	-
31	US	63	?	95	_	127	DEL

〉 Index